A NEW MANUAL
OF
FRENCH COMPOSITION

A NEW MANUAL OF FRENCH COMPOSITION

FOR UNIVERSITIES AND THE HIGHER CLASSES OF SCHOOLS

BY

R. L. GRÆME RITCHIE

CAMBRIDGE
AT THE UNIVERSITY PRESS
1969

CAMBRIDGE
UNIVERSITY PRESS

University Printing House, Cambridge CB2 8BS, United Kingdom

Cambridge University Press is part of the University of Cambridge.

It furthers the University's mission by disseminating knowledge in the pursuit of education, learning and research at the highest international levels of excellence.

www.cambridge.org
Information on this title: www.cambridge.org/9781316603741

© Cambridge University Press 1969

First edition 1941
Reprinted 1947, 1951, 1953, 1959, 1963, 1969
First paperback edition 2016

A catalogue record for this publication is available from the British Library

ISBN 978-1-316-60374-1 Paperback

PREFACE

The *Manual of French Composition* has had a long innings: twenty-six years and not out. It probably owes this happy fate to the quality of the English passages and their suitability for the purposes of French Composition, and seems therefore likely to retain its usefulness unimpaired. But many teachers who have worked through its two hundred passages ask for a further volume, on the same general lines.

The present work contains the same number of PASSAGES, including some sixty tried favourites taken from the now extinct *Supplement* of 1922. These two hundred passages have passed three tests which experience shows to be essential. However promising an English passage seems, it cannot be guaranteed suitable for the special purposes of French Composition till it has actually been used in a written examination and found to 'work out well'; thereafter discussed in class with interested and not easily satisfied students; and finally provided with a 'fair copy' which examiners and teachers, candidates and students can behold without shame or without indignation. The severest of these tests is the last, and we might have had to dispense with it in some cases but for the help of colleagues and friends.

The relative difficulty of the Passages is indicated by asterisks: * Easy [Higher Certificate and Scholarship papers standard]; ** Moderately difficult [University Pass Examinations]; *** Difficult [Final Honours and the highest Civil Service Examinations]; **** Very difficult [More useful as Exercises than as tests in any of the existing Examinations].

While the 'fair copies' were being in the fullness of time achieved—they are published for the use of Teachers in a companion volume entitled *French Fair Copies*—we noted the 'points' brought out by each. They are classified and discussed in the INTRODUCTION. It thus deals not with difficulties which might conceivably occur in the translation of English prose into French, but with difficulties which do occur—and persistently—in our two hundred passages. But as these represent many different types and authors, and were originally selected for examination purposes, there seems little doubt that the Introduction gives the gist of the matter and contains the hints and the information most useful to a candidate confronted with any piece of English prose.

In alternate passages further and more direct help is given in Notes.

An illustration of the principles followed in the choice of variants is given by means of a Model Lesson.

We are privileged once more to print Model Translations kindly written for us by distinguished French scholars. Some of the original contributors happily contribute again. The place of others is worthily filled by their successors in office, that of the late Professor Émile Legouis by his son. As a sign of the times, British scholarship is represented by two contributors, Professors A. J. Farmer and F. C. Roe.

To all these we would express our gratitude—as also to the scholars whose names adorn the companion volume which, but for their valued help, might never have reached a conclusion.

R. L. G. R.

March 1941

TABLE OF CONTENTS

ACKNOWLEDGMENTS

Each extract printed is followed by the name of the Author, the title of the book, and the publisher. Opportunity is taken here to thank those publishers and owners of copyright who have granted permission to make the extracts.

PRINCIPAL ABBREVIATIONS USED

cp.: compare
esp.: especially
F.: French
fig.: figurative
freq.: frequently
gen.: general
intr., intrans.: intransitive
iron.: ironical
Lat.: Latin
lit.: literal, literally
mil.: military
O.E.D.: The Oxford English Dictionary

poet.: poetical
qqch.: quelque chose
qqn.: quelqu'un
relig.: religious
sb.: substantive
s.v.: sub voce
trans.: transitive
Var., var.: variant
vb.: verb.
= : equals, means equivalent to
) (: as contrasted with

N.B. Double inverted commas indicate erroneous renderings.

GENERAL INTRODUCTION

As an Academic exercise, French Composition is both a means of learning the language and a test of linguistic attainment.

As a means of learning French, it is of course only one among many: Grammar, Reading, Translation into English, Free Composition, Oral Work, Stay Abroad. Knowledge of French acquired by one means is improved and extended by others. The part played by Composition is to increase our *active* Vocabulary and make our knowledge of French more *precise*.

To know the meaning of French words and phrases and be able to recognize them when we see them is a passive art, highly useful for many purposes, but not for Composition. In that exercise we have to produce them ourselves—a much more exacting task. One might, for instance, have some difficulty in giving the French for 'Pharaoh', 'the Rich Man in the parable', 'the Field of the Cloth of Gold', 'the League of Nations' or 'the self-determination of peoples', but none in recognizing *le Pharaon, le mauvais riche, le Camp du drap d'or, la Société des Nations* or *le droit des peuples de disposer d'eux-mêmes*. If a student cannot produce exactly the French words or phrases required, it is often because he has not had occasion to use them himself. He may have come across them in his reading, but not *seen* them—till his French Prose is returned, with corrections. Then the scales fall from his eyes. He sees that *Pharaon* is the title of a ruler and not his name, that this particular 'Field' is *Camp* and not *Champ*. His knowledge of French becomes to that extent fuller and more active. If he did not know these words before, he knows them now. If he only half-knew them, he now knows them fully, and returns them to store, well overhauled and with the missing parts supplied. Henceforth they belong to his active vocabulary and are available for practical use. The number of words so treated is relatively small, because practice in French Composition must in the nature of things be limited. But the habit of mind so formed is afterwards applied in the acquisition of other words and in other domains of French study. The faculty of *seeing* words instead of merely glancing at them is indeed as essential for reading French properly as for writing it.

For Composition purposes, to know a French expression may be useless unless one also knows it precisely—the exact words and their order, their spelling and gender, the way in which the expression is used, its literary value and its force. The right word with the wrong gender may be worse than useless. In Composition, incomplete knowledge may be more dangerous than ignorance.

Composition thus encourages us to continue amassing language material in quantity, but at the same time to keep an eye on the quality. It gives us practice in manipulating language material ourselves and skill in performing what is before all things a work of precision. It is not an end in itself; it is an aid to something higher, to a full, precise and active knowledge of French.

As a test of attainment in French, Composition reveals strength and weakness as no other exercise can. Quantity and quality, information and skill, vigilance and readiness all come up for judgment. In examinations Composition is well known to be the most searching part of the French papers. No single test is of course perfect, but within its own limits Composition is the least imperfect—and the least 'subjective'. The candidates who do best in it are those who have the soundest knowledge of the language. There are so many opportunities of making elementary errors that unsound knowledge is inevitably exposed over and over again, and any system of deductive marking which leaves the best French scholars with high marks, automatically leaves the less good with extremely few. No doubt positive marks can be gained by meritorious translations of occasional phrases. But in examinations Composition is in essence a negative art—like the art of war in the field, where the best general is he who makes the fewest mistakes.

To improve one's marks in French Composition it is therefore necessary to improve one's knowledge of the language, but more particularly as regards active vocabulary, exactness and the avoidance of error, i.e. to learn more French, learn it better and learn to write it more carefully. How to achieve these three results is a subject too wide for treatment here and the methods, moreover, are too well known.

There are, however, some aspects of French study which concern Composition more closely than others, and these are considered in the Introduction. The material utilized in it is mainly drawn from the Passages for Translation—a method which has a three-fold advantage. It reduces to practical dimensions what is a formidable, and would otherwise be an unlimited, undertaking. It provides help in the translation of every passage in the book. And it encourages —and rewards—re-reading and consultation of paragraphs whose purpose is to be generally helpful. Except in the annotated alternate passages—and even in them very sparingly—no direct references to the Introduction are given. Discussion of the difficulties, and hints and guidance as to their solution, will be found in the four chapters into which they naturally fall: I, Descriptive Vocabulary; II, Homonyms and Synonyms; III, Grammar; and IV, Style.

DICTIONARIES

French-French

E. Littré, *Dictionnaire*, 4 vols. and Supplement.

Still indispensable: contains a vast number of well-chosen examples from classical authors, with references. The material, however, is not very well arranged, and as a rule time is required to find exactly the information sought. There is an *Abrégé* by A. Beaujean (Hachette).

Dictionnaire de l'Académie française.

Contains well-chosen phrases, exemplifying *the* correct usage of words.

Hatzfeld, Darmesteter et Thomas, *Dictionnaire général de la Langue française* (Delagrave).

The examples given are few, but carefully selected; the etymologies suggested represent the results of modern scholarship.

Bescherelle, *Dictionnaire national de la langue française* (Garnier).

Contains many words too recent for inclusion in Littré or Hatzfeld.

***Larousse du XX⁰ siècle* (Larousse), 6 vols. 1928.**

[An *encyclopædic* Dictionary.]

English-French

Harrap's *Standard French and English Dictionary*, Part II, edited by J. E. Mansion (Harrap), 1939.

Extraordinarily complete, up-to-date and accurate.

Ch. Petit, *Dictionnaire Anglais-Français* (Hachette), 1934.

Excellent and full.

Gasc's *Concise Dictionary*. New Edition with an enlarged Supplement and revised Introduction by J. Marks (G. Bell and Sons), 1938.

Useful as a convenient small-size Dictionary.

French-English

Harrap's *Standard French and English Dictionary*, Part I, edited by J. E. Mansion (Harrap), 1934.

Indispensable; supersedes all existing French-English Dictionaries.

Abel Chevalley and Marguerite Chevalley, *The Concise Oxford French Dictionary* (Clarendon Press), 1934.

Excellent *selective* Dictionary.

Professor F. Boillot, *Le vrai Ami du traducteur anglais-français* (Presses Universitaires de France), 1930.

[Deals fully and amusingly with Homonyms.]

GRAMMAR

R. L. G. Ritchie, *Nelson's French Grammar* (Nelson), 1936.

STYLE

Antoine Albalat, *L'Art d'écrire en vingt leçons* (Colin), 1899; *Le Travail du style* (Colin), 1903.

CHAPTER I

DESCRIPTIVE VOCABULARY

A student 'doing a French Prose' is not just 'making it up'.
He is drawing on a store of remembered fact. Where does his
French vocabulary come from? In the main, from reading.
It is a stock of accumulated lore, a mass of observations
made, often unconsciously, in the course of his reading in
French.

The bulk was acquired without conscious effort. The
strangest thing about language-learning is that it is just
when our attention is riveted on the subject-matter and not
on the form, that we learn new phrases most readily. This
applies as much to speaking French as to reading it. To take
an extreme case, a pronouncement made by a French dentist
at a moment when one feels intense interest in *what* he is
saying and none whatever in *how* he says it, is afterwards
found to have passed mysteriously into one's active vocabulary. The phrases, the exact words used have been learned,
unconsciously, unintentionally, but once and for all. In
like manner, the passages in a French book which teach us
most French are those which, at the time of reading, so
completely absorbed us that we stopped not to think of the
words, or even to think whether we were reading French or
English. But in any form of reading, some French always
sinks in. It finds its way to the store of unconsciously
remembered fact, from which it comes forth during an
exercise in Composition, often much to the owner's surprise.

The surest, most natural, way to increase vocabulary is
by reading. That is '*la manière douce*'. But there is also '*la
manière forte*', which consists in applying to the acquisition
of vocabulary whatever means come to hand, such as learning off lists of words and phrases and making a sustained
effort to discover and fill up blanks. Such methods are only
supplementary, but they are not to be despised. In

particular it is always worth while to re-read well-written passages and to note—and enter in a phrase-book—material likely to be useful for the special purpose of Composition, including of course Free Composition, and consequently also useful for the general purpose of learning French. And what is that material? It consists chiefly of words and phrases which make up any French writer's stock-in-trade. Theoretically there is no limit to the number of French words and phrases required for Composition. But in practice there are limits, laid down by the nature of the exercise. English passages used in class, or set in examinations, fall into a few recognized types, 'Descriptive', 'Portraits', 'Narrative', etc. Vocabulary which is very technical or out-of-the-way is unlikely to bulk largely in an academic exercise intended to afford practice in the general use of French, or in a public examination meant for candidates whose French reading has not been identical.

Thus most of the two hundred passages of this book were originally selected, whether by ourselves or by others, for examination purposes. Going through them and noting and classifying the French vocabulary they required, we found certain words and phrases continually recurring. They turned out to be in the main what might be termed 'descriptive', though they are by no means confined to descriptions of scenery or the like, but occur in passages of every type. To facilitate the acquisition of active vocabulary, they are given here, arranged according to subject, and in the passages reference is made to these paragraphs. The remainder proved to be more abstract and came more naturally under the heading of 'Grammar and Syntax' or 'Style'. They are therefore incorporated in Chapters III and IV.

§ 1. *Orientation*:

S'orienter is to get an idea of the lie of the land, to find one's bearings; hence 'bewildered' may be *désorienté*. A land-mark is *un point de repère*.

North, Northern, etc.: *Septentrional, méridional*, etc., suggest the geographical text-book; 'on the north road' = *sur la route* du nord; 'in all the northern countries'=*dans tous les pays* du nord; 'the western sky' (also the setting sun)=*le couchant*; 'the campaign on the western front'=*la campagne sur le front* ouest; 'the eastern sky'=*le côté* est *du ciel*; 'bounding it *on* the west' =*le bornant à l'ouest*. N.B. *le vent* d'*est* and d'*ouest*, but *le vent* du *nord*, du *sud*.

RIGHT: 'Turn to the right'=*Tournez* à droite; 'to keep to the right'=*tenir sa droite*; 'on the right'=*à droite*; '*on* one's right'=à *sa droite* (He had *on the* right=*Il avait* à sa *droite*); 'at *right angles* to'=à *angle droit* avec.

ROUND: 'Round about', 'all round'=*tout autour*; 'all the country around'=*tout le pays* d'alentour; '*for* several miles round'=à *plusieurs milles* à la ronde; 'a *widening* circle'=*un cercle* grandissant.

SIDE: 'Seen from this side'= *Vu de ce côté*; 'on the side of' (in the direction of)=*du côté de*; '*on* the north side'=*du côté du nord*; '*on* every side'=de *tous les côtés*; '*on* both sides'=des *deux côtés*; but: '*on* three sides'=sur *trois côtés*; 'from side to side'=*d'un côté à l'autre*; 'sideways'=*de côté*. 'The path *runs* (*lies*) *by the side of* a river several yards wide'=*Le sentier* longe *une rivière, large de quelques mètres.*

§ 2. *Distance*:

FAR; FAR AWAY: '*Far* in the pale North-East'=Loin *dans le pâle Nord-Est*; '*far to* the West'=au loin vers *le couchant*; '*far* from land'=loin *de la terre*; 'far beyond the crest'=*bien au delà de la crête*; 'a village *far* in the country'=*situé dans une* lointaine *campagne*. 'The mountains *farthest away*'=*Les montagnes* les plus éloignées.

Loin is an adverb and consequently invariable; *lointain* is the adjective='distant', and therefore agrees. The presence of 'far' and 'away' and 'distant' in the same sentence causes in French an awkward repetition avoidable only by some alteration in the wording: 'the *distant* Jura, like a pale mist, very *far away*'=à une très grande distance, *le Jura, semblable à une pâle brume lointaine*.

'*Away* one could see...'=Là-bas (Plus loin) *on distinguait*....
'The plain stretched *away to* the South...mile after mile'=*La plaine s'étendait* au loin (à perte de vue) vers *le Sud*...pendant *de*

longues lieues; 'situated five miles *away*' = *situé à huit kilomètres*
de là (*à huit kilomètres de distance*); 'a short distance *away*' = *non*
loin de là (d'ici).

§ 3. *Landscape*:

(*a*) 'In the foreground' = *au premier plan*; 'in the middle
distance' = *au second plan*; 'in the background' = *à l'arrière-plan*
(or *au fond*). 'The scene which *presents itself* to the traveller
(which he sees)' = *Le paysage qui* s'offre aux yeux *du voyageur*
(*qui* s'offre à ses regards: *qu'il* aperçoit, découvre, discerne,
distingue); 'when *he comes within sight of X*' = *lorsqu'il* arrive
en vue de *X*, 'is pleasant' = *riant* (gentle, *doux, aimable*; lovely,
merveilleux, ravissant, d'une grande beauté; wild, *sauvage, tour-*
menté). 'The moon *gives him a view* of the ruins' = *La lune* lui
permet de voir *la ruine*. '*The prospect around* is lovely' = Le pays
d'alentour *présente un ravissant coup d'œil*. 'It is a scene *of*
incredible beauty' = *un spectacle* d'une *beauté incroyable*.

(*b*) 'The coast is (not now) in sight' = *La côte* (*n*')*est* (*plus*)
visible; (*ne*) *se distingue* (*plus*). 'The clouds shut out the sky' = *Les*
nuages dérobent le ciel à la vue; 'some object is almost lost in sea
and sky' = *se confond* (*se perd*) *dans la mer et le ciel*; '*merges into* a
confused horizon' = se fond en *un horizon confus*; or '*stands out*
(black) *against*' = se détache (*en noir*) sur; se découpe sur
l'horizon; or 'is clearly marked' = *nettement marqué* (*dessiné*),
'indistinct' = *confus, vague*; or 'has dim outlines' = *contours*
estompés, or 'is shadowy in outline' = *aux contours sombres*. Note
also 'to harmonize with' = s'*harmoniser* avec.

§ 4. *Hills and Valleys*:

Rocks: '*Jagged* rocks *overhanging* a ravine' = *des rochers* déchi-
quetés (dentelés) surplombant *un ravin*; 'overhung with bushes'
= *surplombé de buissons*; 'beneath the rocks' = *au pied des*
rochers; 'in the nooks below' = *dans les recoins d'en bas, en dessous*
dans les coins; 'seen from below' = *vu d'en bas*. Note 'rocky'
= stony, pebbly, *rocailleux*.

Slopes: 'The other side of the valley' = *le versant opposé*; 'on the
steep *sides* of the hills' = *sur les* flancs *escarpés des montagnes*; *un*
village posé (*perché, juché*) au flanc *d'une colline*; 'the hills
opposite' = *les montagnes* d'*en face*; cp. 'the house over the way'
= *la maison* d'*en face*; 'All down the *sides* of the rocks' = Du haut

en bas *des rochers*; 'slope'=*pente* (f.); 'sloping meadows', 'hill-pastures'=*prairies en pente*; 'wooded slopes'=*coteaux boisés*; 'a hill' (on a road), 'gradient'=*une côte*; 'Do not overtake *on the top* of a hill'=*Ne dépassez pas* en haut *d'une côte*, au sommet *d'une côte*; 'half-way down (up)'=*à mi-côte*; 'The meadows *fell away* into the depths of the valley'=*Les prairies allaient* s'enfoncer jusque *dans les profondeurs de la vallée*. 'Along ground of an undulating and varied form'=*Suivant les plis et les accidents du* terrain.

STEEP: 'The ground rose (descended) *sharply (gently)*'=*La terre (Le terrain) s'élevait* en pente raide (brusque, rapide), en pente douce; 'in places almost precipitous', 'sheer'=*par endroits presque à plomb (à pic)*; 'a precipitous gorge'=*une gorge escarpée*.

§ 5. Woods and Trees:

TREES: 'A noble tree'=*un bel arbre, arbre majestueux*; 'century-old'=*séculaire, centenaire*; 'stunted'=*rabougri*; 'twisted' (by the wind)=*tordu, tourmenté*; 'tree trunks'=*des troncs d'arbre*; 'blossom'=*fleurs*; 'in blossom'=*en fleur(s)*; 'withered leaves'=*feuilles flétries, mortes, d'automne.*

'To grow' usually=*pousser*; a verb has often to be supplied: 'the palms *on* the islets'=*les palmiers* qui *poussent sur les îlots*; 'the tall (low) trees that *grow along* the shore'=*les grands (petits) arbres qui* bordent *le rivage.*

WOODS: 'A clump'=*un massif*; 'fir-clump'=*un* groupe *de sapins*; 'grove'=*un bosquet, bocage*; 'sacred grove'=*bois sacré*; 'a *knot* of palm-trees'=*un* bouquet *de palmiers*; 'a *tangle* of ashes'=*un* enchevêtrement (fouillis, labyrinthe) *de frênes; des frênes* enchevêtrés; 'among the beeches'=*parmi les hêtres, dans les bois de hêtres, dans les hêtraies*; 'a glade', 'clearing'=*une clairière.*

'Woodland'=*sylvestre, perdu dans les bois, au fond des bois*; often just *bois*; 'woodland valleys'=*vallées boisées*)(treeless=*déboisé*. 'The woods' often=*la forêt.*

§ 6. Fields, Grass:

FIELDS: 'Gate' (in a field)=*une barrière*; 'gate (ornamental, iron) of a park', etc., also a railing=*une grille*; 'flocks and herds'=*troupeaux* (m.) *de gros et menu bétail; gros bétail*=cattle (including horses, asses, mules); *menu bétail*=smaller livestock;

'a farmer's cattle'=*ses bêtes*; 'a sheep'=*un mouton; une brebis* properly =a ewe; sheep (*pl.*), generally =*moutons*; 'the *bleat* of a lamb'=le bêlement *d'un agneau*; 'to bellow'=*beugler*; 'lowing' =*le mugissement.*

GRASS: '*There is* scanty grass'=*Une herbe rare* y pousse; '(smooth) grass'=*le gazon*; 'blade'=*un brin d'herbe*; 'scented' =*embaumé*; 'giving off scent'=*odoriférant*; 'the bright grass' =*l'herbe vive (fraîche)*; 'soft'=*tendre*. 'The ground was covered with verdure'=*couvert (tapissé) de verdure*. 'The grass was jewelled with glow-worms'=*émaillée de vers luisants*; 'strewn' =*parsemée (de violettes)*. 'The flowers among the grass'=*émaillant le gazon*; (cp. *les prairies émaillées de fleurs*). 'The rank grass'=*Les hautes herbes; Les herbes luxuriantes.*

§ 7. *Water*:

To FLOW ='overflow'=*déborder*; 'to *flow* into the sea'=se jeter *dans la mer*; 'The river of life flows *backward*'=*remonte vers sa source*. 'The tide *flowed* gently over the fine sand'=*La marée montait doucement sur le sable fin.*

RIPPLING: *ondoyant, étincelant; Le vent* ridait *la surface*; 'the gentle *rippling* of the tide'=*la douce* ondulation *de la marée*; 'stretched away in leagues of *rippling* lustre'=*s'étendaient au loin pendant des lieues* en ondulations *étincelantes*; 'a soft murmuring *ripple*'=*un* clapotis *doux comme un murmure*; 'the chilly water *lapping* (rippling) *against* the shore'=le clapotis *de l'eau glacée* sur *le rivage.*

STREAM: *ruisseau (le babil, le doux murmure du ruisseau), un cours d'eau, un affluent*; '(mountain) stream'=*un torrent*; 'current'=*le courant*; 'out in the deep current'=*au plus profond du courant*; 'a thin (narrow) *stream of water*', 'trickle'=*un mince* filet d'eau; 'upstream', 'farther up', 'down'=*en amont, en aval*; 'above the lock'=*en amont de l'écluse*; 'curves', 'bends'= coudes (m.), *sinuosités* (f.).

WAVES: 'The waves (*les vagues, les lames* (f.), etc.; see p. 30, §18) dashed *against* the coast'=*venaient* (see p. 16, §18, To BREAK), *se briser* sur *la côte*; 'foam-flecked'=*marbrées d'écume*. 'The water leaped'=*L'eau jaillit, Les flots bondissaient.* 'The wreaths (The curl) of a wave'=*les volutes* (f.) *d'une lame.* 'Mingled *spray* and rain'=Embrun(s) *mêlé(s) de pluie*; 'a mist of spray'=*une poussière d'embruns.*

§ 8. The Sea, Nautical Expressions:

'At sea'=out at sea=*en mer*; 'on the open sea'=*en pleine mer*; (=as regards the sea, *sur mer*; cp. *sur terre et sur mer*=on land and sea); 'put out to the open (sea)'=*pousser au large*; 'off Saint Malo'=*au large de Saint-Malo*.

'To go on board'=*embarquer*; 'All aboard!'=*Embarquez! S'embarquer* is less technical, more figurative: *s'embarquer dans un train, dans une nouvelle guerre, dans une dissertation sur....* To land is *débarquer*.

'On the ship'=*sur le navire, à bord*; 'on deck'=*sur le pont*; 'to the fore'=*à l'avant du navire*; 'to drift'=*s'en aller à la dérive*; 'to furl a sail'=*amener une voile*; 'to sail towards' =*cingler vers*; 'He was going in a boat from X to Y'=*Il allait en bateau*, etc.

§ 9. Air and Sky:

AIR: 'The clear air'=*l'air pur*; 'clearness'=*la netteté*; 'a dark and misty air'=*l'atmosphère opaque et brumeuse*; 'the dark vapours'=*les sombres vapeurs*. 'Mist *crept* along the water below'=*Le brouillard rampait, là-bas, au long des eaux*. 'Fog *falls upon* the town'=*s'abat sur*.

CLOUDS: 'Clouds gather'=*s'amoncellent*; 'hang over'=*planent sur*; 'pile up'=*s'amoncellent*; 'roll over one another'=*s'enroulent les uns sur les autres*; 'open out'=*s'écartent*. 'On a cloudless day'=*sous un ciel sans nuages*. 'The moon riding clear of the cloud-rack'=*se dégageant des nuages en fuite (chassés par le vent)*.

SKY: 'The broad sky'=*Le vaste ciel*. 'The mountains were silhouetted against the bright sky'=*se silhouettaient sur le fond lumineux du ciel*; 'skies' (technical, artist's term)=*les ciels*; 'the vault (dome, canopy) of heaven'=*la voûte du ciel*; 'the *floor* (the courts) of heaven'=les parvis *du ciel*.

STREAK: *un trait, une traînée, une bande*: e.g. *l'horizon rayé d'un long trait rouge: les traînées violettes qui barraient l'horizon; une bande de lumière verte.*

§ 10. Seasons, Weather:

SEASONS: 'It was winter'=*C'était l'hiver*. 'In spring'=*Au printemps*; 'late-coming springs'=*des printemps tardifs*; 'in summer and winter'=*été comme hiver*; 'the pale spring foliage'=*le pâle feuillage* printanier; 'their *winter (autumn)* colouring'=*leurs teintes* hivernales (d'automne). 'Soon it will be May'=*Bientôt nous serons en mai*; 'The weather is exceptional for the time of year'=*Le temps est exceptionnel pour la saison.* 'Season'(vaguely) =*époque* (f.).

WEATHER: 'One stormy (sultry) day'=*un jour d'orage.*

Note *par*: 'In calm weather'=par *temps calme*; par *un beau dimanche d'été*; 'this cool pleasant afternoon'=par *cette fraîche et agréable après-midi*; 'to lie awake on such nights'=*veiller* par *de telles nuits.*

COLD: 'Coldness' (coolness)=*fraîcheur*; 'cool'=*frais.* 'In the frosty air'=*Dans l'air glacé.* 'The (period of) frost'=*le gel*; 'thaw'=*le dégel*; 'hoar-frost'=*le frimas*; poet.=*les frimas, la gelée blanche*; 'the *ground, sprinkled* with snow'=le sol, saupoudré *de neige.*

RAIN: 'Rainy weather with bright intervals'=*temps pluvieux avec éclaircies.* '*In* rain or sun'=sous *la pluie ou* au *(grand) soleil.* 'The rain was now steady'=*Il pleuvait sans discontinuer*; 'the showers of spring'=*les giboulées (ondées) printanières.*

WIND: 'There was no wind to stir the branches'=*Nulle brise ne* venait (see also p. 16, §18, To BREAK) *les remuer.* 'The wind was very rough'=*Le vent soufflait avec violence.* 'Gusts *swept* over the island'=*Des rafales* passaient *sur l'île.*

§ 11. *Daylight, Moonlight, Stars*:

DAYLIGHT: 'The dawn *came (stole)* through the trees'=*Le jour (L'aurore)* filtrait *à travers les arbres*; 'at sunrise'=*au lever du soleil*; 'As the light grows'=*A mesure que la lumière croît*; 'The sun came out'=*se montra, parut*; 'beat down on me'=*dardait ses rayons sur moi*; '*came slanting* down the slopes'=lançait ses rayons obliques *sur les pentes*; 'where the sun (sunlight, sunshine) *fell on* the trees'=*aux* endroits *où le soleil* frappait *les arbres*; 'the sun was rising *higher*'=s'élevait)(*se levait*=was rising; 'in the bright sunshine'=*au grand soleil*; 'to sun oneself'=*prendre le soleil*; 'at sundown'=*au coucher du soleil; fig.* 'to live in the daylight'=*vivre au grand jour (à la clarté du jour).*

MOONLIGHT: *La clarté de la lune.* 'The moon shone brightly'=*La lune brillait d'un vif éclat*; 'now shone out'=*brillait maintenant de tout son éclat*; 'The moon, pale...'=*la lune, blafarde (blême)*;

'The moonlight fills the open sky'=*Le clair de lune emplit le vaste ciel*; 'The moonlight fell on the dark water'=*La lune tombait (en plein) sur la surface de l'eau sombre*; 'Waving in the moonlight'=*Ondulant au clair de lune.*

STARS: 'The stars had not yet come'=*n'avaient pas encore paru*; 'were out'=*étaient allumées (brillaient).* 'The stars shone out above, brighter than...'=*apparaissaient en haut, plus éclatantes que....* 'To sleep under the stars (out of doors)'=*coucher (dormir) à la belle étoile.*

§ 12. Light and Shadow:

LIGHT: '*There was light enough to see* the road'=Il faisait assez clair pour voir *la route*; 'brilliant in the sun'=*éclatant au soleil, éblouissant*; 'burning'=*ardent, flamboyant*; 'ruddy light'=*une lumière rouge, un rougeoiement*; 'glowing' (red)=*rutilant*; 'a glimmer'=*une lueur (incertaine)*; 'to flicker'=*vaciller.* Very gradual change is expressed by *allait*+participle, e.g. *de moment en moment allait pâlissant.*

'A sheaf of (fire)light'=*une gerbe*; 'to set the world aflame' =*mettre le feu au monde*; 'their flaming villages'=*leurs villages en flammes*; 'the fiery sky', 'sky on fire'=*le ciel embrasé (enflammé).*

SHADOW: 'Shadowy'=*plein (rempli) d'ombre*; *vague.* 'A patch of shade'=*une tache d'ombre*; 'grateful' (shade)=*agréable*; 'in the shade of an ancient oak'=à *l'ombre d'un vieux chêne*; 'in the shadow of the forests'=dans *la pénombre des forêts*; 'to darken the landscape'=*assombrir (attrister) le paysage*; 'darkness'=*les ténèbres* (f.), less poetically, *l'obscurité* (f.); 'It was night'=Night came=*Il fit nuit.* 'It was now full night'=*Il faisait nuit noire.*

§ 13. Colours:

(a) French tends to differentiate colours more exactly than English: 'colour' often=*une teinte (se teinter), une nuance.* The simple term, *vert, rouge*, etc., may seem too crude or too monosyllabic: hence, green=very generally *verdâtre* or *verdoyant*, sometimes *émeraude*; 'threw out a radiance of gold and green' =*rayonnaient d'or et d'émeraude*; 'a red cloud'=*un nuage vermeil* [red hair is *des cheveux roux*]; 'the sea assumed a certain peacock blue shade'=*prenait une certaine nuance bleu paon*; 'the hills lay blue on the horizon'=*bleuissaient à l'horizon*; 'in soft blue shadows'=*en douces ombres bleutées.*

(b) Contrasts which in French might seem violent can be advantageously toned down: 'red and gold' = *rose et or*; 'yellow and red' = *or et rouge*; 'black' = *sombre*. N.B. Purple = *mauve* or *violet*, except in *la pourpre romaine*; crimson or scarlet often = *pourpre*; 'clouds tinged with crimson' = *colorés de pourpre*; *écarlate* is usually a noun, *endosser l'écarlate* (of a Cardinal), *des nuages d'écarlate*, occasionally an adjective, *des rubans écarlates*, *elle devint écarlate*.

(c) Compounds are common. They do not agree with the noun: *une eau vert pâle*; grey-green is *gris-vert* or *d'un gris vert*, but odd compounds like 'green-blue' are better separated (*bleu et vert*). Note *bleu sombre*, more prosaically *bleu foncé*, as opposed to *bleu clair*, light blue; 'dark (bright) green woods' = *des bois d'un vert sombre (vif)*; 'of a bright (staring) colour' = *aux couleurs voyantes (criardes)*; 'light-coloured' = *de couleur claire*; 'snow-white' = *blanc comme neige, d'une blancheur de neige*; 'a layer of dazzling white' = *un tapis éblouissant de blancheur (d'un blanc éblouissant)*; 'clouds of pearl and snow' = *de nacre et de neige*. 'The colour of the clouds *faded* till it was no more than a pink blush' = *se dégradait jusqu'à n'être qu'une lueur rose*.

§ 14. *Sound, Voice*:

SOUND: 'To drown' = *dominer, faire taire, imposer silence à*; 'loud *above* all this tumult' = dominant *tout ce tumulte (vacarme)*; 'an unaccustomed sound' = *un bruit insolite*; 'a faint sound' = *un faible bruit*; 'sound (distant) as of the Ocean' = *la rumeur*; (of waves) 'roar', 'booming' = *grondement*; 'of cannon' (or church bell) = *la voix*; 'reverberate' = *se répercuter*; 'to ring' (of a bell) = *sonner, tinter*; (of a brook) *gazouiller, murmurer; le glouglou*; 'rustle' (of leaves) = *bruissement*, verb *bruire*; 'A sound broke in on the silence' = *vint rompre le silence*; 'quiet' = *tranquille, paisible*.

VOICE: 'In a low voice' = *à voix basse*; 'a little hoarsely' = *d'une voix un peu rauque*; '*said* a few kind words to him' = *lui adressa quelques mots aimables*; 'say a few words' = *prononcer quelques paroles*; 'deliver a speech' = *prononcer un discours*; 'he *whispered* in my ear that...' = *il me dit (chuchota) à l'oreille que...*; 'to shriek' = *pousser des cris perçants*.

§ 15. *Town and Country*:

'Suburb' (immediate) = *le faubourg*; (outer) *la banlieue*; 'in the provinces' = *en province*; 'a country town' = *une ville de province*; 'county town' = *un chef-lieu de département*; 'rich villages' = *des villages prospères*; 'a place' = a district or a village, *un pays*; 'a wall' (stretch of wall) = *un pan de mur*; 'waste land' = *un terrain vague*; 'an open space' = *un espace libre*.

'Mansion' (town) = *hôtel* (*hôtel particulier*); (country) *manoir*, *château*. 'The mansion is a large one' = *Le château est important*; 'feudal castle' = *château fort*. 'That grey stone building' = *Cette maison de pierres grises*; 'built of brick' = *construit en briques*; 'on the ground floor' = *au rez-de-chaussée*; 'first floor' = *au premier*.

'A noble church' = *une belle église*; 'in the aisles' = *dans les bas-côtés*; 'its roof' = *sa voûte* (*la toiture*); 'floor' = *le sol*; 'its door' = *le portail* (pl. *des portails*); 'an ivy-mantled tower' = *une tour revêtue de lierre*; 'ruinous' = *en ruine*; 'the tower rises' = *se dresse* (unexpectedly = *surgit*).

§ 16. *Personal appearance*:

'Physically as well as morally' = *Au physique comme au moral*. 'What is he like to look at?' = *Comment est-il au physique?* 'The family likeness between him and his nephew' = *L'air de famille qu'il y a entre lui et son neveu*.

BEARING: *maintien, manière, contenance*; 'to bend one's back', *fig.* and *lit.* = *courber l'échine*; 'to lean backward' = se renverser *en arrière*; 'to lean forward' = se pencher *en avant*; 'the way he held himself' = *sa façon de se tenir*.

FACE: 'Ill-set features' = *traits mal agencés*; 'in repose' = *au repos, immobiles*; 'receding brow' = *front fuyant*; 'noble brow' = *front pur*; prominent: 'of eyes' = *à fleur de tête*; 'of the jaw' (*la mâchoire*) = *avancée*; 'of the nose' = *proéminent, aquilin, romain*; 'thin-lipped' = *aux lèvres minces*; 'full lips' = *les lèvres fortes*; 'of fair complexion' = *au teint clair*; 'thin (sparse) hair' = *cheveux rares*; (hair) 'straggling' = *en désordre*; 'he has auburn hair' = *il a les cheveux châtains*. 'He is not particularly prepossessing' = *n'a pas l'air particulièrement engageant (sympathique)*.

FIGURE: 'He is a tall thin young man' = *C'est un grand jeune homme mince.* 'He is tall' = *Il est de haute taille;* 'of middle height' = *de taille moyenne.* 'The cook wore too light colours *for her size*' = *portait des couleurs trop voyantes* pour sa taille (corpulence); 'of robust make' = *solidement bâti;* 'well made' = *bien bâti, bien tourné;* (of a woman) *bien faite.* 'He is not bad looking' = *Il est bien de sa personne, il est bel homme;* 'he has short legs' = *il a les jambes courtes.*

§ 17. *Personal Qualities and Defects:*

'A noble action' = *une action généreuse;* 'to perform a task', 'do one's duty' = *s'acquitter d'une tâche, de son devoir.*

BAD, GOOD: 'a good woman' = *une femme de cœur;* 'good people' = *les braves gens; Ce n'était pas une méchante femme.*

IDLE: 'an idle hour' = *une heure de loisir* = 'with nothing to do' = désœuvré; 'her thoughts were not *idle*' = *son esprit ne* chômait *point.* 'It would be *idle* to maintain that...' = *Il serait* vain *de prétendre que....*

KIND: *affectueux, aimable;* 'with his kind smile' = *avec son bon sourire.*

LEARNED: *docte, savant; les érudits.*

MISTAKEN, WRONG: 'You are wrong' = *Vous vous trompez; Vous êtes dans l'erreur.* 'You are *in the wrong*' = *Vous êtes* dans votre tort. 'He took the wrong road' = *Il s'est trompé de chemin.* 'To be wrong about something' = *se méprendre sur;* 'to mistake for' = *confondre avec;* 'a wrong (mistaken) view' = *un point de vue erroné;* 'my watch is wrong' = *ma montre est détraquée.*

CHAPTER II

HOMONYMS, SYNONYMS AND SIMILAR DIFFICULTIES

As languages, French and English are very similar. The differences, numerous and striking though they are, are largely in the detail and the *nuances*. Many common French and English words, especially those directly derived from Latin, are practically identical in form. But these 'homonyms', as they are called, are subtly different in their meaning or their associations. In the early stages of French study it is well to ignore English so far as possible and it is always well to 'think in French'. But it is not possible to proceed far without having to compare and contrast French words with English. Such comparison is not only necessary. It is highly instructive and forms a fascinating subject of study. In Composition the question of the relative values of French and English words is raised in its most acute form. We have to be continually on our guard against real differences disguised as similarities which we might never notice in reading French but which are thrust before us at every moment by the English text.

Another sort of difference must be kept as carefully in mind. It is that between two or more French words of approximately the same sense. They are traditionally called 'synonyms', but no two words ever are completely synonymous. The difference between them may be small, but in translation it is the difference between right and wrong. The accuracy and the merit of a rendering depend largely on a judicious choice between possible variants, and before finally selecting one we must give full consideration to its rivals. The most important of these French synonyms are collected here and, for convenience of reference, classed alphabetically along with homonyms in a single list.

§ 18. **Homonyms, Synonyms, etc.,** are collected in the following list, which must not be taken as exhaustive. It deals exclusively with words occurring in the passages for translation and aims at giving the *fundamental* distinctions. *Homonyms* are printed in italics, **usual translations** in black type.

To ABUSE: *Abuser de* = 'make bad use of'; = 'to revile' **insulter, injurier, couvrir d'injures.**

ACTUAL: 'The actual state of the Reich' = le véritable état du Reich; *actuel* = 'present'; 'at the present day' = à l'époque *actuelle.*

To ADVANCE: *intr.* **Avancer** is the usual word; it denotes simply the action of advancing; **s'***avancer* adds to that some *further idea,* as of dignity, difficulty. Thus *Avancez* toujours; ma montre *avance* de cinq minutes. But Le régiment *s'avance,* musique en tête. With words like *nuit, saison,* etc., both are found: La nuit (s')*avançait.* Note, as a useful phrase, *avancer à pas de géant.*

ADVICE: *Avis* (*m.*) = 'opinion', also a 'notice'; **le(s) conseil(s).**

AGONIZED: **Torturé,** not "agonisé"; *agoniser* (*être à l'agonie*) = 'to be dying'.

To ALTER: **Changer,** *gen.*; *altérer* is 'to change for the worse'; *altéré* = 'impaired'.

AMUSING: **Drôle;** *amusant* = 'mildly amusing', of interest to the mind. See also CURIOUS.

ANCIENT: *Ancien,* see OLD.

ANOTHER: = 'a *further* one', **encore un;** = a *different* one', **un autre;** Donnez-moi *encore une* tasse, j'ai très soif; but, Donnez-moi *une autre* tasse, celle-ci n'est pas propre. 'Others' = **d'autres;** 'of the others' = **des autres.**

APARTMENT. See ROOM.

To APPEAR: **Paraître,** *gen.*; ap*paraître* usually of unexpected, sudden or noteworthy appearance; often = *paraître,* but more *recherché* in tone.

APPEARANCE: *Apparence* (*f.*) = *external* appearance; **apparition** (*f.*) = the action of appearing; **aspect** (*m.*) = the manner in which something presents itself to the eye.

To APPROACH: Approcher = 'to come near'; s'approcher
= 'come nearer', usually personal, but also *la nuit (s')approche*;
se rapprocher = 'to come even nearer'.

ARCH: L'arche (*f.*), of a bridge (also 'ark', *l'arche de Noé*); but
'triumphal arch' = un arc de triomphe.

To ASCEND: Monter, grimper; "ascendre" does not exist,
though *une gradation* ascendante (= 'climax') does.

To ASSIST: Aider, *gen.* secourir, of urgent need; *assister* when
it means 'to assist financially' = giving charity; *assister à* = 'to
attend', 'be present at'; *assister à* la première représentation.
N.B. *Les assistants* = 'spectators', 'bystanders', but *un assistant*
may be 'an assistant'.

ATHEIST: Athée (*m.*); "athéiste" is not French now.

AUDIENCE: L'auditoire (*m.*), les assistants, l'assistance (*f.*),
at theatre, etc.; *l'audience (f.)* = 'sitting of a law court',
'hearing'; solliciter une *audience* (of a king).

BALL: Balle (*f.*) = 'a bullet', or *e.g.* a *tennis* ball; ballon (*m.*)
= an *inflated* ball, *e.g.* a foot-ball; boule (*f.*) larger than *balle*
and usually *solid, e.g.* for a bowling-green; boulet (*m.*) = a
cannon-ball; la bille = *billiard*-ball.

BANK: See SHORE.

BELL: Cloche (*f.*) = a *big* bell; clochette (*f.*) = a *small* bell, *e.g.*
a cow-bell or the 'bell' of a flower; grelot (*m.*) = a small,
metallic, spherical bell, containing a metal 'pea' (on harness,
sledge, cat); timbre (*m.*) = a bell which is struck, not shaken,
e.g. on a bicycle or office table, etc.; sonnette (*f.*) = a bell *in a
house*. To ring the bell, simply sonner.

BLINDNESS: Cécité (*f.*) = physical; aveuglement (*m.*) = moral.

BOAT: Bateau (*m.*) *gen.*; barque (*f.*) often = a *fishing*-boat;
canot (*m.*) = a rowing-boat; embarcation (*f.*), any (small) craft;
navire (*m.*) = a 'ship'; vaisseau (*m.*), often a war-ship; voilier
(*m.*), sailing ship; paquebot (*m.*) = a *liner*, or a Channel packet.

BOY: Garçon (*qualified*) = 'boy', *e.g. petit garçon*; (*unqualified*)
is used only in direct opposition to fille, 'girl': *Collège de
Garçons*; gamin = 'urchin', 'youngster'; élève = 'boy' (*in class*);
collégien = 'boy at school'; jeune homme = 'lad'; enfant
= 'child'; gars = 'country lad', 'big strong fellow', etc.,;

mousse = 'ship's boy'; in military use, *Mes enfants!* = 'Boys !', cp. *Les enfants perdus* = 'the forlorn hope'.

BRAIN: **Cervelle** (*f.*) = physical, *e.g. se brûler la cervelle*; **cerveau** (*m.*), usually metaphorical = 'intelligence'.

To BREAK: **Briser** = 'shatter', gen. including poetic diction (*le cœur brisé*); **casser** is said particularly of a sharp fracture, of something fragile, to '*snap*' (*casser un verre*); **rompre** = breaking *through*, not a 'clean' break (*rompre une canne*), implies resistance, effort, time (cp. Avant que la corde d'argent se *rompe*, que le vase d'or se *brise*, que la cruche se *casse* sur la fontaine, *Ecclés.* xii, 8); **fendre** = to split, cleave (wood, etc.). N.B. The sense of *briser* and *rompre* is often completed by *venir*: Les vagues qui venaient *se briser sur la côte*; Rien ne venait *rompre la monotonie*.

To BRING: **Apporter** = to *carry* to; **amener** = to *lead* to.

BRUTAL: **Féroce**; *brutal* = 'blatant', 'unrefined'; 'the plain truth' = la vérité *brutale*.

BUILDING: gen. **bâtiment** (*m.*); (public) **monument** (*m.*), **édifice** (*m.*); 'a range of buildings' = un corps de **bâtiments**.

To BURY: *Lit.* **enterrer**; **ensevelir** = to deposit in a grave, to bury under something; **enfouir** = to place in a hole in the ground and cover up with earth, *e.g.* a treasure.

CAN, *v.*: **Pouvoir**, of physical ability; **savoir**, of knowledge, skill; thus: 'Je ne *peux* pas nager' [there is not enough depth])('Je ne *sais* pas nager' [I have never learned]. See also §51, CAN.

CANDLE: **Bougie** (*f.*) = the ordinary word = a stearic (until recent times, wax) candle; **chandelle** (*f.*), the word with older associations, specifically = *tallow*-candle; **cierge** (*m.*) = *wax*-candle, 'taper' (*ecclesiastical*).

CART, WAGGON: **Charrette** (*f.*), the usual word; **chariot** (*m.*) = esp. a *farm*-cart or waggon; **fourgon** (*m.*) = military cart for baggage or provisions; **tombereau** (*m.*) = a *tip*-cart. N.B. **Char** (*m.*) = 'chariot'; **wagon** (*m.*) = 'railway carriage'; cp. *wagon-restaurant* = 'dining-car'.

CHANCE: *Chance* (*f.*) = 'luck'; le hasard, l'occasion (*f.*).

CHANGE, *sb.*: *Change* (*m.*) = 'exchange' (of foreign money); **monnaie** (*f.*) = 'small change'; **changement** (*m.*).

CHARIOT: See CART.

CHINK: La fente, l'interstice (*m.*); la crevasse = a cleft in a flat surface; la lézarde = an irregular crack in masonry, recalling a lizard (*un lézard*) running up the wall.

CHURCH: Église (*f.*), *gen.*; mosquée (*f.*), Mahommedan. A French *Protestant* church = temple (*m.*).

CITY: Ville (*f.*), *gen.*; cité (*f.*), specifically = the oldest part of the town; cp. *L'Île de la Cité* in Paris; also, in elevated style, = 'town'.

CLERGYMAN: See PRIEST.

CLIFF: Falaise (*f.*), by the sea only; rocher (*m.*), *gen.*, often inland. Précipice (*m.*) = not 'precipice', but a *void*, a *chasm*, 'abyss'; cp. *tomber* dans *un précipice*)(Eng. 'to fall *over*...'. 'Huge precipices of naked stone' = D'immenses murailles de pierre à nu.

To CLIMB: Monter, *gen.*; escalader, properly, of a *wall*; grimper = to clamber up, not used in elevated style; to climb trees, *grimper* aux *arbres*. Beware of "*ascendre*"; there is no such word in French.

CLOCK: *Cloche* (*f.*) is a bell; pendule (*f.*) = a small clock, standing on the mantelpiece or on a piece of furniture; horloge (*f.*) = a clock in a tower or one in a tall case standing on the floor.

CLOUD: Nuage (*m.*), *gen.*; nue (*f.*), usually *fig.*, implies great height; nuée (*f.*), of clouds in regard to *contents*, 'ready to break', a cloud of locusts, *une* nuée de sauterelles.

COACH: Carrosse (*m.*), voiture (*f.*); = stage-coach, *diligence*.

COAT: Habit (*m.*), usually = *dress*-coat; pardessus (*m.*) = *over*-coat; redingote (*f.*) = frockcoat; veste (*f.*) = jacket; veston (*m.*) = *lounge*-jacket.

COMFORTABLE: *Confortable* [note spelling], said of furniture and houses; 'to be comfortable' = être bien; 'Make yourselves comfortable' = Mettez-vous à l'aise; 'in comfortable circumstances' = *aisé*.

To COMMAND: *Commander* often = to 'order', *e.g.* of a customer in a shop; ordonner. *Fig.* 'Our elders *commanded* no respect' = Nos aînés ne nous *inspiraient* pas de respect.

COMPLAINT: *Complainte* (*f.*) = a 'lament' (elegy, dirge); plainte (*f.*), sujet (*m.*) de plainte, réclamation (*f.*).

CONFIDENCE: Confiance (*f.*)=trust, reliance; confidence (*f.*), used when one confides private matters to another.

To CONQUER: *Conquérir*=to *acquire* by conquest; now usually vaincre; Guillaume, ayant *vaincu* Harold, *conquit* l'Angleterre.

CONTENT, *adj.*: Satisfait='content'; *content*='pleased'. Se contenter+*de* often gives the best translation.

COULD: See above under CAN, and also § 51.

COUNTRY: Campagne (*f.*), like Lat. *rus*='country' as opposed to 'town'; *contrée* (*f.*)=a stretch of country (*geogr.*); patrie (*f.*)='native land'; pays (*m.*), country town; ville (*f.*) de province, *gen.* = 'village', 'district' or 'nation'.

COURSE: Usually le cours (*d'un fleuve, de la vie*); *au cours d'un voyage*; *un cours de physique*; la course = the action of running, race; *une course en voiture*; *faire des courses*, to go errands.

To CROUCH: Se tapir=to *hide* behind by making oneself as small as possible; se blottir, to curl up so as to occupy the smallest possible space; 'crouching'=tapi, blotti, accroupi.

CURIOUS='strange', 'odd', étrange, bizarre; =inquisitive or interesting (to see or know), *curieux*; =funny, *drôle*; a strange (funny) figure=*une drôle de figure*; *Quelle drôle d'idée!*

DAWN: Aube (*f.*) (Lat. *alba*, white), originally the *whitening* of the sky, *early* dawn; aurore (*f.*) (Lat. *aurora* [*aurum*, gold]) =the dawn *in full splendour*; le point du jour=the '*break*', 'peep' of day.

DAY: Jour (*m.*), *gen.*=the day considered as a point in time; journée (*f.*)=the day considered in regard to *duration, contents, happenings.* Similarly *année, matinée, soirée.*

DAYS: *Pl.*=époque (*f.*), temps (*m.*); *e.g.* 'In my predecessor's days'=Du *temps* de mon prédécesseur; 'in those days'=*dans ce temps-là*; 'in the olden days of travelling'=dans les voyages du *temps* jadis.

DEATH: Mort (*f.*); décès (*m.*), the legal or official term or a euphemism; archaic or poet.='passing', trépas (*m.*).

DEFORMED: *Déformé*=distorted; difforme; informe=formless.

DEPLORABLE: *Déplorable*=to be pitied more than to be condemned, cp. '*le déplorable Oreste*'; lamentable.

DESTINY: See FATE.

DEVOTION: *Dévotion* (*f.*)=religious devotion, devoutness; **dévouement** (*m.*).

DILIGENCE: *Diligence* (*f.*)='speed' (also 'stage-coach'); **application** (*f.*).

DRESS, TO DRESS: **Vêtir** (**le vêtement**), to clothe; **habiller** (**un habillement**) implies suitable clothes with some pretension to style; **revêtir**=put on special garment (*e.g. revêtir la pourpre*); **les habits** (*m.*)=*top* clothes.

EDGE: **Bord** (*m.*); of a wood or field, **lisière** (*f.*); along the edge of=**en bordure de**; of a wood only, **à l'orée** (*f.*) **du bois.**

To EDUCATE: *Éduquer*, of *moral* upbringing; **instruire, élever.**

EDUCATION: *Éducation* (*f.*)=moral upbringing; **instruction** (*f.*); **pédagogie** (*f.*)=the science of teaching;=Board of Education, **Ministère** (*m.*) **de l'Éducation Nationale** (formerly, *de l'Instruction publique*).

EMPHASIS: *Emphase* (*f.*)=bombast, pomposity; **force, énergie** (*f.*).

EMPHATIC: *Emphatique*=bombastic; **catégorique, énergique;** emphatically, **très certainement, avec conviction, etc.**

END: **Bout** (*m.*), **fin** (*f.*); often **extrémité** (*f.*); Le couvent est à l'*extrémité* du village.

To ENJOY: **Jouir** (**de**), *gen.*; (oneself)=**s'amuser;** when='to appreciate'=**goûter, trouver;** cp. 'Comment avez-vous *trouvé* la pièce?' **Se plaire** = to take delight in (**à**+infin.).

To ESCAPE: **Échapper à**=evade, *e.g. échapper à la mort*; **échapper de**=to save oneself from, run away from, *échapper de prison*; **s'échapper de** is also used in the latter sense.

EVENING: **Soir** (*m.*), **soirée** (*f.*); see DAY.

EVIDENCE: *Évidence* (*f.*)=ce qui est *évident* (='obvious'); **témoignage** (*m.*).

EXALTED: *Exalté*='excited'; **élevé.**

EXCITING: *Excitant*=stirring *up*, provoking; **captivant,** *e.g. un livre captivant.*

EXERTIONS: [No such word in French.]=**Efforts** (*m.*), **fatigues** (*f.*).

EXPENSE: **Frais** (*m. pl.*) *lit.*; *aux frais de l'expéditeur*='at the sender's expense', 'carriage paid'; to recover one's expenses

2-2

=s'indemniser de ses *frais*; rentrer dans ses *frais*; **dépens** (*m. pl.*), *fig.*; Tout flatteur vit *aux dépens* de celui qui l'écoute.

EXPERIENCE: **Expérience** (*f.*); also='experiment'. Often *sensation*.

FACE: **Figure** (*f.*), usually; **visage** (*m.*), esp. with reference to the *expression*, and in *literary* use; **face** (*f.*), *relig.*, *poet.* (sometimes *iron.*); se voiler la *face*; la *face* de la terre, de la lande, etc. Very often **tête** (*f.*), *e.g.* Les Mahométans prient la *tête* tournée vers la Mecque.

To FAIL: **Manquer de faire quelque chose**=to omit to do a thing; **manquer à**=to fail in one's duty to; for *manquer* see also § 51, WANT; **ne pas réussir (parvenir) à**+infin.=not to succeed; *absolutely*, **échouer**, il a *échoué* dans sa tentative, son entreprise a *échoué*, *échouer* à un examen (au baccalauréat, etc.)

FAMOUS: **Célèbre**, usually; **fameux** often='notorious', '*too famous*' (sometimes *iron.*).

FATAL: **Fatal**='destined', 'inevitable', cp. *fatalement*=inevitably (sometimes=Eng. 'fatal'); **funeste**='bringing destruction'; **mortel**=causing death.

FATALLY: **Blessé à mort**; *fatalement*='inevitably'.

FATE: **Destin** (*m.*)=the unseen power which rules our 'fate'; **destinée** (*f.*)=the 'fate' meted out by that power; **sort** (*m.*)='lot' has both senses.

FAULT: **Défaut** (*m.*)=defect; **imperfection** (*f.*)=slight blemish or shortcoming (in one's character, etc.); **faute** (*f.*)=error (in conduct, etc.).

FIELD: See MEADOW.

FIGURE: *Figure* (*f.*)=the face; **taille** (*f.*)='shape', 'waist'; **chiffre** (*m.*)=a figure in arithmetic; une **silhouette (forme)** humaine. See also FACE and NUMBER.

FLAG: **Drapeau** (*m.*), *gen.*=the national emblem; **pavillon** (*m.*) (*maritime*).

FOUNDATION: **Fondement** (*m.*), solid ground or base on which a building rests; also *fig.*; **fondation** (*f.*), the action of founding a town.

FUNNY: See CURIOUS.

GATE: **Porte** (*f.*); ornamental, iron, leading to grounds, etc., **grille** (*f.*); in fields, **barrière** (*f.*).

GEM: See JEWEL.

GENTLEMAN: **Gentilhomme** (plural *gentilshommes*) = 'of *noble* birth'; **monsieur** = a man of some *social* standing, indicated by his *dress*; often translated by *un homme bien élevé, un galant homme, un homme comme il faut*; in seventeenth-century *un honnête homme*; in recent French use, **un gentleman.**

GHOST: **Fantôme** (*m.*) = an *unsubstantial* apparition; **ombre** (*f.*) = 'a shade'; **revenant** (*m.*) = a spirit that *comes back* from the tomb; **spectre** (*m.*), *gen.* = an *awe*-inspiring vision.

GIRL: **Fille** only when used in direct opposition to *garçon* (*École de Filles*), or when *qualified* (*une jolie fille*); in all other cases = **jeune fille.**

GRAVE: **Fosse** (*f.*), the actual excavation; **tombe** (*f.*) = originally *la fosse* with a stone slab over it, more *gen.* and *poet.* than either *fosse* or *tombeau*; **tombeau** (*m.*) properly = the *monument* raised over the grave; **sépulcre** (*m.*) [note spelling], properly *relig.*, chiefly Biblical and of the ancients.

GUEST: **Invité** (*m.*), **hôte** (*m.*); **le convive,** someone invited to a meal; *l'hôte* can also = host; *hôtesse* = usually 'hostess' only.

HABIT: *Habit* (*m.*) = a coat, see p. 17; **habitude** (*f.*), **coutume** (*f.*).

HAGGARD: *Hagard* [note spelling] = wild-looking, wild-eyed, does not imply fatigue; hence 'haggard' (of the face) often; = **défait, décomposé; les traits tirés.**

HAIR: **Les cheveux** (*m.*), on head, of human beings; = plentiful (mass of) hair, **chevelure** (*f.*); **le poil,** *not* on head, also of animals generally; **crin** (*m.*) of *mane* or *tail* of a horse.

HARDY: *Hardi* = 'bold'; **robuste, vigoureux.**

HEAP: **Tas** (*m.*) often miscellaneous; *des tas de* = piles and piles of; **monceau** (*m.*).

HEART: **Ame** (*f.*), esp. of *religious* or *sentimental* feeling; **cœur** (*m.*), esp. of *affection* or *courage*; cp. *un homme de cœur* = 'a man of courage'; **esprit** (*m.*), of the *intellect.*

HIDE: See CROUCH.

HOLIDAY: Congé (*m.*) = leave of absence, an *occasional* holiday; fêtes (*f. pl.*) = 'festivities', public holiday; vacances (*f. pl.*) = the regular (and longer) 'holidays'.

HOME: Foyer (*m.*) (freq. plural) = properly 'hearth', hence home circle, home life; intérieur (*m.*), le chez soi; pays (*m.*); come home, *rentrer*, bring home, *rentrer les blés, ramener, rapporter*. At home, *chez nous, à la maison*.

HONEST: *Honnête* = 'honourable'; droit, intègre, loyal.

HUMOUR: Humeur (*f.*) = spirits; good humour (temper), *bonne humeur*; *montrer de l'humeur* = show ill temper, *avec humeur* = testily; as opposed to wit (*l'esprit*), *humour* (*m.*).

To IGNORE: *Ignorer* = not to know; ne pas tenir compte de, faire semblant (affecter) de ne pas (re)connaître (voir).

IMPOSE: 'They imposed upon him' = abusaient de lui.

IMPRESSIVE: = *Impressionnant*. "Impressif" is not a French word.

INDUSTRIOUS: *Industrieux* = ingenious, clever; diligent, travailleur, laborieux. ('Laborious' = *pénible*.)

INFANT: *Enfant* = child, boy; petit enfant, bébé.

INGENUITY: *Ingénuité* (*f.*) = ingenuousness; ingéniosité (*f.*).

INJURY: *Injure* (*f.*) = abuse; blessure (*f.*).

JEWEL: Bijou (*m.*), the commonplace word; joyau (*m.*), esp. of *hereditary* or Crown jewels, or *fig.*, *e.g.* of fine buildings.

LABOUR: *Labour* (*m.*) = 'tilling'; *labeur* (*m.*) (*poet.* and elevated style) = 'toil'; travail (*m.*).

LABOURER: *Laboureur* (*m.*) = field-worker, ploughman; ouvrier agricole, terrassier (*m.*).

LADY: Dame; une femme du monde, une femme comme il faut, bien élevée, de bonne famille; young lady, demoiselle, now usually jeune fille.

LAMP: *Lampe* (*f.*), used in a house; lanterne (*f.*), used outside; fanal (*m.*), *e.g.* of a locomotive; phare (*m.*), of a motor-car 'head-light'; un bec de gaz, 'gas-lamp'.

LANGUAGE: Langage (*m.*) = '*diction*', choice of words, the way in which one expresses one's thoughts; langue (*f.*) = the *tongue* (of a nation).

LAP: Usually = **sur les genoux de**...; **giron** (*m.*), *ecclesiastical*; cp. *le giron de l'Église*.

LAST: Often **suprême**, in referring to the end of life (cp. *'le suprême sacrifice'*).

To LEAVE, *trans.*: **abandonner** = 'to desert', 'to leave to its fate'; **laisser**, to leave *behind one*; **quitter** = to take leave of; *intr.*, **partir, s'en aller**.

LECTURE: *Lecture* (*f.*) = reading; **conférence** (*f.*).

LIBRARY: *Libraire* (*f.*) = (now) 'bookseller's shop'; **bibliothèque** (*f.*).

LIGHT: **Lumière** (*f.*), *gen.*, often abstract; **lueur** (*f.*) = 'gleam', 'glimmer', or a subdued, distant glare; **jour** (*m.*), opposed to *nuit*, = *day*light; **feu** (*m.*), of a lighthouse; **les feux**, of a ship, town, railway; **clarté** (*f.*), pure, clear light; **éclat** (*m.*), strong brilliant light.

LINE: **Ligne** (*f.*), of prose; **vers** (*m.*), of poetry.

LOOK, *sb.* and *vb.*: See § 51.

LUXURY: *Luxure* (*f.*) = 'lust'; **luxe** (*m.*).

MARRIAGE: **Noce** (*f.*) usually = wedding festivities, jollification; **mariage** (*m.*) [note spelling] = the state of matrimony, or the ceremony.

To MARRY: **Épouser**, of the bride or bridegroom; **marier**, of the officiating clergyman, or the parents, = 'to perform the ceremony' or 'to give in marriage'; = 'to get married' = *se marier*.

MEADOW: **Pré** (*m.*), **prairie** (*f.*), often just **champ**.

MERCHANT: **Commerçant**, *gen.* = *anyone* in business, *e.g.* 'shop-keeper'; **marchand** = a *small* dealer, *e.g.* 'coster'; **négociant** = trader on a *large* scale, *e.g.* 'wholesale dealer'.

MIND: See HEART.

MIST: **Brouillard** (*m.*) = 'fog'; **brume** (*f.*) = *'mist'* (esp. sea-fog). But these words are often interchanged. **Buée** (*f.*), esp. on window-panes; 'a mist of spray' = *une buée d'embrun.*

MORNING: **Matin** (*m.*), **matinée** (*f.*); see DAY.

NATIVE, *adj.*: **Natif** = (1) 'born in', *e.g. natif de Rouen*; (2) **argent natif** = silver found in a pure state; **natal**; une institutrice origi-naire de Dôle; sa ville **natale**; native customs, **les mœurs indi-gènes**. *Sb.*, **Indigène**, chiefly of coloured people; **habitant**.

NEW: Neuf = 'brand-new' (absolute); nouveau = 'fresh '(relative).

NEXT: **Prochain**, of the immediate future; **suivant**, often in the *past*. 'The *next* week he was dead' = *la semaine* suivante *il était mort*. 'Next day' = *le lendemain*, 'next evening' = *le lendemain soir*. See also under To-MORROW, p. 61.

NIGHT: **Nuit** (*f.*) = any time after bed-time; **soir** (*m.*) = any hour between mid-day and bed-time. 'Last night' = *Hier soir*; 'the preceding night' = *la veille au soir*.

NUMBER: **Chiffre** (*m.*) = a figure (*e.g. le chiffre* 7); **nombre** (*m.*) = quantity (*cardinal*); **le numéro** (*ordinal*), the number of each object in a series; 'A large number of people think that...' = Quantité de gens pensent que....

To OBSERVE, REMARK: = look at, **observer, remarquer**; = say, **dire, faire observer, faire remarquer, faire la remarque.**

OFFICE: **Bureau** (*m.*), *gen.*; **étude** (*f.*), of a notary or a solicitor; = position, function, **charge** (*f.*); *office* (*m.*), often = religious service; **office** (*f.*), a pantry, servants' room.

OLD: **Vieux,** *gen.*; **ancien,** either = 'going back for generations', or = 'former', 'ex-'; **antique** = 'old-fashioned', 'old-world'; **âgé,** of the 'time of life'.

OPPORTUNITY: *Opportunité* (*f.*) = 'opportuneness'; **occasion** (*f.*).

OPPRESS: **Oppresser** = (of weighing on the mind, chest, etc.); **opprimer** (*un peuple*).

To ORDER: See COMMAND.

OTHER: See ANOTHER.

To OVERTAKE: (a vehicle) **dépasser**; *fig.*, **surprendre**; La mort l'a *surpris*.

PAIN: *Peine* (*f.*) = 'effort, trouble'; also mental pain; *faire de la peine* à *qqn*; **douleur** (*f.*), **souffrance** (*f.*); to cause pain, **faire souffrir.**

PAINFUL: = *un contraste* **pénible**; *une opération* **douloureuse.**

PARENTS: Usually = **père et mère**; also **les parents**, which, however, usually = relations, *e.g. prévenir les parents* = inform the next-of-kin.

PART: **Partie** (*f.*), the general word; **parti** (*m.*) = *political* party, also = a *resolution*; he resolved, *il prit* son *parti*)(*il prit le parti de*, made up his mind to...; **portion** (*f.*) = portion; **rôle** (*m.*)

=role, part played; **part** (*f.*) = 'share'; also in *prendre part à, avoir part à, pour ma part* (as for me, for my part), *faire part de qqch. à qqn.*, to inform. . . .

PARTICULAR, *adj.*: *Particulier* = 'private'; **certain.** *Sb.*, **détail** (*m.*).

PAVEMENT: (Of the street) **trottoir** (*m.*). **Dalle** (*f.*) = a stone slab; **pavé** (*m.*) = a causeway, or a place paved with stone.

PENCIL: *Pinceau* (*m.*) = painter's 'pencil'; **crayon** (*m.*).

PENURY: *Pénurie* (*f.*) = lack; une *pénurie* de documents; **misère** (*f.*); **pauvreté** (*f.*).

PEOPLE: *Peuple* (*m.*) = populace, nation; tous les *peuples* du nord; 'the people of Oxford' = les **habitants** d'Oxford; = 'folks', **gens.**

To PERCEIVE: **Apercevoir**, with the eye; s'*apercevoir*, with the *mind's* eye.

PETROL: *Pétrole* (*m.*) = paraffin; **essence** (*f.*) (for cars).

PETULANCE: **Humeur** (*f.*); **irritabilité** (*f.*), **esprit chagrin**; *pétulance* (*f.*) = liveliness.

PHYSICIAN: *Physicien* = 'a scientist' (Natural Philosophy); **médecin.**

PINNACLE: **pinacle** (*m.*), *architectural* = *clocheton*; **cime** (*f.*), **pic.** *Fig. Au* **sommet** *de la gloire.*

PLACE: **Endroit** (*m.*), *gen.*; 'spot'; **emplacement** (*m.*) = 'site'; **lieu** (*m.*), to be used charily; note *avoir lieu*, to take place)(*tenir lieu de* = take the place of, replace; **place** (*f.*) = 'position', 'seat' (in a theatre).

PLEASING: *Plaisant* = 'amusing', 'joking'; **agréable.**

POINT: **Point** (*m.*) (mathematical), freq. = 'dot', 'speck'; **pointe** (*f.*) = the sharp end of something.

POSITION: = 'place' (*mil.*), *prendre position*; = office, see OFFICE.

POST: = 'situation', **le poste**; = G.P.O., **la poste, le courrier.**

PRAIRIE: **Savane** (*f.*); also *prairie*, which usually = meadow.

PRECIPICE: See CLIFF.

PREJUDICE: *Préjudice* (*m.*) = 'detriment'; **préjugé** = preconception.

PREPARATION: *Préparation* (*f.*) = the *action* of preparing; **préparatif** (*m.*).

PRESENT, *adj.*: *Présent*='here and now present'; actuel. See also ACTUAL.

To PRETEND: *Prétendre*=to lay claim to; also=to maintain; faire semblant (de).

PRIEST, CLERGYMAN: Abbé=*anyone* in Holy Orders (R.C.), a *cleric* of any status, as opposed to a layman; curé=the incumbent of a parish (R.C.); pasteur=a *Protestant* clergyman, esp. in France; prêtre=a 'priest', with reference to his function; vicaire=a priest assisting the *curé* of a parish.

PROSPECT: See VIEW.

PROUD: Altier, of hard aloofness; fier, of legitimate pride; hautain='haughty'; orgueilleux='puffed up'; superbe, of pomp and grandeur—only in literary use; vaniteux='vain'. Note F. *vain*='empty'; cp. *de* vaines *paroles.*

To REALIZE: *Réaliser*=to convert into reality, *e.g. un rêve,* to turn into money; se rendre compte (*de qqch.*).

To RECOVER: Recouvrir=to cover *again* or to cover *up* (entirely); recouvrer=to recover, get back. Note also se rétablir (guérir)=to recover health.

To REFLECT: Réfléchir, to give back the colour or light; refléter, to send back the image; renvoyer more general.

REFLECTION: *Réflexion* (*f.*) [note spelling] corresponds to *vb. réfléchir,* reflet (*m.*) to *vb. refléter.* See above, REFLECT.

To REFRESH: *Rafraîchir*=to cool down (*trans.*); se reposer, se récréer.

To REMARK: *Remarquer*='to notice'; =to 'say', see OBSERVE.

To REMEMBER: Se rappeler (*qqch.*), of *active* remembrance; se souvenir (*de qqch.*), of *passive* remembrance. Often=ne pas oublier. 'I remember reading a story'=Je me rappelle avoir lu une histoire.

RESPECTABLE: *Respectable*=worthy of respect; convenable.

REST, *sb.*: Les autres, usually; le reste=the remnant, what is left over.

To RESUME: *Résumer*=to sum up; reprendre, continuer, se remettre à, etc.

To RETURN: Rentrer=to go or come *home*; retourner=to go *back*; s'en *retourner*=to go *back* to one's own *country*; revenir

= to *come* back; cp. 'Il va au fond de l'eau, il *revient*, il *retourne*, il *revient* encore' (Mme de Sévigné).

To RISE: **Se lever** = to rise *from a lying* or *sitting* position; **s'élever** = to rise *clear*, to rise into the air, often *fig*.; **se soulever** (*contre quelqu'un*) = to rise in *insurrection*; **surgir** = to rise up (suddenly) before one, *lit*. and *fig*.

RIVER: **Fleuve** (*m*.) = a river which you *sail* across; **rivière** (*f*.) = one which you *ford*; **ruisseau** (*m*.) = one which you *jump* across. The distinction is chiefly one of *size*.

To ROAR: **Rugir**, of lions; **mugir** (properly = 'to bellow'), of the sea, wind, etc.; **gronder** (with implied menace) of the sea, thunder, etc.; of the voice, **hurler**.

ROCK: **Écueil** (*m*.), specifically, a 'reef' in the sea; **roc** (*m*.), in reference to *hardness* or *stability*; **roche** (*f*.) = a block of stone, sometimes isolated, rising above the surface of the soil; **rocher** (*m*.), esp. in reference to *height*, = 'CLIFF', which see.

ROMANCE: **Romance** (*f*.) = a (sentimental) drawing-room song; **roman** (*m*.).

ROMANTIC: **Romanesque** = removed from prosaic reality (usually of personal temperament, often slightly *iron*.); **romantique** = instinct with romance; specifically, of the Romantic school in literature. Often **chevaleresque**.

ROOM: **Pièce** (*f*.), *gen*.; = living-room, **salle** (*f*.); = (bed)room, **la chambre** (à coucher); classroom = **classe** (*f*.); un *appartement* de cinq pièces = 'a five-roomed flat'.

SAILOR: **Marin**, (1) a sailor, in respect of *seamanship*, (2) a man-of-war's man; **matelot** = an A.B. seaman.

SATIRICAL: **satyrique** = in literary history (*le drame*) *satyrique*; = 'sarcastic', **moqueur, mordant**.

SCENE: **Paysage** (*m*.), used of the natural features of the *landscape*; **scène** (*f*.) = what the spectator sees (including *persons*); **les lieux** (*m*.) = the 'scene', *e.g.* of a murder; 'arrived on the spot' (scene) = *sur le lieu* (de l'incendie); le **théâtre** d'une guerre; **perspective** (*f*.) = 'vista'; **site** (*m*.) = a fine locality, a 'beauty' spot, a 'view'; **milieu** (*m*.) = surroundings; 'life in a new scene' = la vie dans un *milieu* nouveau.

SCHOLAR: **Écolier** = 'school-boy'; **élève, savant, homme d'étude**: scholars = **les érudits**.

SENSIBLE: *Sensible* = 'sensitive'; sensé, de bon sens.

To SHINE: **Briller**, *gen.*, of *steady brilliancy*; **étinceler** = to '*sparkle*'; **luire**, of a dull *gleam* or a glossy *sheen*; **reluire**, of an object *reflecting* the light; **miroiter** = to reflect the light from a *moving* surface, *e.g.* from 'rippling' waters; **resplendir**, of a *glorious* or *dazzling* light.

SHIP: See BOAT.

SHOP: **Magasin** (*m.*) = large shop, stores; **boutique** (*f.*) = small shop.

SHORE, BANK: **Bord** (*m.*), *gen.*, = 'edge, margin'; **côte** (*f.*) = the coast seen from the *sea*; **plage** (*f.*) = a sandy beach; **rivage** (*m.*) of sea or large river; **rive** (*f.*) = the bank of any stream; **berge** (*f.*) = steep bank of river or canal; **grève** (*f.*) = *shingly* beach.

SILVER, SILVERY: (of objects) **argenté**; (of sounds) **argentin.**

SITE: Often **site** (*m.*), see SCENE; **emplacement** (*m.*).

SORROW: **Chagrin** (*m.*) = domestic affliction; **douleur** (*f.*), **peine** (*f.*).

SOUND: **Son** (*m.*), more limited in meaning than 'sound', of musical tone; **bruit** (*m.*).

SPOT: See SCENE.

SQUADRON: *Mil.* **escadron** (*m.*); *naval*, **escadre** (*f.*); *air*, **escadrille** (*f.*).

STAR: **Étoile** (*f.*), *gen.*; **astre** (*m.*), a heavenly body, often the *sun* or *moon*; often *fig.*

STORM: **Orage** (*m.*), a thunder-storm, rain-storm; **tempête** (*f.*), a *wind*-storm.

STORY: **Histoire** (*f.*); = narrative, **récit** (*m.*); of a play, **intrigue** (*f.*).

STRANGE: See CURIOUS.

STUDY, *sb.*: **Étude** (*f.*); **cabinet** (*m.*) d'étude.

To SUCCEED: *Succéder* (+ *à*) = to come after; **réussir**. Georges II ayant *succédé* à Georges Ier, ce ministre ne *réussit* pas à se maintenir au pouvoir. Il fut *remplacé* par X.

SUDDENLY: = in a sudden fashion, **soudainement**; = abruptly, **brusquement**, cp. a sudden attack = *une attaque brusquée*; = unexpectedly, **à l'improviste.**

To SUPPORT: **Maintenir** = to keep a thing in its present position; **soutenir** = to keep in position something which *otherwise would fall*; **supporter** *(moral)* = to 'endure', to 'bear up under'.

To SWELL: **Enfler**, of an unequal, temporary, or accidental swelling; **gonfler**, of symmetrical and regular distending, *e.g. un ballon.*

To TELL: **Dire**; = 'to inform', often **prévenir**; Hettie est venue me *prévenir*; cp. to inform the next-of-kin, *prévenir* les parents; 'He told them of it' = Il le leur **fit savoir**; = relate, **raconter**. 'I told him my adventure' = Je lui *racontai* (or *Je lui fis le récit de*) mon aventure.

TEMPLE: Often *temple (m.)*; see CHURCH; **tempe** *(f.)*, of the brow.

THIN: **Maigre** = 'lean', often *iron.*)(*gras*; **amaigri** = 'emaciated'; 'having *become* thin'; **mince** = 'slim', 'slight')(*gros*; **grêle** *(rare)* = 'fragile', of the voice = 'thin-sounding'; **svelte** = 'willowy', 'slender'; **rare**, of the hair; **fluet** = very slim; **grêle** (of voice *only*).

To THROW: **Jeter**, *gen.*; **lancer**, with some notion of *force* or *aim* = to 'hurl'.

TIME: **Époque** *(f.)* = a *period* of time, in much more common use than 'epoch'; **heure** *(f.)*, esp. with reference to the *clock*; **moment** *(m.)*, a *point* of time, and more precise than *heure*; **temps** *(m.)*, *gen.*

TINT: **Teint** *(m.)* = *natural* tint; **teinte** *(f.)* = *dyed* tint.

TRAFFIC: *Trafic (m.)* = trading; also of railway traffic; of streets, **circulation** *(f.)*.

To TRAIN: *Traîner* = to drag; **élever**, of persons; **dresser**, of animals.

TRAP: **Piège** *(m.)*, of a snare or trap for animals, or *fig.* for persons; 'trapped' = **pris au piège**; **guet-apens** *(m.)* = an ambush.

To TREAT: *Traiter* **en** = to treat as; *traiter* **de** = to call (names); To *call* such a man ambitious ! **traiter** *d'*ambitieux un tel homme !

To TROUBLE: *Troubler* = to disturb, make muddy (as in 'troubled waters'); **déranger**, **agiter**, **embarrasser**. *Sb. trouble (m.)* = embarrassment, confusion, sentimental disturbance; **peine** *(f.)*.

To USE: *User* = to use *up*, wear out; **employer**, **se servir de**, **profiter de**, **user de**.

Vapour: *Vapeur* (*f.*) = 'steam', also 'vapour'; **miasme** (*m.*), **exhalaison** (*f.*).

View: **Perspective** (*f.*) = 'prospect'; **panorame** (*m.*), **échappée** (*f.*) = a vista, glimpse; **vue** (*f.*) = extent of what can be seen from any spot; cette maison a une belle *vue*; also *fig.* See Scene.

Vineyard: **Vigne** (*f.*) = a *field* of vines; **vignoble** (*m.*) = a stretch of country planted with vines.

Visitors: Hardly ever *visiteurs*; **voyageurs, du monde, touristes, clients,** etc.

Vivid: **Vif, vivant, saisissant, net;** "vivide" does not exist in French.

Waggon: See Cart.

To Wake, Awake: Éveiller, réveiller are both used in the literal sense; éveiller is also *fig.*, *éveiller des soupçons*.

Wall: **Mur** (*m.*), *gen.*; **muraille** (*f.*), a stretch of wall; **un pan de mur;** the walls (*e.g.* of Chester), **les remparts.**

Wave, *sb.*: **Vague** (*f.*), *gen.*; **flots** (*m. pl.*), more poetical; esp. in the *open sea*; **brisant** (*m.*) = 'breaker'; **houle** (*f.*) = 'swell', 'ground-swell'; **lame** (*f.*) = a long *ridge* of wave, a heavy 'sea'; **onde** (*f.*), *poet.* = properly the curving wave, often = 'water' of fountains and streams.

Way, Road: **Chemin** (*m.*), *gen.*; **route** (*f.*) = the highway, *e.g. le Code de la Route;* **sentier** (*m.*) = a 'pathway'; **voie** (*f.*), used only in certain expressions, *e.g. la voie ferrée, une voie fréquentée, par la voie des airs,* etc.; **rue** (*f.*) = street, road, *in town;* **ruelle** (*f.*) = 'lane', 'alley'; **allée** (*f.*), of a 'walk' with trees on both sides.

Wild: **Sauvage,** *gen.* = 'uncivilized', 'uncultivated'; **farouche** = 'shunning the haunts of men'; **fauve** = 'resembling the *bêtes fauves*' (= 'wild beasts'); **hagard** = '*wild-eyed*'. Often to be translated by *violent, tourmenté.*

Window: **Fenêtre** (*f.*), *gen.*; **croisée** (*f.*) = an *old-fashioned* type of window, a *casement*-window; often, however, interchangeable. N.B. *La croisée* is properly the *frame* of the window, not the glass; *casser les fenêtres,* but not *casser les croisées.*

Window-pane: **Carreau** (*m.*), originally *diamond-shaped*, now *gen.*; **vitre** (*f.*), larger and less precisely described; **vitrail** (*m.*)

[*pl. vit*raux], also **verrière** (*f.*)=a stained-glass **window** in a *church*; **vitrine** (*f.*)=the 'glass', *e.g.* of a glass case.

To Wonder: **S'étonner**=to be *surprised*; **se demander**=to *ask* oneself.

Word: **Mot** (*m.*), the word considered as an *objective* thing; **parole** (*f.*), *subjective*, the word considered with regard to its *import*, properly the spoken word, =connected words; Histoires sans *paroles*; Ses dernières *paroles* étaient...; La *parole* est un assemblage de *mots*.

Work: **Travail** (*m.*) *gen.*; **tâche** (*f.*)=a particular job; **besogne** (*f.*)=unpleasant labour, drudgery; **œuvre** (*f.*) (of a writer) his achievement; *ses œuvres complètes*)(*un de ses* **ouvrages**=a separate work.

Year: **An** (*m.*), **année** (*f.*). See Day. 'Year in, year out', d'*année* en *année*, d'un bout de l'*année* à l'autre; 'lapse of time', la fuite des *ans*.

CHAPTER III

GRAMMAR AND SYNTAX AS AFFECTING COMPOSITION

Composition is the practical application of grammatical knowledge. In translation from English into French some difficulties of Grammar and Syntax naturally recur much more persistently than others. These are dealt with here in the order of the Part of Speech concerned. It does not of course at all follow that because the English writer has used one part of speech, the translator must use it too. It often happens that French normally expresses the idea by a different part of speech, and examples of this abound in the present chapter. The fact none the less remains that both languages are on the whole similar in their Grammar and Syntax, and that the most convenient system to follow is the traditional grammatical order. Since in Composition we are proceeding from English to French, Grammar and Syntax are treated so far as possible in the order of the *English* parts of speech.

Section I. The Article

§ 19. (*a*) The **indefinite article**, which English uses sparingly in phrases like 'of *a* remarkable beauty', is regular in French, 'A woman of great beauty' = *une femme* d'une *grande beauté*; 'fine rain' = une *pluie fine*; 'brownish smoke' = une *fumée rousse*.

(*b*) Sometimes 'a' is *le* (*la*): 'to run *a* race' = *faire* la *course*; 'with *a* smile on his lips' = le *sourire aux lèvres*. 'It is almost a definition of *a* gentleman to say', etc. = *C'est presque définir* le *gentleman que de dire*. 'There was not *a* trace of' = *Pas* la moindre *trace de*.

(*c*) 'a', 'an', is not to be translated in some stock expressions which have the value of a single verb: 'to put *an* end to' = *mettre fin à* = *terminer*, 'to seek *a* refuge' = *chercher asile* = *se réfugier*, 'to take *a* wife' = *prendre femme* = *se marier*. The omission is constant after *avoir* and *faire*: 'to have *a* good memory'=*avoir bonne mémoire*, 'to make *a* sign'=*faire signe*;

or, usually, in apposition: *C'était à Mégara*, faubourg de Carthage;

or when a noun is used adjectivally: 'Each leaf was first *a* torch and then *an* emerald'=*Chaque feuille était tour à tour flambeau, puis* émeraude. So also 'in the form of *a* cross'=*en forme* de *croix*;

with *quel* in exclamations: 'What *a* fool he had been!'=*Quel* idiot *il avait été!*

in sentences like 'I had never seen *a* more delectable evening' =*Jamais je n'avais vu* soir *plus délicieux (pareil spectacle, chose pareille, chose semblable,* etc.).

§20. (*a*) The **definite article** may have to be translated *ce* for emphasis or clarity: 'As Englishmen worthy of *the* name'= *En Anglais dignes de* ce *nom*; 'the pride which is generally associated with it'=*cet orgueil qui l'accompagne généralement*.

(*b*) It is not found in French

in many old stock expressions:'to come out of *the* ground'= *sortir* de *terre, contre terre, sous terre; sur mer*;

after *en*: 'in *the* shape of a cross'=en *forme de croix*; 'at *the* same time'=en *même temps*; 'in *the* open sea'=en *pleine mer*, en *pleine campagne*, en *plein moyen âge*, etc.; 'during *the* week'=en *semaine*—except in a few traditional phrases like *en l'air, en l'absence de*. N.B. en *Afrique* but dans l'*Afrique du Nord*, dans la *France d'outremer*, etc.;

or in the phrases corresponding to '*the* more': Plus *obscure est la nuit (et)* plus *l'étoile y brille*; 'all *the* more because'=*avec* d'autant plus *d'énergie...que*.

It is freely omitted in enumerations: *Officiers et soldats; Hommes, femmes, enfants*, etc.

§21. The **definite article is required** in French in many cases where English does not require it: 'to go into action' is *aller* au *feu*; 'to go to dances, theatres'=*aller* au *bal*, au *théâtre*; 'This gave him time to do it'=*Cela lui donnait* le *temps de le faire*. N.B. 'You are welcome'=*Vous êtes* le *bienvenu*; St John's Day=la *Saint-Jean*; On a mild St Valentine's morning=*Par une douce matinée de* la *Saint-Valentin*; so, la *mi-été*. In particular, French requires the definite article:

(*a*) with nouns used with a generic sense: l'*or est un métal précieux*; le *tabac*, les *vins*; 'as is usual in *dreams*'=*comme il arrive dans* les rêves;

(b) with abstract nouns (la *vertu*, le *vice*, etc.), except when they are mentioned as names rather than discussed as qualities: 'They are for ever speaking about "liberty".' = *Ils nous parlent toujours* de liberté: 'He cared little for poetry' = *Il ne se souciait guère* de poésie, *i.e.* Poetry was not in his mind at the time of speaking [)(*Il aime* la *poésie* = 'He is a lover of poetry']; 'He made every sacrifice both of *pride and passion* which could interfere with it' = *sacrifiait tout ce qui pouvait le contrecarrer, orgueil aussi bien que* passion;

(c) with names of countries, except when *de* + substantive = adjective: *les vins* de France = *French* wines, *la grande plaine de Bourgogne*;

(d) with names of towns when qualified: l'*Athènes du Nord*, la *Rome impériale*, le *Paris du seizième siècle.* Sometimes the article is a part of the name itself: *Le Bourget, Le Caire,* Cape Town, *Le Cap, Le Havre* [originally *Le Havre de Grâce*], and cannot be omitted; *e.g. Il est né* au *Havre.*

§22. (a) The **Partitive Article** can be omitted with a phrase which is adjectival: 'It is *mere pose*' = *C'est* pure pose; 'The world is *labour and vanity*' = *Le monde n'est que* labeur et vanité. *Dans la ville tout était* inexpérience et confusion. And, rhetorically: *Nous recherchons le bonheur et ne trouvons que* misère et mort.

(b) As regards the omission of the article after *pas*, two cases must be distinguished: (1) *Je n'ai pas de pain*; (2) *Ce n'est pas du pain.* In (1) *pas* negatives only *pain*, and *de* is prepositional; in (2) *pas* negatives the verb, and *du* is partitive. Positive: *c'est du pain*; negative form of the same sentence: *ce n'est* pas *du pain*; so, *L'enfant craint* les *vaches*, ne *craint* pas les *vaches*; *a peur* des *vaches*, n'*a* pas *peur* des *vaches*.

Note also: *d'autres* = some others; *les autres* = the others; therefore '*of* the others' is des *autres*.

SECTION II. THE NOUN

§23. **Gender** is perhaps the most fruitful source of error in French Composition. But the whole mystery is disclosed in a few pages of any French Grammar (pp. 40–63 of *Nelson's*), and the secret can be mastered in a few hours, after which, however, constant vigilance and frequent verification in the Dictionary will be required. The best way to remember genders is to associate the noun with an adjective: *un* grand *arbre, le* Saint *Empire* Romain, *sous des auspices plus* heureux; his rustic dupes = *ses dupes* campagnardes. Nouns showing gender, *e.g. rival, rivale,* should be used in the appropriate form: *Venise (f.) et sa* rivale. Names of ships, especially geographical, create a difficulty which has given rise to much controversy (? *le* or *la Normandie, le* or *la Ville d'Alger*). The French naval authorities announced in 1985 that, so far as they are concerned, the gender is that of the Proper Name: *la Normandie, la Jeanne d'Arc,* etc.

§24. Plurals in English may be singulars in French: 'at right *angles*' = *à* angle droit (but also plural); 'houses under their snowladen *roofs*' = *sous* leur toit *chargé de neige*; 'The ruins' [= ruined castle, etc.] = *la ruine*; 'on Sundays' = *le dimanche*; 'his trousers' = *son pantalon*; so, *son pyjama*; 'cosmetics' = **du** *cosmétique*; 'dialectics', 'politics', 'tactics', etc. = *la dialectique, la politique,* etc.

Or *vice versa*: 'The air' often = *les airs*; 'The birds were chasing each other high *in the air*' = *se pourchassaient tout en haut* dans les airs; *des forêts suspendues* dans les airs; (travel) by air = *par la voie* des airs; applause = *des applaudissements*; fruit = *des fruits*; 'the gilding of the room' = les dorures *de la pièce*; by his *side* = *à ses* côtés; to achieve one's purpose = *arriver à* ses fins (ses desseins); 'slander and gossip' = *les* médisances et *les* potins; 'snow', 'water' are sometimes best translated, *les neiges, les eaux.*

Note: (*a*) 'every' + singular noun (see p. 38, §30, EVERY) usually = *tous les* + plural.

(*b*) *le blé* = grain, *les blés* = standing corn, corn-fields; so *les orges*, etc. Similarly *foin: une charrette chargée de* foin, but *ramener* les foins.

§25. Proper Names. (*a*) When English names of persons have a direct equivalent in French, *e.g.* Maggie, *Margot,* it should be given unless reasons can be shown for the contrary, such as local colour or historical accuracy. For most well-known names there is of course a French form and we must be careful to use it: Elijah, *Élie*; Tiberius, *Tibère*; 'Elizabethan' = *du temps d'Élisabeth.* Note: the (ancient) Germans = *les Germains,* as opposed to *les Allemands.*

(*b*) Historical personages, famous writers, politicians, etc., are commonly referred to in French by their *full* name: *Christophe Colomb,* and often with a hyphen: *Jules-César, Tite-Live, Marc-Aurèle.* Some distinguished Italian names take the definite article: *l'Arioste,* Primaticcio, *Le Primatice, le Tasse,* but *Dante* is more correct, and is becoming more usual, than *Le Dante.*

§26. **Place-Names** should be given their French form even when they are those of English towns: *Cantorbéry, Douvres, Édimbourg.* The chief place-names occurring in our Passages are: *les monts albains, le Mont d'Albe, les Îles Borromées, la Campagne (romaine),* Capreae, *Caprée, l'Île d'Elbe, Gênes, La Haye,* Leghorn, *Livourne, les Îles Marquises* or *les Marquises,* Navarino, *Navarin, Saint-Germain, Saint-Malo* [the word *Saint* is not abbreviated in place-names], *Tandjore, Varsovie.* N.B. The German Ocean = *la Mer du Nord.*

Such names as 'High Street' may be translated (*la Grand' rue*), or left as they stand, according to circumstances. In the latter case, the gender attributed will be that of the usual French equivalent, *e.g. la* 'High Street' because 'Street' naturally suggests **la** *rue.* Our counties and districts are treated as masculine and require the article 'in Surrey' = *dans* le *Surrey, les industries* du *Lancashire, les montagnes* du *Lauderdale.*

SECTION III. THE ADJECTIVE

§27. **Agreement** with the noun, especially with a distant one, must always be kept in mind, and it is well worth while to check the agreement of adjectives (and participles) throughout the whole exercise at a final revision. Compounds expressing colour (see p. 10, §13, (*c*)) remain unchanged: *une eau vert-pâle.* Some adjectives agree, though adverbial in sense: 'newcomers' = *des* nouveaux *venus;* 'the newly wed' = *les* nouveaux *mariés; la* nouvelle *mariée;* 'with the windows *wide* open' = *les croisées grandes ouvertes.* Irregular forms must not be overlooked: *un* bel *homme, quelque* nouvel *obstacle, mon* vieil *ami; des vents* glacials.

§28. The **position** of the adjective is a matter on which it is difficult to lay down definite rules. The most practical rule is to keep constantly in mind that either position is usually possible, and to ask oneself, especially at a final revision, whether one has chosen the better order.

The answer depends on considerations of style and sound, and (apart from the numerous special cases discussed in the Grammars) on individual taste. Note also intentional archaisms, e.g. 'human nature' is generally *la nature humaine*, but often (with reminiscences of Montaigne), *notre humaine nature*.

When there are two adjectives qualifying the same noun, one which normally precedes, should precede as usual, e.g. 'the long warm summers' = *les longs étés chauds*; 'the long stiff leaves' = *les longues feuilles raides*. In other cases both may be placed after the noun and connected by *et*: 'huge black masses' = *des masses énormes et noires*. Difficulties can often be met by the use of another part of speech: 'Dusk fell in *a sultry and expectant silence*' = *Le crépuscule tombait dans* un silence lourd d'attente.

§29. **Adjectival phrases** like 'with the red roofs', or formed from a past participle, 'red-roofed', are translated by *à*+article+noun; *la ville aux toits rouges*; 'a *one-legged* beggar' = *un mendiant à la jambe de bois*; 'a *red-legged* regiment' = *un régiment aux culottes rouges*; 'the *stone-brimmed* swimming pool' = *la piscine au rebord de pierre*.

When = 'with *a*', the French phrase usually takes no article: 'a gold-headed cane' = *une canne à pommeau d'or*.

§30. Some **indefinite adjectives** require special attention because they may occur in almost any sentence and because French usage diverges so widely from English that they have to be variously translated.

ALL, WHOLE: 'all day' = *toute la journée* = the livelong day, *tout le long du jour*; *pendant la journée entière*; 'all night' = *toute la nuit*; *la nuit durant*; 'the whole of humanity' = *tout le genre humain*; 'on the whole' = *en somme*. See also p. 42, §36, ALL pron.

ANY, *adj*,: often simply *un*; 'at any time of the day' = *à toute heure du jour*; 'without any reason whatsoever' = *sans aucune raison, sans raison aucune*; 'in any new aspect' = *sous n'importe quel aspect*; not...any: 'You do not generally associate him with any social class' = *On ne le rattache généralement pas à une classe sociale*; 'He had never done anyone *any* harm' = *Il n'avait jamais fait de mal à personne*; 'He never had *any* trouble with his men'

= *Il n'avait jamais* d'*ennuis avec ses hommes*; 'in the absence of *any* landmark' = *en* l'*absence* du moindre *point de repère*. See also ANY, *pron.*, §36.

EVERY: *chaque* (pronoun *chacun*) restricts the sense very definitely, often to that of 'each', and is appropriate when the reference is to a number which is very limited or has already been specified: '*every* island' = chacune *de ces îles*; '*every* one of us' = *chacun de nous.* Hence 'every', when it applies to an unlimited number, is often *tout*: '*every* thinking man' = tcut *homme qui pense,* or *tous les*: '*every* afternoon' = tout les *après-midi*; '*every* night' = tous *les soirs.* '*Every* calamity which is incident to our nature' = Tous les *malheurs qui peuvent accabler notre humaine nature.*

MANY: See MUCH.

MUCH, MANY: *Beaucoup* is never qualified by *si* or *très*; 'very much' is simply *beaucoup*; 'so much' = usually **tant**; when slightly depreciatory = *autant*; 'hammers falling like *so many* earthquakes' = *marteaux qui s'abattaient comme* autant de *tremblements de terre*; 'with *much* precision' = *avec* une grande *précision*; 'I never felt *so much* affection for' = *Je n'ai jamais éprouvé* une si grande *affection pour*; **maint**: chiefly in stock phrases: *mainte(s) fois, en maintes occasions, à maintes reprises,* etc., and in elevated style: '*many* a pleasant grove' = maint *bosquet riant*; '*many* a poet' = plus d'*un poète*; 'for *many* years' = *depuis* bien des *années,* de longues *années (semaines)*; '*many* (large numbers of) books are useless' = quantité de *livres ne servent à rien*; un grand nombre de; '*many* pillars' = de multiples *piliers, des piliers* innombrables; '*many* houses were empty' = De nombreuses *maisons étaient vides.*

NECESSARY: usually = *il faut.* After *nécessaire* the construction is: (1) *La respiration est* nécessaire à *la vie*; (2) *Il est* nécessaire de *travailler*; (3) *Le travail est* nécessaire pour *réussir.*

ONE, *adj.* and *pron.*: '*One* shower I remember' = *Je me rappelle* (une) certaine *ondée*; 'now in *one* place, now in another' = *tantôt à* tel *endroit, tantôt à* tel *autre*; '*one* principal event in my story' = un des *principaux événements de mon récit*; '*one* of them' = l'un *d'eux*; 'carrying a letter in *one* hand' = *portant dans* une de ses mains; 'He was educated a Presbyterian and remains *one*' = *et il* le *reste.*

OTHER: See p. 34, §22 (*b*).

OWN: See p. 40, §32.

SAME: 'at the same time'='simultaneously'=*en même temps*; ='nevertheless', *cependant*. 'He will find it the *same as* he left it'=dans l'état où *il l'a laissé*; 'It *is the same with* his writings' =*Il* en est de même de *ses écrits*; 'Everybody did *the same*'= *Tout le monde* en *fit* autant.

SOME, FEW: 'some' often simply *un*: 'some stranger'=*un étranger*; frequently *un je ne sais quel*; 'to *some* extent'=*jusqu'à* un certain *point*; 'dear to *some* hearts'=*chers* à certains *cœurs*; 'in *some* measure'=*dans la mesure* du possible; *adv.*=approximately, *quelque* without *s*: quelque *dix francs*. For SOME... OTHERS, see p. 43, §36.

A few, *quelques*: '*A few* stars were out'=De rares *étoiles brillaient*; '*a few* women there'=quelques-unes des *femmes qui étaient là*.

'Few (Not many) people believe it'=*Peu de gens le croient*. 'Few of them'=*Peu d'entre eux*; 'a few years ago'=*il y a quelques années*.

SUCH: 'in *such* contrast'=*dans* ce *contraste*; 'on *such* occasions' =*en* pareilles *occasions*; 'a sea *such as*'=*une mer* comme celle qui; 'on *such* a day as often follows heavy thunder'=*un jour* comme on en voit *souvent après les grands orages*; un de ces jours qui suivent *les grands orages*. 'Did you ever taste *such a* cup of tea *as* Miss Gibbs is this moment handing to Mr Pilgrim?'=*Une tasse de thé* comme *Miss Gibbs* en *tend* une (celle que *Miss Gibbs tend) en ce moment à M. Pilgrim?* 'There is no *such* journey in the world as'=*Il n'est pas de voyage au monde* comparable à. '*Such* people as were there'=Les rares gens *qui se trouvaient là*. '*Such* poignant and *such* terrible effects'=*des effets* si poignants et si *dramatiques*.

VERY, *adj.*: See p. 59, §54, EVEN.
WHOLE: See ALL.

§31. Adjectives in UN- and -LESS are rendered as follows:

(*a*) UN- by *peu*: 'unattractive'=*peu intéressant*; 'so unmanly' =*si peu digne d'un homme*;

by *sans*: 'uninteresting'=*sans intérêt*; 'unmindful of'=*sans se préoccuper de*; 'unmitigated'=*sans mélange*; 'unrelated with' =*sans aucun rapport avec*; 'the unruffled water'=*l'eau sans ride*;

by *in-* (*im-*, *ir-*): 'unearthly'=*irréel* (also *surnaturel*); 'unintelligible'=*inintelligible*; 'unnecessary'=*inutile* (also *superflu*);

'unnoticed', 'unobserved'=*inaperçu*; 'unseen'=*invisible*; 'unwary'=*imprudent*;

or by *dé-, dés-*: 'unpleasant'=*déplaisant, désagréable.*

But sometimes quite a different word is required: 'unobtrusive'=*discret*; 'unvarying'=*uniforme*; 'not unmingled with horror'=*non exempt d'horreur.* 'It is not unlike'=*ressemble assez à.* '*Unscared* by the thunder of the artillery'= Sans se laisser émouvoir *par le tonnerre de l'artillerie.*

(b) -LESS: as for UN-, *e.g.* 'careless'=*peu soucieux, insouciant*; 'countless'=*innombrable*; 'hopeless'=*désespéré*; 'motionless'= *immobile*; 'restless'=*toujours en mouvement*; 'senseless'=*insensé, absurde*; 'spotless'=*sans tache* (also *immaculé*).

§32. 'His own', etc. The **Possessive Adjective** in English is less strictly 'possessive' than in French. 'His', 'her', etc., thus often require to be supplemented by 'own', where French says only *son*. It follows that 'own' can be very generally omitted in translation: 'in my *own* opinion'=*à* mon *avis*; 'in her name and in my own'=*en son nom et au mien.* For emphasis, *propre* can be used, although it is apt to over-emphasize: 'of their own accord'=*de leur propre gré*; other phrases may be more suitable: 'peculiarly his own'=*n'appartenant qu'à lui*; 'motives of her own'=*des motifs qui lui étaient particuliers*; 'his own room'=*la pièce qu'il occupait lui-même.* Or *à lui, à elle*, etc., can be added: 'Not a single *letter of his own* had been preserved'= *Pas une seule de* ses lettres à lui *n'avait été conservée.* This device is in regular use when it would not otherwise be clear to which noun *son* refers: '*His* mother had known *her* father'=*Sa mère* à lui *avait connu son père* à elle. 'He brought them down to *his own level* '=*Il les ramena à* son niveau à lui.

§33. 'His', 'her', etc., are rendered by the definite article: 'with *his* hands in *his* pockets'=les *mains dans* les *poches*; *ils ont dû perdre* la *tête*; accompanied sometimes by the dative of the personal pronoun: 'She bit *her* lips'=*Elle* se *mordit* les *lèvres*; 'that great writer whose works are as a thorn in *their side* '=*ce grand écrivain dont les œuvres* leur *sont comme une épine* au flanc.

In reference to things, French prefers *en*: *cette affaire est délicate, le succès* en *est douteux*='its success'; 'unconscious of what *its* real meaning was'=*sans savoir quelle* en *était la vraie signification.*

'His'+adj.+noun cannot readily be rendered in French: 'his smallest movement' is *le moindre de ses mouvements* rather than *son moindre mouvement*; 'their thirst for news' is *leur soif de nouvelles*, but 'their *general* thirst for news' would be rather *la soif des nouvelles* qu'ils ont tous.

Note: 'a friend of his'=*un de ses amis*; 'every book of his'= *chacun de ses livres*.

Section IV. The Pronoun

§34. **As regards form**: (a) It is obvious when one comes to think of it, which one does not always do, that the French pronoun must take the gender and number of the French noun, not of the English one: 'the ship...she'=*le navire...il*; 'the cat...she'=*le chat...il* (or *la chatte...elle*). 'The Cabinet met yesterday....*They* have decided...'=*Le Conseil des Ministres s'est réuni hier....Il a décidé*, etc. It should also be borne in mind that where 'he' is perfectly clear, *il* may mean 'it'; in such cases the noun should be repeated, or 'he' should be rendered by *celui-ci* or *ce dernier*.

(b) The stressed form is used after a preposition, e.g. with verbs of motion: 'She went up *to him* '=*Elle alla vers lui*; *Si la montagne ne vient pas* à nous, *il faut aller* à elle; and with reflexive verbs: 'He joined *them*'=*Il se joignit* à eux. It may be used as subject of a sentence when there is a sharp contrast: *Lui est parti*, eux *sont restés*.

(c) 'Of him', etc., often=*son, sa*; 'at the sight *of him*'=*à son aspect, à sa vue*. 'To him', etc., is often expressed by a special phrase: e.g. 'They were so grateful *to him* '=*éprouvèrent tant de reconnaissance* à son égard; 'went to meet *him*'=*allèrent* à sa rencontre; 'rushed *after him*'=*se lancèrent* à sa poursuite; 'about him'=*à son propos*; 'about you'=*à votre sujet*.

(d) '-self' is often to be omitted: 'worthy of himself'=*digne de lui*; 'for himself'=*quant à lui, pour ce qui était de lui, pour sa part*; 'itself'=*even* (see p. 59, §54) is usually *même*; 'Do they live in the town itself?'=*Habitent-ils la ville même?* N.B. 'self-command', 'self-discipline'=*la maîtrise de soi*.

§35. **Pronoun added in French.** (a) Where English leaves a pronoun to be understood, French, being by its nature more explicit, often inserts one: 'Yes, he said'=*Oui*, lui *dit-il*.

This is especially marked with *en* and *y*: 'did not think of blaming her' =*ne songea pas à l'en* [=for it] *blâmer*; 'In less time than *it takes* to write it' = *En moins de temps qu'il ne* m'*en faut pour l'écrire; des boutiques telles qu'on* en *voit* encore *en province*; 'He took as good as he gave' = *Il* en *prenait autant qu'il* en *donnait*; 'It was always so' = *Il* en *était toujours ainsi*; 'before he left Wales, never to return' = *avant qu'il ne quittât le pays de Galles pour ne jamais y* [=to it] *revenir; Plus obscure est la nuit et plus l'étoile y brille.*

(*b*) A pronoun is generally added to complete the sense of a verb: 'As had been foreseen' = *Comme on* l'*avait prévu.* One is often inserted to prepare the way for a noun following at some distance: 'I could have asked the bell-ringer for his blessing' = *J'aurais voulu* lui *demander sa bénédiction* à ce sonneur de cloches. Sentences of the type, *Nous* l'*avons eu*, votre Rhin allemand, Il *est gentil*, votre frère, are very frequent, especially in vivacious style.

§ 36. **Pronouns requiring care in translation are:**
ALL: (*a*) 'All *of* us know' = *Nous savons* tous; (*b*) 'The barking of a dog was *all* that disturbed the silence' = *L'aboiement d'un chien troublait* seul *le silence*; 'He told us *all* he knew' = *Il nous dit tout* ce qu'*il savait*; (*c*) 'All who...' = *Tous* ceux *qui....* See also p. 37, § 30, ALL, *adj.*

ANY, ANYBODY, ANYONE: 'They never did *any* of these things' = *Ils ne faisaient jamais* rien *de tout cela.* 'I wonder whether *anybody* ever saw it before' = *Je me demande si* personne *a jamais vu pareil spectacle.* See also ANY, *adj.*, § 30. 'Anyone who' = *Celui qui*; see also p. 44 § 37 (*d*).

BOTH: = *Tous deux*, tous les deux, l'un et l'autre; use whichever of these forms makes the meaning clearest. See also p. 67, § 58, BOTH, *conj.*

IT: (*a*) 'It is' + adjective. 'It is difficult to learn French' = *Il est difficile d'apprendre le français* ['*C'est difficile d'apprendre le français*' is informal or conversational in tone]. But: '*It* (referring vaguely to some noun, *e.g.* to 'French') is difficult to learn' = *C'est difficile* à *apprendre.* Here the construction is the same as in *Comprenez-vous cela?—Non*, c'*est difficile* à *comprendre.* Similarly: Il est *agréable* de *la regarder. Elle est agréable* à *regarder. Il est* is often dropped in vivacious style: *Impossible de continuer.*

A different case is 'it is'+noun. This requires *ce*: 'It is a weakness to seek revenge'=C'est faiblesse (que) de se venger; the use of *que* is optional. 'Nor would it be honest to portray him as an adventurer'=Ce *serait manquer à la vérité que de le représenter comme un aventurier*.

(*b*) The vague 'it' in, *e.g.* 'Was it the sea?' is *ce*: *Était-ce la mer?* In *e.g.* 'Strange as it may seem', 'it' is *cela*: *Si étrange que* cela *puisse sembler*;

(*c*) *Ce* is often used to strengthen *est*: *Et le résultat* c'est *qu'il était là*. But this *c'est* must be employed sparingly. Thus 'The first circumstance was...' is *La première circonstance était* [not 'c'était']. With any other verb than *être*, this vague 'it' is not *ce* but *cela*: *Une promenade*, cela *vous ferait du bien*.

'It' is not to be translated in the type of sentence: 'We did not think *it* possible to see the town'=*Nous ne croyions pas possible de voir la ville*. 'God had not given *it* them to be English' =*Dieu ne leur avait pas donné d'être Anglais*.

SOME, OTHERS. 'Some were sleeping, others playing'=Il y en avait *qui dormaient, d'autres qui jouaient*.

SOMETHING, NOTHING: *Quelque chose* (always in two words)+*adj.* always requires *de*: *Quelque chose* de *nouveau*. So also *rien*: 'There is nothing easier'=*Rien* de *plus facile*. 'Nothing' is sometimes translated by other words than *rien*. 'He takes notice of *nothing* but what produces an effect'=*ne s'attache* qu'à ce qui *produit de l'effet*. '*Nothing* but experience can...'=Seule *l'expérience peut....*

THIS: after a long enumeration... 'is not this'=*n'est-ce pas là?* Similarly '*This* is an elegant solution' or '*This* solution is an elegant one'=C'est là *une solution élégante*. 'This' referring to something about to be mentioned is usually *ceci*; referring to something already mentioned, *cela*: 'After *this* the rumour spread that...', 'It was soon confirmed by *this*: that...'=*Après* cela *le bruit se répandit que*, etc. *Il fut bientôt confirmé par* ceci: que, etc.

§37. **The Relative Pronoun.** (*a*) The objective case of *qui* Relative, dependent on a verb, is *que*, which becomes *qu'* before a vowel. The objective case of *qui* relative dependent on a preposition is *qui* for persons, *lequel* for things: *L'homme* à qui *j'ai parlé*; *Des habitudes* auxquelles *il faut renoncer*. 'Of whom' is *de qui* only in phrases such as *aux ordres de qui*; otherwise it is *dont*, *duquel. Lequel* is used to avoid ambiguity, *e.g.* where *qui* might be taken to refer to either of two antecedents: *Il y a* une edition *de* ce livre **laquelle** *ne se vend pas.* Even then a change of order allowing *qui* to come next its antecedent is preferable to the clumsy *laquelle*: *Il y a de ce livre une* édition qui *ne se vend pas.* A preposition + 'which' is often rendered by *où*: 'the period *at which*...' = *l'époque* où....

(*b*) The relative pronoun takes the gender, number *and person* of the antecedent: 'It was you who said it' = *C'est vous qui l'*avez *dit.* In French it must be placed immediately after its antecedent, wherever it may happen to stand in the freer order of English. It is not usually tacked on directly to *Nul,* etc.: 'None who has seen' = *Nul* parmi ceux *qui ont vu.*

(*c*) It should be remembered that in a relative clause inversion is frequent (see p. 49, §50), and that in a simile the conditional tense will be required (see p. 50, §46).

(*d*) WHO = 'Anyone who' = *Celui qui.* Note: 'I am one whom men love not' = *Je* suis de ceux *qu'on n'aime pas.* 'I am not among those who think...' = *Je ne suis pas* de ceux *qui pensent....*

§38. WHAT = THAT WHICH = *ce* **qui**, when subject of the verb in the relative clause; = *ce* **que**, when object of the verb, e.g. *Ce* qui *me plaît, c'est ce* que *vous m'avez dit*;
    in comparisons, etc. = *Ce que* as a neuter form acting as a complement to the verbs *être, devenir, rester,* etc.: 'The sound of the waves was to the ear *what* the landscape was to the eye' = *Le bruit des vagues était pour l'oreille* ce que *le paysage était pour les yeux* [cp. 2 : 4 :: 4 : 8 = 2 *est à* 4 ce que 4 *est à* 8]. 'What that journey was [= meant], nobody has been able to say' = Ce que fut *ce voyage, personne n'a pu le dire.*

(*adj.*) in exclamations = *Quel.* '*What* was his surprise,' usually negatively = Quelle *ne fut pas sa surprise.* '*What* a fool he had been!' = Quel *idiot il avait été!* Or *Qu'il avait été imbecile!* Or *Sot qu'il avait été!*

Referring to a whole phrase: 'If—*what* seems to me very doubtful—he had really...' = *Si*—ce que *me paraît très douteux*—*il avait réellement....* So also WHICH in, *e.g.,* '*which* was not often' = ce qui *n'était pas souvent.*

§39. THAT used vaguely = *Que* (predicative). 'The great poet *that* Racine was' = *Le grand poète* qu'*était Racine*; 'He died like the gallant soldier he was' = *Il mourut en brave soldat* qu'*il était*. This *que* may connect two phrases, and provides then an idiomatic translation of 'who were', 'which were', *e.g.* 'Those two white specks *of* huts in the distance' = 'which the huts were' = *ces deux points blancs* qu'*étaient les huttes*.

SECTION V. THE VERB

§40. Verbs **transitive** in English may be intransitive in French and *vice versa*: *changer* d'*habit*. 'The road changed its character' = *changea* de *caractère*; 'to decide it' = en *décider*; *ce qui va décider* de *l'issue de la lutte*; 'to display an energy' = *témoigner* d'*une énergie*; *jouir* d'*une bonne santé*; 'to resist' = *résister* à; 'to succeed' = *succéder* à; *Henri III succéda à Charles IX*; *il ne survécut pas longtemps à son frère*. If a passive form is required, another verb or verbal phrase must be found, *e.g.* 'The attack, repeated and *resisted* so bravely, slackened in its fury' = *L'attaque renouvelée et* soutenue (reçue) *si bravement perdit de sa force*; 'Fear was *succeeded by* fascination' = *La frayeur* fit place à *l'ensorcellement*.

Vice versa: 'to flee *from* death' = *fuir la mort*; 'to trample *on* something' = *fouler quelque chose aux pieds*.

N.B. 'to climb trees' = *grimper aux arbres*; 'to touch' = *toucher*, *e.g. la harpe*)(*toucher à* = 'meddle with', *N'y touchez pas, il est brisé*.

§41. Construction of **Reflexive Verbs**: The reflexive pronoun may be the direct object and therefore in the accusative case: *se voir* = 'to see oneself'; or it may be the indirect object and therefore in the dative: *se parler* = 'to speak *to* oneself'. The past participle agrees with the reflexive pronoun in number and gender, when it is the direct object: *elles se sont* vues, but not when it is the indirect object: *elles se sont* parlé. Hence *les générations qui se sont* suivies, but *les générations qui se sont* succédé.

To make it clear that the reflexive means 'each other' and not 'themselves' it is usual to add *mutuellement*, or the formula *l'un l'autre*: *Ils s'encourageaient* mutuellement; *ils se critiquent* les uns les autres.

Many verbs can be used reflexively or not. The reflexive form is generally more personal: *e.g.* 'to take a bath' is *se baigner*; 'the dipping branches (of a tree)' = *les rameaux* baignant *dans l'eau*;

'to creep'=se *glisser*; *e.g. se glisser dans son lit*; 'to slip', 'glide'=*glisser*. N.B. 'to sink' (general) is s'*enfoncer*; 'to sink into mud, sea', etc.=*enfoncer*.

§42. The English **passive** is often translated (*a*) by the active, especially with *on*: 'It *was said* that...'=On *disait que*...; 'They were *left to* their own devices'=On les laissa *à leurs propres ressources*. The active is unavoidable in French when the French verb is one which is intransitive only: 'He *was distrusted* by everyone'=*Tout le monde* se défiait de *lui*.

(*b*) by the Reflexive: 'to be drowned'=se *noyer*; 'The ridge of the mountains *was silhouetted* on the grey sky'=*La crête des montagnes* se découpait *sur le ciel gris*; 'That *is* not done'=*Cela ne* se fait *pas*; 'Its influence *was* felt'=*Son influence* se faisait *sentir*; 'A dreadful sound *was* heard'=*Un bruit effroyable* se fit *entendre*;

(*c*) by means of *voir*. The English *passive infinitive*, when it is governed by another verb, is in French **active**; 'I have seen this play *acted*'=*J'ai vu* jouer *cette pièce*. This use of *voir* translates a passive and is useful for avoiding a cumbrous form: *e.g.* 'I desire his life *should be prolonged*'=*Je désire* voir prolonger *sa vie*; 'If you go to their house, you *will be expected* to jump the baby'=on s'attendra à vous voir *faire sauter le dernier-né sur vos genoux*; 'Conditions which one cannot expect *to be kept*'=*qu'on ne saurait s'attendre* à voir respecter; 'The Church wanted to have Latin spoken by everyone'=*voulait* voir *tout le monde parler latin*; 'in expectation of more work for her cause'=*dans l'attente de se* voir *confier d'autres tâches pour sa cause*. *Voir* also provides a convenient means of strengthening a passive: 'I *was obliged* to go'=*Je* me vis forcé *de partir*.

§43. (*a*) **Agreement of Tenses.** The rule is that a **Primary** tense in the Main clause must be followed by a **Primary** in the Subordinate clause; a **Historic** must be followed by a **Historic**. Thus, *Je* **veux (voudrai)** *que vous* **fassiez (ayez fait)** *cela*. *Je* **voulais** (*voulus*, **ai** *voulu*, **voudrais**, **aurais** *voulu*) *que vous* **fissiez, eussiez fait** *cela*.

In French Composition the rule should be observed, except in conversational passages, but it may be safely relaxed to avoid ill-sounding forms like -*assions*, -*assiez*. French does not, however, permit the free English use: 'If it *rains*, I *should* not go out'. This must be expressed with either: *S'il* pleut je ne sortirai *pas*, or else: *S'il* pleuvait, *je ne* sortirais *pas*. In Composition awkward situations should be prevented from arising, whenever this is possible, *e.g.* 'The gentlemen replenished their glasses, Mr Pilgrim attempting to give his the character of a stirrup-cup by observing that he "must be going"'. We should here have to choose between a very pompous '*qu'il* fallait *qu'il s'en* allât' and the free-and-easy '*qu'il* fallait *qu'il s'en* aille'. The situation is saved by a change to Direct Speech: '*il* faut *que je m'en* aille': *Ces messieurs remplirent leurs verres, M. Pilgrim essayant de donner au sien le caractère de coup de l'étrier en remarquant "Il faut que je m'en aille"*.

§44. **The English Past.** In translating an English Past one must always think of the different mood or tense which French syntax may require: 'They found nothing which *resisted* them' = *Ils ne trouvèrent rien qui leur* resistât.

As a rule the tense is in French the Past Indefinite or the Past Continuous ('Imperfect') or the Past Historic. The Past Indefinite may be used in any circumstances except formal narrative style to describe an action which took place at any time in the past: *J'ai vu mon ami l'autre jour*. The Past Continuous *describes*, the Past Historic *relates*. The Past Continuous is much overworked by English students and is a constant source of error. It is true that impressionist writers use it very freely, but imitation is dangerous. The practical rule is: when the action takes a new step forward, use the Past Historic; when the tone is that of description, use the 'Imperfect'. In familiar style the Past Historic is never used: 'Yesterday we saw'=*Hier nous avons vu*. On the other hand, it is required much more often in French Composition than students well trained in oral practice are apt to assume—and not only in formal narration or in very 'historical' contexts. For example, it is obligatory in Passage 105. Its most characteristic use is of an action thought of as a single fact, as a unit, as a result or as something which took place in a period of time considered past and ended, *e.g. Bonaparte ne connaissait pas, il ne* connut *jamais les Anglais* = 'did not know [at the time referred to], the English and *never did know* them' [his career being viewed as a complete unit in the past].

N.B. If the verb of the Main clause is in the Past Historic, the tense in a Subordinate Clause introduced by *quand, dès que*, etc., will be the Past Anterior: 'When he *understood* it, he called for his friends' = *Quand il l'eut compris, il appela ses amis.*

§45. **The English Future** is translated:

by *aller* when the reference is to an immediate future: 'I will tell you what has happened' = *Je* vais *vous dire ce qui s'est passé*; 'You are about to hear' = *Vous* allez *entendre.* So also the Future in the Past: 'the functions he would be [= was about to be] called upon to fulfil' = *les charges qu'il allait être appelé à assumer*;

by a *Present* Subjunctive after verbs of fear, etc.: 'I am afraid it *will* rain' = *J'ai bien peur qu'il ne* pleuve. 'They can have no success which *will* last' = *Ils ne peuvent avoir de succès qui* soit *durable.*

In translating 'will', care is required to distinguish 'will' = 'wish' and 'will' merely expressing the future, especially after 'if'. See p. 67, §59, IF.

§46. **The French Conditional** (Future in the Past) can be used in statements the truth of which is not guaranteed: *D'après les journaux une crise ministérielle* serait *imminente.* In translating 'would have', it must be remembered that the tense in the Main Clause is required also in Subordinate Clauses introduced by *lorsque*, etc., and in Relative Clauses: 'Anyone who *had* seen him would have thought him mad' = *Celui qui l'aurait vu l'aurait pris pour un fou.* In Relative Clauses depending on a noun used in a simile, this use of the Conditional is constant, *e.g.* 'the first hours of a sudden sorrow when the human soul is *like* one who *has been* deposited sleeping among the ruins of a vast city and *wakes up* in dreary amazement, not knowing', etc. = *les premières heures d'une douleur soudaine, où l'âme d'un homme* ressemble à *un être qui, déposé endormi parmi les ruines d'une vaste cité,* serait *à son réveil plein de morne stupéfaction, ne sachant,* etc.

§47. **The English Present Participle** is often translated: (a) by a Past Participle, when denoting physical positions: 'clinging' = *accroché, cramponné*; 'hanging' = *suspendu*; 'leaning' = *accoudé, appuyé, penché*; 'lying' = *couché, étendu*; 'kneeling' = *agenouillé*; 'sitting' = *assis*; 'sleeping' = *endormi*;

or (b) by a different part of speech: '*hoping* to reach the frontier' = *dans l'espoir de gagner la frontière*; '*purposing* to do so' = *dans l'intention de le faire*; 'the *rejoicing* trees' = *les arbres en liesse*; 'the *retreating* soldiers' = *les soldats en retraite*'; '*struggling* armies' = *des armees aux prises*; 'a good man *struggling* with adversity'=*un homme de bien* aux prises *avec l'adversité*; '*succeeding* generations'=*les générations* qui se sont (s'étaient) succédé; '*aspens waiting* for the breeze'=*des trembles* dans l'attente *de la brise*; '*weeping* multitudes'=*des multitudes* en pleurs;

or (c) by *dont*—whether to avoid an unpleasant succession of -*ant*'s or to make a sentence more French: 'the factories, their smoke *blackening* the sky, clashed and flamed'=les usines, dont *les fumées* noircissaient *le ciel, éclataient et flamboyaient*.

§48. **The verbal form in -ing** is usually rendered: (a) by the Infinitive: 'I saw him *coming*'=*Je l'ai vu* venir; (b) by a Relative Clause: *Je l'ai vu* qui venait; (c) by *à+infin.*, 'He remained *gazing*'=*Il restait là* à regarder. 'There is a good deal of satisfaction *about feeling* miserable'=*On a une certaine satisfaction* à se sentir *foncièrement triste*. 'Merely by looking at him' =*Rien qu'à le regarder*.

§49. **The English Past Participle** is often elegantly turned by a relative: '*Influenced by* such speeches, Cromwell...'= *Cromwell*, qu'influençaient *de tels discours*...; or by *sans+infin.* (see p. 39, §31, UN-), Sans *se* laisser *influencer par* or by another part of speech, especially when in French the participle might refer to the wrong word: 'shaded by'=*à l'ombre de*. It should be noted here (see also p. 61, §54, ONLY) that a past participle cannot be modified by *ne...que*.

§50. **Inversion** is obligatory in French in such short parentheses as 'It is said'=*dit-on* [note the useful variants: *ajouta-t-il, demanda-t-il, s'écria-t-il, fit-il, reprit-il*] and in sentences introduced by *peut-être* (except when used with *que*), *aussi, toujours* [='nevertheless'], *à peine, en vain*. In the case of the latter two, a better translation is often given by *c'est à peine que, c'est en vain que*.

In a Relative Clause, inversion is usually an elegance: 'a town which so many great men have made famous'=*ville qu'ont rendue célèbre tant de grands hommes*. This is especially desirable when the verb is monosyllabic or only a part of *être*—which would make a very feeble ending. Inversion also occurs in indirect questions and in sentences introduced by *c'est...que*: *ce n'est pas pour lui que chantent les oiseaux, que*, etc.

But it is rarer in French than in English, and we must beware of carrying into French purely English (or German) customs of inversion: 'Nor could he,' 'Never did I see,' etc. Thus 'So cool and easy had his mind become' is *Son esprit avait atteint un tel calme et une telle aisance.*

N.B. 'Great though he was, Chatham yet...' is rendered by *si* or *quelque* + subjunctive: Si *grand* (or Quelque *grand*) *qu'il fût, Chatham...pourtant.* 'Rich as he is' (or 'However rich he is') = Tout riche qu'il est (or *soit*).

§51. Some Verbs and Constructions.

To ASK: 'To ask a question' = poser (or *faire*) *une question.* 'To ask *for* bread' = demander *du pain.* 'Ask someone the way' = *demandez le chemin à quelqu'un.* 'I ask (permission) to speak' = *Je demande à parler,* occasionally with *de, e.g. Il demande de ne pas nous accompagner* = 'to be excused from going with us'. 'To ask someone to do something' = *demander à quelqu'un de faire quelque chose.*

To BECOME: Never use *devenir* + adjective when a specific term is available, *e.g.* 'to become accustomed to' = *s'accoutumer à;* so *s'enrichir, pâlir, vieillir.* 'The road *became* little better than a lane' = n'était plus *guère qu'un sentier;* 'become' sometimes = *se transformer en.*

To BEGIN: *Commencer* usually takes *à* before an infinitive— except where *à* would cause a hiatus: *L'eau* commençait à *tomber; Une cloche* commença de *tinter.*

To BELIEVE: *Je puis à peine* y *croire* = 'believe it is real'; le *croire* = 'give credence to it'. *Je crois* en *Dieu. Croyez-vous* aux *revenants?—Non, je n'*y *crois pas.*

CAN: *Je* ne saurais *vous le dire.* Often 'can' is to be omitted, especially with *comprendre, entendre, voir.* 'I *cannot* understand it' = *Je n'y* comprends *rien. Je vous* entends, *mais je ne vous vois pas. Je ne* retrouve *pas mon chapeau.* See also p. 16, §18, CAN. *Possible* is a useful variant: 'There *can* be no certainty on such a point' = *Aucune certitude n'est* possible *là-dessus.*

To CONSIST: *Consister* takes *en* (*dans*) before a noun, *à* before an infinitive: 'The cottage *consisted of* only one dark narrow room' = *ne consistait qu'en une salle étroite et obscure;* 'His defence *consists in* denying the facts' = *consiste à nier les faits.*

COULD: This may mean either 'was able' or 'would be able' and may be *pouvait, pourrait, a pu,* or *put,* according to the sense of the English. In Indirect Speech the proper form is most easily

determined by asking oneself what the Direct form would have
been: 'He was speculating on what sort of shelter the birds *could
find*' [=peuvent-ils *trouver?*, therefore in the past tense, *pouvaient*] = *Il se demandait quelle sorte d'abri les oiseaux* pouvaient
trouver. 'I have done what I *could*'=*J'ai fait ce que* j'ai pu.
'I stayed as long as I *could*'=*J'y restai aussi longtemps que je le*
pus.

'Could', like 'can', need not be translated in *e.g.* 'On the right
we could see,' etc.=*A droite on* voyait. 'All at once he could
see...'=*Tout d'un coup il* vit. It may sometimes be best rendered by a different turn of phrase: 'after doing all he *could* to,'
etc.=*après avoir fait* tout son possible *pour*. 'I *could* not sleep
because of the noise'=*Le bruit m*'empêchait de *dormir*. 'I *could*
not get to sleep'=Impossible de *dormir*.

N.B. 'She wished she *could* lie down to sleep upon the waves'
=*Elle aurait voulu* pouvoir *s'étendre sur les flots*.

'I *could have* done it, but...'=*J'*aurais pu *le faire, mais....*
'You would have paid everybody if you *could*'=*si vous* aviez pu.

To DARE: 'I dare say'=*J'ose dire, Je croirais bien, Je me figure
bien.*

To DECIDE:'We had *decided to* stay'=*Nous avions* décidé de
rester. 'That telegram *determined me to* start'=*Cette dépêche* m'a
décidé à *partir*. 'At length I *decided to* tackle him'=*Enfin je* me
suis décidé à *l'aborder*. 'We *are* quite *decided to* stay on'=*Nous
sommes bien* décidés à *rester*.

N.B. The Active form means merely to 'decide', the Reflexive
means to come to a decision after some hesitation or with some
reluctance.

To DEFY: 'Had *defied* the authorities *to*'=*avait* défié *les
autorités* (*avait* mis *les autorités* au défi) de.

To DOUBT: The construction is usually with *que*; 'to doubt
if...'=*douter que....* [+ Subjunctive]. 'No doubt but that':
'There was no doubt *but that* the spring had come at last'=nul
doute que *le printemps* ne fût *enfin* venu.

To ENABLE: 'Which enabled me'=*grâce auquel*.

To EXPECT: 'I *expected* to see you'=*Je* m'attendais à *vous voir,
Je* comptais *vous voir*. 'What *do you expect* of him?'=*Qu'*atten-
dez-vous *de lui?*

To FEEL: 'He *would have felt* inclined to'=*Il* se serait senti

4-2

disposé à le faire. 'We *feel* as though we could'=Il nous semble que *nous pourrions.*

To FIND: 'I *find* myself growing more careful'=*Je* me prends à *devenir plus soigneux.* 'I *find* that that way is cheaper'=*Je* constate *que....*

To GET: 'To get caught'=*Se faire pincer;* cp. *se faire pendre, tuer,* etc.

To GLANCE: See LOOK.

To HAPPEN: *Avoir lieu, se produire, survenir.*

To HELP: 'I can't *help* thinking'=*Je ne puis* m'empêcher de *penser.*

To INSIST: 'They *insisted on* my baggage being weighed first'= *Ils* insistèrent pour qu'*on pesât mes bagages les premiers.*

To LACK: See WANT.

To LEAVE: See p. 23, §18.

To LIKE: 'I should *like* her to be happy'=*Je* voudrais *la* voir *heureuse.* 'How do you *like* my hat?'=*Comment* trouvez-*vous mon chapeau?* 'He *likes* talking to the neighbours'=*Il cause* volontiers *avec les voisins.*

To LOOK, GLANCE, STARE, WATCH, etc. (*vb.* and *noun*): Turned sometimes by a verb, *e.g. regarder,* sometimes by a noun, *e.g. air, regard* or *œil (yeux).*

(*a*) 'To take a last *look* at it'=*le* regarder *une dernière fois;* 'to *stare at* someone'=*le* dévisager, *le* regarder fixement; cp. contempler quelque chose *avec stupeur;* '*glancing* towards them'=*les* regardant *à la dérobée;* '*looking* mild reproach at him'=*le* regardant *d'un air de timide reproche;* 'He looked away'= *détourna ses regards.*

(*b*) '*peers down* at him'=glisse *sur lui* un regard (*e.g. timide*); 'he kept *peering* warily about him'=*il* jetait *sans cesse autour de lui* des regards *inquiets;* 'if we *look back* at it'=*à y* ramener nos regards; 'he *looked* into the darkness'=*il* plongea ses regards *dans...;* 'to *look back* into another age'=plonger du regard *dans un autre siècle.*

(*c*) 'He *looked* round him'=*Il* jeta les yeux *autour de lui;* 'I had *looked up* to the stars'=*j'*avais levé les yeux *vers les étoiles;* 'to *stare*' (*intrans.*), *ouvrir de grands yeux;* 'to *look at* (*watch*) someone's movements'=*le* suivre des yeux.

Notice also various other turns of phrase: 'The King, who *looked* bronzed...' = qui paraissait *bronzé à la suite de sa courte croisière à bord du* Victoria et Albert; 'She *looked* tired' = avait l'air *fatiguée* [*avoir l'air* is treated as if = *paraître*, and the participle agrees]; 'was grim-*looking*' = présentait un aspect *sévère*; 'the window *looks on to* the street' = *la fenêtre* donne *sur la rue*; 'eyes which *look through* the blast' = sondent *la tempête*; 'one must *look back on* the palace' = *il faut* se retourner pour contempler *le palais*; 'I turned *to look for* the mountains' = *je me tournai* pour retrouver *la montagne*; 'eyes *peering through* the fog' = *qui* scrutent *le brouillard*; 'made them *look like* = *leur* donnait l'apparence de. 'To watch: = be on the look-out for' = *guetter*: 'snakes *watching* their prey' = *serpents* guettant *leur proie*; '*on the watch* (watching) for a chance to' = guettant *l'occasion de*— Infinitive; = 'to keep an eye on', *surveiller*; 'to watch' *intr.* = not to sleep, *veiller*. 'Two *anxious-looking* gentlemen' = *deux messieurs* à l'air soucieux.

To MAKE + Infinitive: *Je l'ai fait boire*)(*Je lui ai fait boire du vin*; 'made her forget her worries' = lui *fit oublier ses soucis*. 'It made the windows flame' = faisait rutiler *les fenêtres* or *Les fenêtres* en rutilaient. So *voir, entendre, laisser.*

+ Noun: 'made me an author' = *fit* de moi *un auteur*; 'Policy made him the ally of France' = *La politique fit* de lui (*or* en *fit*) *l'allié de la France.* 'Our elders, whom a trick of fate had made our betters' = *Nos aînés*, dont *un caprice du sort avait* fait *nos supérieurs.*

+ Adjective: 'make rich', 'make stronger', etc., *enrichir, fortifier; rendre* should never be used when such verbs as these are available.

'This deportment made the back of his jacket hang' = *faisait que*... + Indicative.

MAY, MIGHT: 'I *may have been* mistaken' = Il se peut que *je* me sois *trompé* or *J'*ai pu *me tromper*; 'he avoids topics that *may* irritate' = *il évite les sujets qui* risquent de *froisser*; 'they *may* well detain our attention' = méritent de (peuvent bien) *retenir notre attention*. Sometimes rendered by *peut-être*: 'He thought the birds *might* shelter under the leaves' [Direct Speech: 'They may' = *s'abritent peut-être*] = *s'abritaient* peut-être.

To MOVE: *Intr. se mouvoir, se remuer, se déplacer, bouger; trans. avancer, reculer; lever, soulever; remuer* = 'shake', 'stir'. N.B.

déménager = 'to move out of a house')(*emménager* = 'to move into'.

MUST: (*a*) indicating probability: 'That *must* be true' = *Cela doit être vrai*; 'You *must have* made a mistake' = *Vous avez dû vous tromper*. There is a subtle distinction between *a dû* and *doit avoir*. *Il a dû finir* = 'Probably he has finished'. *Il doit avoir fini* = 'His work must be over now'. The first stresses the action; the second, the resulting state.

(*b*) denoting compulsion: 'I *must* go this evening' = *Je dois partir ce soir*; also *Il faut que je parte ce soir*.

Often = a future: 'I *must* find an easier job' = *Il me faudra trouver un emploi moins fatigant*.

OUGHT: 'You *ought* to tell me' = *Vous devriez me le dire*. 'You *ought to have* told me' = *Vous auriez dû me le dire*, *Il aurait fallu me le dire*. The distinction between *Il aurait dû finir* and *Il devrait avoir fini* is as above, MUST (*a*).

To PREFER, RATHER, etc.: 'I *prefer* you not to stay', 'I had *rather* you didn't stay' = J'aime mieux *que vous ne restiez pas*; 'I *would rather* die than *do* so bad a thing' = J'aimerais mieux *mourir que de faire une si mauvaise action*.

To SEE: Were seen, *paraissaient*. 'The costume I was used to *seeing him in*' = *Le costume que j'avais l'habitude de lui voir*.

IT SEEMS: = (*a*) *Il paraît que...* = 'I am told that, It is said that...'; (*b*) *Il semble que...* = 'The appearances are that...'; (*c*) *Il me semble que...* = 'My opinion is that...'. In (*a*) and (*c*) the Indicative is used, in (*b*) generally the Subjunctive. (*d*) Beware of making *sembler* personal; 'I *seem* to know you' is *Il me semble que je vous connais*. 'One *seemed* to hear' = *On croyait entendre*; 'I *seem* to be looking through'... = J'ai l'impression *de regarder à travers*....Cp. 'It [the town] *seems* gloomy' = *Elle donne une impression triste*. (*e*) 'It would seem' usually = *Il semble*, simply. (*f*) 'It seemed as if nothing moved' = *Rien ne semblait bouger*.

To SIT: 'Mary *sat* at her window watching the stars' = *Marie, assise à sa fenêtre, regardait les étoiles*. 'There *sat*, enthroned behind the counter, a splendid mature Arlésienne' = *Derrière le comptoir, trônait une splendide Arlésienne d'âge mûr*. 'To *sit* for an artist' = *poser*. 'He bade them *sit down*' = *Il les fit asseoir*; to sit = take one's place at table, *prendre place*. 'Speaking from where he *sat*' = *de sa place*. See also p. 48, §47.

To STAND: Usually *se trouver*, unless a standing position is definitely intended, = standing and not sitting; *se tenir* (*debout*) is personal; *se dresser*, *dressé*: 'angels *standing* like flames about his death-bed' = *anges* dressés *comme des flammes autour de son lit de mort*; *être debout*; 'They *stood* side by side' = *Ils étaient* debout *côte à côte*. 'I must *stand* for a moment and look at' = *Il faut que je* m'arrête *un moment et que je regarde*.

To STARE: See LOOK.

To TAKE: To *take place*, see HAPPEN. 'To take *one's* place' = *s'installer*; (*mil.*) *prendre position*. 'To *take* a walk, a step' = faire *une promenade, un pas*; 'to *take* one's dinner' = manger *son dîner*; '*Take* this letter to the post' = Portez *cette lettre à la poste*; '*Take* these gentlemen to the office' = Conduisez *ces messieurs au bureau*; 'He is *taking* the horses to the water' = *Il* mène *les chevaux à l'abreuvoir*; 'to take away' = 'carry away', *emporter*; = 'lead away' = *emmener*; 'How long do you *take to* get here?' = *Combien de temps* mettez-vous à *venir?*

To TELL: See p. 29, §18.

THERE ARE, HAVE BEEN, etc.: (*a*) The verb is always singular: *il y avait*, also *il est* (literary or poetical) and *il était*, which is restricted to the fairy-tale formula 'There was once upon a time' = *Il était une fois une bergère*, etc. N.B. *Il y a* eu [not '*été*'].

(*b*) 'There was' frequently indicates a new step forward in the narration and is therefore Past Historic in French: '*There was* a sudden silence' = Il y eut *un silence subit*. '*There was* a noise' = Il y eut (On entendit) *un bruit*. It is a point only too easily overlooked in translating.

(*c*) For the colourless *il y avait*, etc., careful writers substitute a more expressive verb, with or without the impersonal *Il*: 'In the middle of the grass there was a tree' = *poussait* (or *se dressait*) *un arbre*; 'In the street *there is* a monument' = *Dans la rue* se dresse *un monument*; '*There was* there that damp smell which...' = Il régnait *là cette odeur humide qui....*

(*d*) To be distinguished from *Il y a*, etc., is the rather subtle use of *C'était*, etc., in, *e.g.*, *Ce* n'étaient que *parfums et concerts infinis*, where *Ce* refers to something not yet expressed, to the state of matters about to be described = '*We perceived* only perfumes and harmonies unending.' This usage takes the place of verbs like *apercevoir, entendre, sentir, voir*, and provides a neat idiomatic translation of, *e.g.*, 'Next *comes* the sea' = *Puis* c'est *la mer*. 'Then *came* Chicago' = *Puis* ce fut *Chicago*; '*All the talk was of* entertainments' = Ce n'étaient que *fêtes et bals*.

To WAIT: 'To wait for someone' = *attendre quelqu'un*; 'waiting to be called' = *attendant* d'être *appelé*.

To WANT, To BE IN WANT OF: 'He was in want of money' may be expressed in three ways: *Il* avait besoin *d'argent*; Il lui manquait *de l'argent*; *L'argent* lui manquait. 'I didn't *want* [= wasn't anxious] to see him' = *Je ne* tenais *pas* à *le voir*. For *manquer* see also p. 20, §18, FAIL.

To WATCH: See LOOK.

To WELCOME: *Accueillir, souhaiter la bienvenue à quelqu'un*; 'to be welcome' = *être le bienvenu*.

WILL, *vb.*: See p. 67, §59, IF.

WOULD: (*a*) As auxiliary; Past tense of 'will' = *future in the past*; (*b*) Verb = 'resolved': 'He *would* not go' = declined to go, *Il ne* voulut *pas aller*; (of persistent refusal) *se refuser* à; (*c*) Imperfect of Repetition: 'He *would* often say' = *Il* disait *souvent*. N.B. 'Guiding them *as he would*' = *à son gré*.

SECTION VI. THE ADVERB

§52. Verb + Adverb (or + **Preposition**). The use of adverbs—and of prepositions—to modify or supplement the sense of a verb, especially a verb of motion, is one of the most striking characteristics of English.

Similar uses do exist in French, *e.g.* in *s'en aller* the old adverb *en* (Lat. *inde* = thence) corresponds exactly to 'away'. This *en* may be required where there is nothing corresponding to it in English: *e.g.* to reach the point = en *venir à l'essentiel*; en *finir avec la vie*. The adverb is often included in the verb itself: 'to go *down*' = descendre; 'to carry *away*' = *emporter*; 'The post *carried with it* the title of King' = com*portait le titre de roi*; 'The minutes went *by*' = *s'écoulaient*; and phrases like *jeter* en bas = 'to cast down', are not uncommon in French; cp. 'She stole *out* from the tent' = *Elle se glissa* hors *de la tente*.

But as a rule English verb + adverb must be rendered:

(a) by choosing a verb which contains in itself the full meaning. Thus 'to break *through*'=*percer*; 'to go *up*'=*monter*; 'drawn *on*'=*attiré*; 'The citadel *looks down* upon the city'=*La citadelle* domine *la ville*; 'The river *sweeps round* it'=*la* contourne; 'winding *in and out*'=*serpentant*; 'The fence was *blown over*'=*La palissade fut* renversée *par le vent*; 'to make up'=*compléter, composer*. So also prepositionally: 'to run (walk, ride, etc.) across' are just *traverser* ('A weasel *ran across* the path'=*Une belette* traversa *le chemin*); 'to swim across' is *traverser à la nage*; 'He *took* him *through* the village'=*lui* fit traverser *le village*; 'Birds *passed through* the air'=fendaient *l'espace*; 'he *followed* him *up* the steps'=montait derrière *lui les marches*;

or (b) by transposing; thus '*ran in and out*'=entra et sortit *en courant*; cp. prepositionally, Daudet, *La Mort du Dauphin*: "*Des chambellans* montent et descendent en courant *les escaliers de marbre*"='are *running up* and *down* the marble stairs'. 'A beetle *went swinging by*'=*Un hanneton* passait d'un vol lourd; 'the gondola *shot out* into the open lagoon from...'=*la gondole*, sortant *de...*, s'élançait *dans...*. Prepositionally: 'The dark rolling column *pressed on and up the hill*'=*La sombre colonne roulante* poursuivit sa marche et gravit la colline; 'who *limped* gloomily *up the gangway*'=*qui, l'air sombre*, gravissait en boitant la passerelle.

§53. The adverbial form in -**ment** is convenient. But it is heavier than English -*ly* and soon becomes intolerable, *e.g.* in the translation of a sentence containing several adverbs and a few participles in -*ant*. Partly for that reason a different mode of expression often produces better French. Thus:

(a) **avec**+Noun: 'bravely'=*avec courage*; 'carefully'=*avec soin*, as well as *courageusement* and *soigneusement*; 'cautiously' =*avec précaution* (*prudemment*); 'indignantly'=*avec indignation*; 'lovingly'=*avec amour*; 'miraculously'=*par miracle*; 'temperamentally'=*par tempérament*.

(b) **de façon**, etc.: 'disagreeably'=*de façon désagréable*; 'The birds had sung *erratically* and spasmodically'=de façon *intermittente et spasmodique*. Also *d'une façon, d'un air, d'un ton, d'une voix*, à pas *rapides, lents*, etc.

(c) by the adjective:
'disconcertingly odd'=d'une *bizarrerie déconcertante*; 'Clive was in a *painfully anxious* situation'=*dans une situation* pénible

et dangereuse; 'Shadows crept *slowly* here and there'=*Des ombres* lentes *rampaient çà et là*; 'he died *early*'=*il mourut jeune.*

Note also (*d*) 'definitely'=*pour de bon (définitivement)*; 'equally'=*non moins*; 'the *equally* Italian palace'=*le palais* non moins *italien*; 'the *equally* honest waggoner'=*le* non moins *honnête charretier*; 'fitly'=*à juste titre*; 'intensely: *intensely* conscious of one thing'=*conscient* au plus haut degré *d'une chose*; merely: 'a crowd which collected *merely* for amusement' =*une foule réunie* dans le seul but *de s'amuser*; 'quietly'=*à loisir*; 'rarely'=*Il est rare que*+Subjunctive; 'secretly'=*en cachette*; 'strangely'=strange to say, *chose étrange*; 'successively' =*les uns après les autres, tour à tour (successivement).*

§54. Some Adverbs.

ABOUT: 'just *about* long enough for a man to'=à peu près *le temps qu'il fallait à un homme pour*; 'when *about* to leave'=au moment de *partir*; sur le point de *s'en aller.* 'You are *about* to hear'=*Vous* allez *entendre.*

AGAIN: Often neatly rendered by prefixing re- to the simple verb: 'He sat down *again*'=*Il se rassit*; 'He opened his eyes *again*'=*Il rouvrit les yeux*; 'passing over and over again'=*passant et repassant.* When the idea of 'again' is more or less implicit in English, French generally makes it explicit: *Je ne retrouve pas mon chapeau*; 'to take breath'=*reprendre haleine*; so, *retomber.* N.B. 'Once again'=*Une fois de plus.*

ALL: *tout*='quite', 'all' is invariable before a vowel, but agrees before a feminine adjective beginning with a consonant: '*Quite* astonished, *all* trembling, she replied...'=Tout *étonnée*, toute *tremblante, elle répondit....*

AT LEAST: (*a*) Making a restriction: *Il le croit*, du moins *il le dit.*
   (*b*) Stating a minimum: *Il gagne* au moins *mille francs par semaine.*

AT ONCE: *tout à coup, tout d'un coup, au premier abord, d'emblée*; = 'once and for all', *une bonne fois, une fois pour toutes.*

AWAY: See p. 3, §2.

BEFORE: Remember *auparavant*: 'He speaks French better than *before*'=*Il parle le français mieux qu'*auparavant.

EVEN: usually *même*, or *jusqu'à*, which also render 'very': '*even* the look of (the *very* look of) the heath' = *l'aspect* même *de la bruyère*; '*even* (the *very*) climate' = jusqu'au *climat*. *Même* often comes after: '*even* those who' = *ceux même qui*. N.B. 'She was the *very* opposite of her sister' = *elle était* tout l'opposé *de sa sœur*.

EVER, NEVER: = *Toujours*; sometimes = *un jour*; *sans cesse*; *sans répit*; *sans trêve*. '*If* ever...' = *Si* jamais. 'For ever' = *à jamais, perpétuellement*. 'And *never* more so than' = *et surtout*.

FAR: = 'distant', see p. 3, §2; '*far* into the night' = avant *dans la nuit*; '*far from* numerous' = peu *nombreux*; 'So far from...' = Loin de, bien loin de: '*So far* from helping them, their tactics do them harm' = Bien loin *de les avancer, leur tactique leur fait du tort*.

HALF: = *à moitié* or *à demi*: e.g. *à moitié mort, à demi mort*; 'What we had but *half*-felt before' = *ce que nous n'avions auparavant éprouvé qu'*à demi; 'was *half* inclined to believe' = *n'était pas* loin de *croire*; '*half* an orb... now a whole one' = une moitié d'orbe... *puis un orbe entier*.

HARD: 'to work hard' = *travailler ferme*; 'drink hard' = *boire sec (ferme)*; 'running *as hard as he could*' = *courant* à toutes jambes.

HARDLY: *difficilement*: 'I can *hardly* believe it' = J'ai peine à *y croire*; *ne...guère*; 'such as the earth can *hardly* parallel' = presque *sans pareil sur la terre*.

HERE: often *là* rather than *ici*: 'Is Mr X *here*?' = *M. X est-il* là? 'There is nobody *here*' = *Il n'y a personne* là. 'Here' is often emphatic and is then C'est *ici* (*là*) que.

HOW: 'How is it that...?' = *Comment se fait-il que...*? In narrative style: 'You will remember *how* once upon a time', etc.; simply *que*.

HOWEVER + *adj*.: See §50.

JUST: '*just* as far' = tout *aussi loin*; '*just* in the middle of the wood' = juste *au milieu du bois*; 'on *just* such a night' = *par une nuit* en tout point (toute) *semblable*; 'with *just* sufficient talent to' = *avec* juste *assez de talent pour*; = 'barely' = *tout juste*: colloq. *tout simplement*.

LIKE: See p. 65, §57.

LITTLE: 'He cares *little* for appearances' = ne *se soucie* guère *des apparences*; 'his work is *little else* than...' = *n'est*, à peu de chose près, *que*....

MEANTIME: = 'in the interval' = *en attendant*; = 'while this was going on' = *sur ces entrefaites; pendant ce délai.*

MERELY: See ONLY.

MORE: 'of *more than* common height' = *d'une taille* qui dépassait *la moyenne*. 'The more...the more' = *Plus...plus*: Plus *on a d'argent*, plus *on a d'amis*. See also p. 33, §20 (*b*). Note the use of *ne* after a comparative: *plus beau que je* n'*avais* (also ne l'*avais*) *pensé*. When the main clause is negative, *ne* is not used: *Cela n'est pas aussi facile* qu'on croit.

MOST: 'In a most violent way' = either (*a*) *D'une façon* très *violente*, or (*b*) *D'une façon* des plus *violentes*, or (*c*) *De la façon* la plus violente. [Never 'd'une façon la plus violente', which is not logical enough to be French]. After a superlative the preposition required is *de*: 'the most splendid region *on* the globe' = *la plus belle région* du *globe*.

MUCH: See p. 88, §80.

NEVER: See EVER.

NOT: *pas* is omitted with some verbs: *Je ne puis (saurais), Je ne savais où,* and in rhetorical questions: *Qui ne connaît ce tableau? Que de fois ne l'a-t-on décrit?*; 'not to be equalled upon earth' = *qui n'a pas son pareil au monde.* 'Not that...', 'Not but that...' = *Non que, Non pas que* + Subjunctive. 'Not less than' = *non moins que*.

   'not', when used parenthetically, is *non pas* or *non point*: *Car c'était*—non pas *son frère*—*mais lui-même*; in this use, '*and* not' is et non, or et non pas. [Not 'et pas', though *pas* alone may be used, more or less colloquially.] Before an infinitive ne pas: *Pour ne pas mentionner....* It often improves a sentence to avoid the negative form; *e.g.* '*not* to mention' = *sans parler de, sans compter*; 'a woman of *not more than* thirty-eight' = *de trente-huit ans* au plus. 'The lake glittered, but *not* so brightly as the stars' = avec moins d'éclat *que les étoiles.* 'Who is so happy as *not to know* these feelings? = *Qui est heureux au point d'ignorer ces sentiments?*

NOW: See TO-MORROW.

OFTEN: The sense is sometimes eked out by *arriver*: 'They *often* leave the matter where it was' = Il leur arrive souvent *de laisser le sujet là où il en était.*

THE ADVERB 61

ON: 'It went *on* snowing=*Il neigeait* toujours; 'They marched *on*' = *marchaient* toujours (*continuaient à marcher*); 'He *rode* slowly *on*' = continua *lentement sa route*.

ONLY: *Ne...que, seulement, uniquement, si ce n'est*; = 'barely'; see JUST.

Ne...que is not used with past participles; 'a bank founded *only* five years ago' = *une banque fondée* il y a seulement cinq ans. When 'only' modifies a verb, *faire* is required with *ne...que*. 'She *only* smiled' = *Elle ne* fit *que sourire*; also *Elle* se contenta de *sourire*. 'She did not speak, but *only* went up to him' = *ne dit rien mais alla* simplement *vers lui*.

Notice also *d'autant*: 'which *only* made the heat more welcome' = *ce qui rendait la chaleur* d'autant *plus agréable*.

OVER: 'When the dance was over' = *Lorsqu'on avait fini de danser*. 'All is over' = *Tout est fini*.

PERHAPS: is used more loosely than *peut-être*: 'perhaps fifty' = environ *cinquante*; sometimes *le cas échéant*.

RATHER: = 'fairly', *assez*; = 'if anything', *plutôt*: 'rather troublesome' = *plutôt gênant*.

So: *tellement*: 'so very much smaller' = tellement *plus insignifiant*; 'so early' = *d'aussi bonne heure*; '*So* is it when...' = *Il en est de même quand*...; 'so doubtful did it seem to me' = tant *cela me paraissait douteux*.

SOON: *bientôt* is not qualified by *si* or *très* (cp. *beaucoup*); say *si tôt, très tôt*: 'soon after sunrise' = peu après *le lever du soleil*. 'He will *soon* be back' = *Il* ne tardera pas à *rentrer*. *Il va revenir*.

TO-MORROW, YESTERDAY; Now, NEXT: Speaking from the standpoint of to-day, use *demain, hier, maintenant, jusqu'ici, prochain*. Speaking from the standpoint of some day in the past, use *le lendemain, la veille, alors, jusqu'alors, suivant*. 'I *now* understood' is, according to the speaker's standpoint, Maintenant *je comprenais*, or *C'est* alors *que je compris*. 'The next minute' = *Un instant après*)(*L'instant d'après*. 'The *next* train' = *le train* suivant; *la gare* suivante.

'Now' is often = *A présent, déjà, aujourd'hui, à l'heure actuelle*, or, when = from now onwards, *désormais*; now...now is *tantôt...tantôt*.

Too: 'was *too* glorious *to be* distinctly *seen*' = était trop *éblouissant* pour qu'on pût le voir *distinctement*; '*La guerre est une chose* trop *sérieuse* pour qu'on *la* laisse *aux militaires.*' Briand.

WHERE: *Où* (except interrogatively) should be used only in reference to an antecedent already expressed, *e.g. l'endroit* où; otherwise, use *là* où: '*Where* you see my white plume' = La où *vous verrez mon panache blanc.* [Tense as for WHEN.]

YESTERDAY: See TO-MORROW.

SECTION VII. THE PREPOSITION

§55. **French Prepositions,** notably *à* and *de,* **are weaker** than their usual English equivalents. They will not stand as much strain and may require to be strengthened by additional words: 'the path *to* the threshold' = qui mène jusqu'*au seuil*; 'the cut *on* his forehead' = *la coupure* qu'il avait *au front*; 'Gaston *in* his forest costume' = vêtu de *son costume de forêt*; 'They do not throw lights *from* unexpected quarters' = *ne jettent pas de lumières* venant de *points inattendus*; 'I learned to speak *from* my family' = *J'ai appris à parler* en écoutant *ma famille*; 'my own idea *of* poetry' = *l'idée* que je me fais *de la poésie*; 'the confusion *of* his mind' = *la confusion* qui régnait dans *son esprit*; 'his bulldog growling *at* his distant voice' = *son bouledogue qui grondait* en entendant *sa voix lointaine*; 'Intent on the gain and glory *of* new conquests' = *Avide des richesses et de la gloire* que lui vaudraient *de nouvelles conquêtes.*

Such expansion is particularly necessary in translating a sentence where *de* could mean either 'of' or 'from'. Thus 'the view *from* the walls' should be *la vue* du haut des *remparts* in contexts (*e.g.* in the title of a passage) where the reader might understand *la vue des remparts* to mean 'the sight of the walls'.

§56. **A following preposition,** usually omitted in English, must be inserted in French (*e.g.* 'forgetful of everything except the danger which...' = *oublieux de tout sauf* du *danger qui...*), unless the two ideas are very closely linked (*e.g.* swearing to *conquer or die* = *en se jurant* de vaincre ou mourir = Death-or-Victory).

The English practice of making a noun depend on two different prepositions is un-French. The noun is usually given with the first preposition and a pronoun with the second: 'He is useful *to*, and beloved *by*, his children' = *Il est utile à ses enfants et il en est aimé.*

§57. Some prepositions. French and English differ every moment in their use of prepositions. It seems impossible to state general rules which will be helpful; *e.g.* the French preposition for 'towards' may turn out to be anything except *vers*: 'He set his dilapidated hat on with a knowing inclination *towards* the left ear' = *Il mettait son chapeau délabré avec une inclinaison maligne sur l'oreille gauche.* Cp. a colloquy between two workmen putting up a telegraph pole: '*Est-il d'aplomb? — Non, il penche sur la droite.*' But it is at least possible to enumerate some very common uses, as follows:

ABOUT: 'About this time' = Vers *cette époque*; '*About* two o'clock in the afternoon' = Vers *deux heures de l'après-midi*; 'my anxiety *about*' = *mon inquiétude* au sujet de; for *about him* = *à son sujet, à son propos, à son endroit*, etc., see p. 41, §34 (*c*); 'the people *about* him' = *les gens* (*personnes*) qui l'entouraient (de son entourage); 'There is something unpleasant *about* them' = Ils ont *quelque chose de déplaisant.* See also, p. 58, §54, ABOUT, *adv.*

AFTER: 'Closing the door *after* him' = *Fermant la grille* derrière lui; 'running *after* them' = *leur courant* après.

AGAINST: 'The waves dashing *against* the shore' = *qui venaient se briser* sur *la grève*; against (of colours), *sur, sur le fond de.*

ALONG: '*Along* the path' = Le long du *chemin*; '*along* (= *alongside*) the sea' = en bordure *de la mer*; often the meaning is rendered in the verb: 'Stretching his arms *along* his body' = *A*llongeant *les bras sur le corps.* 'Then he *walked along* the pool' = *Puis* il longea *la mare.*

AMONG: 'As long as he was *among* us' = *Aussi longtemps qu'il* fut des nôtres; *au nombre de.*

AT: '*At* the same time' = En *même temps*; = at one and the same time, *à la fois*; '*at* normal times' = en *temps normal.*

BECAUSE OF: *à cause de*: 'He was very unpopular *because of* his pride' = *Il était très impopulaire* à cause de *son orgueil*; = as a consequence of, *par suite de*; '*Because of* his misfortunes, he gave up his social ambitions' = Par suite de *ses malheurs, il renonça à....*

BEFORE: of place, *devant*; of time, *avant*.

BELOW: *au-dessous de*; more distant or less concrete, *en dessous de*.

BY: '*By* the light of'=à *la lumière de*; 'by the look of'=à *l'aspect de*; 'One recognized him *by* (*from*) his walk'=*On le reconnaissait à sa démarche*; 'That is seen *by* (is apparent *from*) his attitude'=*Cela se voit à son maintien*; 'a play *by* Rostand'= *une pièce* de *Rostand*; 'the post is held *by* this precarious tenure' =en vertu de *cette précaire tenure*; 'to howl *by* the hour'=*hurler des heures* durant.

EXCEPT: *excepté, sauf, à l'exception de*; often *si ce n'est*.

FOR: 'Peace was not to return *for yet another year*'=*ne devait pas être rétablie* avant un an, *ne devait être rétablie* qu'un an après, *ne devait pas revenir* d'une année encore; '*for* miles and miles, not a human habitation'=pendant *des milles et des milles pas une seule habitation humaine*; 'Tom had not heard from home *for* some weeks'=Depuis *quelques semaines Tom n'avait pas eu de nouvelles de chez lui*.

FROM: (*a*) '*From* 1870 to the present day'=Depuis 1870 *jusqu'à nos jours*; (*b*) '*From* his childhood (onwards)'=Dès *son enfance*; (*c*) '*From* the walls'=Du haut des *remparts*; (*d*) 'Tell him *from* me'=*Dites-lui* de ma part; 'more emphatic declarations *from* the British Cabinet'=*des déclarations plus catégoriques* de la part du *Cabinet britannique*; 'to hide something *from* someone'= *cacher quelque chose* à *quelqu'un*; so *arracher* à.

IN: *Dans* is of very restricted sense, almost=inside: *tenir un crayon* dans *la main*)(*l'épée* à *la main*. '*In* the castle'=au *château*)(dans *le château*='inside' (cp. '*in* Paris'=à *Paris*)(dans *Paris*=within the city boundary); so au *salon*, au *lit*, au *milieu de*; '*in* the service of Germany'=au *service de l'Allemagne*; auquel *cas*, au cours de *mon dernier voyage*; '*in* the sun'=au *soleil*, also, sous les rayons du *soleil*; '*in* Morocco'=au *Maroc*; '*in* his stead'=à *sa place*; '*in* his opinion (eyes)'=à *son avis*, à *ses yeux*; '*in* time to be present at'=à *temps pour assister à*; '*in* spring'=au *printemps*; 'to take an interest *in*'=*s'intéresser* à.

'*In* this way'=de *cette façon*; 'Paris is the most beautiful city *in* the world'=*Paris est la plus belle ville* du *monde*; 'About two o'clock *in* the afternoon'=*Vers deux heures* de *l'après-midi*.

Used of time, *in*=at the end of=*au bout de, dans*: *J'irai à Londres* dans *huit jours*; =within the space of is *en*: *Les maçons ont construit ce mur* en *huit jours*.

Sous: 'to see things *in* a new light'=*voir les choses* sous *un jour nouveau*; '*in* the rain'=sous *la pluie*; 'disappearing *in*'= *disparaissant* sous; '*in* the reign of Louis XIV'=sous *le règne de Louis XIV*.

Sur: 'one *in* a hundred'=*un* sur *cent*; 'I saw it *in* the newspaper' (prospectus, etc.)=*Je l'ai vu* sur *le journal (la brochure)*. 'He saw *in* him a friend who'=*il reconnut* en *lui un ami qui*.

INTO: Since *en* is vaguer than *dans*, it is much more likely to be the translation for 'into', especially after *se changer (transformer), se fondre*, etc. But as *en* is not used with *le* (see p. 33, § 20) 'into the...' will be *dans le...*; e.g. 'merged *into* a confused horizon'=*se fondaient* en *un horizon confus*)(*se fondaient* dans *le flamboiement de la mer*.

'To fall *into* the hands of'=*tomber* entre *les mains de*; 'Throw it *into* the fire!'=*Jetez-le* au *feu!*

LIKE: *Comme, pareil à, ressembler à, fait penser à*; is not unlike, *ressemble assez à*. *Tel, On eût dit, On dirait*; 'woman-like'=à la manière des *femmes*; 'dream-like'=*en pays de rêve*; *féerique*; 'lakelike'=semblable à *un lac*; *partir* tel (or *telle) une flèche*; *de même que*.

NEAR: *Près de, auprès de quelque chose*. Often to be rendered by an adjective, *proche*: 'the rifts *near* the summits'=*les crevasses proches des sommets*.

OF: '*Of* all days in the year, on Christmas Day'=Entre *tous les jours de l'année, le jour de Noël*; 'in this *of* all places'=*dans ce lieu* entre *tous*.

OVER: ='above', *au-dessus de*; ='upon', *sur*. See also p. 61, §54, OVER, *adv*.

TILL: See p. 67, §59, TILL, *conj*.

TO: often *jusqu'à*: *les voix arrivaient (parvenaient)* jusqu'à *nous*.

TOWARDS: *envers, à l'égard de*: 'indulgence *towards*'=*indulgence* à l'égard de.

WITH: (*a*) Omitted: 'He listened *with* folded arms'=*Il écoutait, les bras croisés*; (*b*) **de** is just as likely to be the equivalent as *avec*: '*With* all his heart'=De *toute son âme*; 'he held on *with* one hand'=*s'y cramponna d'une main*; (*c*) expressing comparison= compared with, *auprès de, à côté de, au prix de*; (*d*) *ayant*: 'a house *with* a garden'=ayant *un jardin*; (*e*) often turned by an adverb, *e.g.* '*with* safety'=*impunément*; or (*f*) by *dont*: 'epigrams *with* the point everywhere'=*des épigrammes* dont *la pointe* est *partout*; or by *où*: 'the lake *with* the gliding boat' = *la nappe* où glissait *le bateau*. N.B. 'I could say *with* truth' = *Je pourrais dire* en *toute vérité*; 'to find fault *with* something' = *trouver à redire à quelque chose*.

Section VIII. The Conjunction

§58. Conjunctions repeated in French. When there are two co-ordinate dependent clauses, the first of which is introduced by a conjunction, *que* must be used to introduce the second clause: *Il dit* que...*et* que..., **Parce** que...*et* que..., **Quand**...*et* que.... When *que* is substituted for *si* in a second (conditional) clause, the verb must be in the subjunctive.

§59. Some conjunctions.

ALTHOUGH, THOUGH: *Bien que* and *quoique* **always** take the subjunctive: 'He appears stupid, although he *is* in point of fact very clever' = *Il a l'air bête, quoiqu'*en réalité *il* soit *très intelligent*, also *tout en étant* (which is often a neat way of turning 'although'). For 'though' in, *e.g.* 'Rich though he is', see p. 50, §50, HOWEVER. For 'even though' see IF.

AND: See p. 77, §67.

As: omitted: 'a glitter *as* of steel' = *un éclair d'acier*; 'silence *as* of death' = *un silence de mort*; '*as* pale as death' = *pâle comme la mort*; '*as* blue as sapphire' = *d'un bleu de saphir*. '*As* late *as* yesterday' = *Pas plus tard qu'hier*. 'Two is to four *as* four is to eight' = 2 *est à* 4 ce que 4 *est à* 8; 'are *as* powerful *as*' = *ont* autant *de pouvoir* que; 'he is not *as* good *as* his brother' = *il ne* vaut *pas son frère*. 'Shakespeare is at least *as* good *as* Corneille' = vaut *bien Corneille*; 'serve *as*' = *servir* de; *e.g.* 'serves him *as* a riding whip' = *lui sert* de *cravache*; 'known *as*' = *connu (désigné)* sous le nom de.

Tandis que, à mesure que: '*As* the day went on' = A mesure que *le jour s'avançait*.

'As...so' = *De même que...de même (ainsi)*.

As if. 'It seemed as if' = *il semblait que. On eût dit que*.

BECAUSE: 'All the more because' = *d'autant plus...que*.

BEFORE: *Avant que* (*ne*) + Subjunctive: *Je vous reverrai* avant que vous ne partiez, but, whenever possible, *avant de* should be used, *e.g.* when the *avant que* clause would have the same subject as the main verb: 'I shall see you again before *I* leave'=*avant de partir.* N.B. 'It was not long before he came'=*Il ne tarda pas à venir*; also simply *Peu après.*

BOTH: 'Both...and'=*Et...et*; when simultaneity is implied, à la fois...et.

IF: (*a*) *Si*, except when it introduces an indirect question, is not used with the *future* or the *future in the past*: 'If Monday *will* suit you, we shall come then'=*Si lundi vous* convient, *nous viendrons ce jour-là.* 'If Monday *would* suit you'=*Si lundi vous* convenait. When 'will' clearly means 'wish', *vouloir* is required: 'If he *will* not go away'=*S'il ne* veut *pas s'en aller.*

(*b*) 'If' is often to be rendered by other words than *si*: 'If so...' =*Dans (En) ce cas,* as well as *S'il en est ainsi*; '*if* one looks at it closely'=à *y bien regarder*; '*if* only for a moment'=*ne serait-ce qu'un instant*; 'Here *if* anywhere'=*Dans ce lieu* entre tous. Note also the double Conditional: 'If I *were* rich, I should buy that house'=*Je* serais *riche, j'*achèterais *cette maison.* So also 'If I had' or with inversion 'Had I had', *e.g.* '*Had I had* companions, still we should have kept silence'=Aurais-je eu *des compagnons, nous aurions gardé le silence*; '*Even if* I were offered that post, I should not take it'=Quand *on m'*offrirait *ce poste,* je *ne l'*accepterais *pas.*

NOR: '*Nor* had he'=De plus, Au surplus, *il n'avait pas.* Inversion (see p. 49, §50) after 'nor' is not paralleled in French: '*Nor would it* be honest to portray him as an adventurer'=Et ce serait *manquer à la vérité que de le représenter comme un aventurier.*

OR: *Ou* is strictly alternative: 'His income is six *or* seven hundred a year'=*Il gagne* de *six à sept cents livres par an*; *ou* might imply that the income is either exactly £600 *or else* exactly £700; cp. *Un enfant âgé* de *sept à huit ans* [not, usually, '*sept* ou *huit ans*']. For additional clearness or for harmony *ou* is often expanded to *ou bien.*

THAT: 'That *he* should...'=*Dire que lui....*

THOUGH: See ALTHOUGH.

TILL: *Jusqu'à ce que* (which now always takes the subjunctive) is a cumbrous expression often best avoided: '*until* his brother arrived'=jusqu'à *l'arrivée de son frère.* A new sentence with *enfin* is much neater; so also is *pour*+Infinitive: 'The fields run down *till* they lose themselves in the links' = pour se perdre *dans la lande.* Sometimes 'till' is better expressed by other conjunctions, *e.g. tant que* or *au point que: tant qu'à la fin;* 'You need not trouble *till* you are quite well again' = *Inutile de vous tracasser* tant que *vous ne serez* pas *remis;* 'the hills huddle together *till* the waters can scarce find a passage' = *se resserrent* au point que *les eaux trouvent à peine un passage;* often *avant que* or *avant de:* 'He will not touch it *till* he has fed his horses' = *Il n'y touchera pas* avant d'*avoir donné leur provende à ses chevaux;* 'I could not get to sleep *till* I finished the book' = avant de *l'avoir fini;* 'No one can understand Shakespeare *until* he has...' = *Nul ne peut...* avant d'avoir...; 'I did not know it *till* later' = *Je* ne *l'ai su* que *plus tard;* 'Nobody thinks of making reforms *till* it is too late' = *Personne ne pense à faire des réformes* que lorsqu'*il est trop tard;* also *jusqu'au moment où,* with indicative; *en attendant que;* 'to wait *until*' is always *attendre que,* never *jusqu'à ce que.*

UNLESS: *A moins de* + infinitive may be neater than *que* + subjunctive.

WHEN: Often *alors que;* in some sentences *que quand* does not sound very well; say *que lorsque.* 'It was noon-day when' = *Midi était passé* lorsque.

The verb of the clause introduced by the French equivalent of 'when' must be in the same tense as the verb of the principal sentence (or in the corresponding compound tense), *e.g.* 'When it rains, we shall use our umbrellas' = *Quand il* pleuvra, *nous nous* servirons *de nos parapluies;* 'When you have finished talking I shall begin to speak' = *Quand vous* aurez *fini de causer, je* prendrai *la parole.*

It is neater to do without Conjunction + Verb: '*When* he *wakes* up' = *A son réveil;* '*When* night *fell*' = *A la nuit tombante.*

'When' is often *où:* 'at a time *when*' = *à une époque* où; *quand, lorsque,* etc., are not readily used in direct relationship with a noun and their place is taken by *au moment où, le jour où,* etc.

WHILE: *Pendant que,* of simultaneous actions; *tandis que,* of two contrasted actions.

CHAPTER IV

STYLE

The chief concern of style is with the choice and order of words. The best writer is he who uses the best words in the best order. In translation both choice and order are largely pre-determined by the original. The 'best' French words for the translator to choose are those which are most likely to convey the precise sense and general tone and colour of the English passage and to harmonize with the rest of his French sentence. The most suitable order in which to place them will usually be that which the English author freely selected for his own purposes—for the marshalling and expression of his ideas.

French and English being very similar as languages, an accurate translation of good English prose—i.e. one which conveys the precise and entire sense in a manner not unworthy of the original and which keeps as close to the English text as the genius of the French language permits—is good French prose, except in some details. As a rule, the improvements which will make it read like a piece of natural, spontaneous French will be effected by minor changes: removal of stray Anglicisms; occasional concessions to the laws, which are often unwritten laws, of French usage; substitution here and there of words or phrases, or of a word-order, which are more appropriate, more harmonious or more characteristically French:—

§60. **Appropriateness.** In our choice of French phrases we must let ourselves be guided in the first instance by their exactness as equivalents of given English terms. But they are not exact unless they are also appropriate.

Thus, 'I am going to my Father's' is exactly *Je vais chez mon père* in many circumstances but not in all—not, for instance, in Passage 77, where the writer is Bunyan and the speaker Mr Valiant-for-Truth. The French is not the sort of thing a Monsieur

Vaillant-pour-la-Vérité would say in the circumstances described. *Je vais à la demeure de mon Père* would be more exact, because more appropriate to the speaker and in better harmony with the rest of the French translation. A French phrase may not be of such wide application as the English. When in some impassioned description of dawn or sunset we come upon 'the curtains of God's tabernacle' we may write down *rideaux* and hope for the best. But a feeling for French leaves a lurking doubt whether the matter-of-fact, up-to-date, domestic *rideaux* is quite right. Unhappily a feeling for French does not tell us what the right word is. Reference to the French Bible shows that 'les tentures *du tabernacle de Dieu*' is the appropriate phrase. What is the French for 'Leave me alone'? That depends on who makes the remark; if a perplexed, world-weary Cromwell (Passage 128): *Laissez-moi en paix*; if a young man in a hurry: *Laissez-moi tranquille*, or worse.

The above instances are occasions for the exercise of the tact acquired in the course of wide reading in French. They indicate subtle discrepancies between the English and French languages. Words may have the same sense in both, but the conventions governing their use may be utterly different. These discrepancies, when not merely accidental, have profound causes, such as a difference in the mental make-up of the two nations. For instance, the French mind being sharp, analytical, somewhat matter-of-fact, tends to express itself in concrete and objective terms.

Hence perhaps the French tendency to put things personally: 'A rap *was heard* at the door' = Nous entendîmes *frapper à la porte*, and to avoid metaphors which might be taken too literally. 'For two hundred yards nothing met his eye' = *Sur deux cents mètres rien ne frappa*—assuredly not *son œil*, nor yet *ses yeux*, merely—*ses regards*. Where 'feet' seems a normal expression, *pieds* may sound *too* precise and have a slightly comic effect; 'a clatter of *feet* on the stones' is *un bruit de* pas *qui résonnaient sur les pierres*; 'marked out by *the feet* of generations' is *marqué par* les pas *des générations successives*. Or, again, 'A band of white vapour hung round the *shoulders* of the mountain' = *Une écharpe de vapeur blanche s'accrochait*—shall we say *aux* épaules *de la montagne*? If we do, it personifies the mountain very distinctly, and more so, perhaps, than the English warrants; the singular is safer, because less personal: à l'épaule *de la montagne*.

English vagueness allows us to say things which, when translated literally into French, are apt to be startling. 'I always stare anew', says Kinglake (in Passage 16), 'because that a poor boat, with the brain of a man and the hands of a boy on board, can match herself so bravely against black Heaven and Ocean.' English can say such things with impunity. French cannot— and seeks refuge in abstractions: l'intelligence *d'un homme et* la manœuvre *d'un mousse.* '"Yes", said little Nell to her grandfather,...and so (Passage 146) bringing her lips closer to his ear': *pour pouvoir lui parler à l'oreille* is quite close enough, as a translation. Failure to make sufficient allowance for English vagueness and French precision often produces odd effects. In students' French, parts of the human frame seem to become strangely detached and give an impression of anatomical specimens or bits of broken statuary.

§61. Harmony. It is the tragedy of translation that the joy of finding the exact equivalent, *the* word, *the* phrase, is often followed by the sorrow of being unable to use it. Admirable in itself, it so clashes with its neighbours that on further reflection we find that either it or they must go, and all efforts to dislodge them fail. The dissension may be only one of sound, but the translator must retreat before it, for wise old Boileau counsels well:

> Il est un heureux choix de mots harmonieux;
> *Fuyez* des mauvais sons le concours odieux.

As to what constitutes an intolerable clash, French takes a stern view. The Briton can praise 'the patient resignation of this ancient nation' unblushingly and without remonstrance from anyone. The Frenchman must be more careful, for his hearers have a sensitive ear and a sharp tongue. Thus 'British public opinion' figures of course as *L'opinion publique britannique* in the French newspapers, unless there are too many other *-ique*'s in the offing, whether adjectives (*pudique*) or verbs (*communique*). But in more careful and more leisurely Academic prose *l'opinion publique anglaise* or *en Angleterre* is preferable—for euphony, though not for historical or geographical accuracy. In translation into French the finishing touches on a final draft consist partly in altering one or other of two words which are correct but jar with each other: 'the Englishman, the perfection of mankind' (Passage 145) = *l'Anglais, le type achevé de l'humanité* [say *parfait*]. For 'however fair they be', *si beaux qu'ils soient* is a good phrase;

but when there are other *s*'s round about, tout *beaux qu'ils soient*
is a better one. 'Yarrow singing her ageless song for evermore'
(Passage 52)=chantant sans cesse sa chanson séculaire [say *tou
jours*; and if the alliteration still seems excessive, *murmurant*].

§62. **Avoidance of repetitions.** This comes partly under
'Harmony', but it is often a matter more of pleasing the eye
than of pleasing the ear. The French reader's eye is particularly
sharp in noting the reappearance of a word already used. Unless
the repetition is clearly intended for rhetorical or other effect, it
is taken as a sign of careless writing or meagre vocabulary.
Hence, in weekly exercises, the familiar design in blue pencil,
which puts rings round the repeated words and links them all up
together in silent self-condemnation. But even in careful revision the writer himself remains strangely deaf to cacophony and
blind to what catches the reader's eye at once. Pascal, in his
profound remark on this matter of repetition, perhaps failed to
notice his own lapse, the double 'on trouve': *Quand, dans un
discours*, on trouve *des mots répétés et qu'essayant de les corriger*,
on les trouve *si propres qu'on gâterait le discours, il faut les laisser.*
Once noted, inadvertent repetitions can be removed: *Il se
défendit deux fois* contre *les attaques publiées* contre *lui dans la
presse*; say dont il était l'objet *dans la presse.* 'When I travelled
in France as a tourist'=*Lorsque je voyageais* en *France* en
touriste; say *parcourais la France.*
   But the cause may not be inadvertence. The writer may be
painfully aware of the blemish but unable to remove it, *e.g.* when
the English text contains several different words normally translated by one French word or its compounds, such as 'very' and
'self'=*même* and *eux-mêmes* or 'far', 'distant', 'remote'=*loin,
lointain, éloigné.* In that case we can only employ with what
success we may such devices as those enumerated in §2. But
before admitting defeat, we must make sure we have exhausted
the resources of synonym. Since no two words are ever exactly
synonymous, we may in the end have to choose the less appropriate one and sacrifice some part of the sense on the altar of
euphony. On the other hand, the further reflection entailed by
the necessity of avoiding repetition may result in the discovery
of a better term than either. The difficulty is often of our own
making. The French word which we are so anxiously endeavouring
to avoid repeating may not be that which comes most naturally
to a French writer unobsessed by the cares of translation. It may

be pressing itself on a mind hypnotized by the English text or suffering from the *idée fixe* that the French for so-and-so is *always* such-and-such. The following translations—and similar examples will be found in most of our sections—may not occur to us at the critical moment. They are, nevertheless, often the normal French equivalents of the English words:

to begin, *débuter*; beginning, *début, seuil, au* seuil *d'une époque nouvelle*; custom, *habitude*; to destroy, *anéantir, réduire à néant*; end, *extrémité*; to enter, *pénétrer*; except, *sauf*; full, *rempli*; to go, *se rendre*, 'They used to go regularly' = *Ils* s'y rendaient *régulièrement*; to hide, *dissimuler*; to kill, *assassiner, massacrer, mettre à mort*; to show, *révéler*; a sign, *un indice*; in spite of, *en dépit de*. Phrases of the type 'for days and days', though they can be paralleled in French, have not the same vogue as in English; 'for days and days' is usually *des journées entières*; cp. 'for hours and hours' = *des heures durant*; 'for years and years' = *pendant de longues années*; for 'hundreds and hundreds' one *des centaines* is enough. 'Artless' repetitions, 'very, very', etc., are appropriate only in familiar or colloquial French.

§ 63. **Frenchness.** It is easy to push a sound doctrine too far and reject excellent French phrases merely because they happen to exist also in English. But when choosing between two variants equally appropriate and equally harmonious, it is generally well to select the one which seems the more 'French'—and the less 'English'. Other things being equal, there is a certain improvement to be obtained by preferring a type of phrase which is by its nature more French than English. For example, of the following variants the second seems on that ground preferable: 'every night' (1) *chaque soir*, (2) *tous les soirs*. There are, of course, cases where (2) is wrong: 'Chaque soir, *espérant des lendemains épiques*', but generally (2) is preferable. 'I could not enjoy its peace' (said of a beautiful evening): (1) *Je ne pouvais* jouir de sa paix, (2) en *goûter* la *paix*; 'an uneasiness I could scarce explain': (1) *une inquiétude que je ne* pouvais *guère expliquer*, (2) *que je* n'arrivais *guère à* m'*expliquer*.

In particular, the more characteristically French way of expressing an idea may be by means of a different part of speech. For instance, one could translate 'It was his *task* to' just as well by *Il avait la charge de* as by *Il lui* incombait (appartenait) *de*, but on the whole the second expression seems the more French, the more idiomatic and therefore, in some contexts at least, preferable. Similarly: 'A musing *touch* of her harp-strings drew the intruders...'=*Elle* effleura *rêveusement les cordes de sa harpe*, ce qui *attira les intrus*. 'Further *progress* up the river was impossible'=*Il était impossible de* remonter *plus loin la rivière*.

Or the English noun may correspond to the French adjective and vice versa, so that the elegant solution is to transpose: 'too complaisant indulgence'=*une complaisance par trop indulgente*; '(grass) that narrow point of feeble green'=*cette étroite pointe faible et verte*, or: *cet étroit ruban de faible verdure*.

Likewise the English adjective may in more characteristic French be a noun: 'very useful'=*très utile*, better *d'une grande utilité*; 'absolutely sincere'=*d'une sincérité absolue*; or an adverb: 'for so *short* a time'=*pour si* peu *de temps*; or a participle: 'at *short* intervals'=*à intervalles* rapprochés.

§64. **The order of words.** Sometimes a change in the order of the words in the English text is inevitable. It so happens that English says 'the other five', and French says *les cinq autres*; 'come and go' is normally *vont et viennent*, and nothing that any writer can do will alter such facts. There are stereotyped phrases in both languages and it would be remarkable indeed if the order of words in them were always identical. But when no such compelling reason intervenes, the translator should at least make an honest effort to retain the order of words which the English author must in fairness be assumed to have adopted for good and sufficient reason. Example: 'To argue against these opinions would have been idle' could be easily rendered by *Il eût été vain de discuter de telles opinions*. But had the English author so desired, he could have expressed himself in that way. What he did say would be more faithfully reflected by : *Discuter de telles opinions aurait été en pure perte*. Very often the English order can be retained in French by adding a supporting word: 'so deafening was the noise which...'=*tant* il *était assourdissant le vacarme qui....* 'The real force of France, which keeps her at the forefront of the nations'=*la vraie force de la France*, celle *qui la maintient au premier rang des nations*; 'It was Empire, this resistless subjugation of all this central world', etc.=*C'était l'Empire* que *cette irrésistible conquête*, etc.

§65. **Justifiable alteration of English order.** A sound rule is to follow the order of words in the English text except when we can clearly show that something is gained by departing from it. Thus: (*a*) A phrase may be given a more typically French turn: '*one or two rogues* of his acquaintance' = un fripon ou deux *de sa connaissance*. 'Fine rain is falling' = *Il tombe une pluie fine*. 'He did not go to Genoa, he went to Venice instead' = Au lieu d'*aller à Gênes, il alla à Venise*. 'I loved and feared its solitude' = *Sa solitude me plaisait en même temps qu'elle me faisait peur*. 'What a curious old legend that is' = *Qu'elle est curieuse, cette vieille légende*.

(*b*) A phrase may be saved from jerkiness: 'Suddenly the rumour of his resignation spread' = *Soudain le bruit de sa démission se répand* is an awkward sentence, with a subject too long for its verb. Inversion would restore the balance: *Soudain se répand le bruit de sa démission*;

or from cacophony: 'square and heavy' is *carré et lourd*, but, to a purist at least, the hiatus is unpleasing; say *lourd et carré*; 'in the sunshine far aloft' = *bien* haut au *soleil*: say *au soleil tout à la cime*;

or from the reproach of banality: 'The cold earth slept below' is *La terre froide dormait en bas*. But this is commonplace, whereas in the proper context the English has rhythm and emotion—the author in fact is Shelley—and the phrase amply merits the honour of inversion: *En bas dormait la terre froide*.

(*c*) A strained metaphor may be eased by the ancient rhetorical device known as 'Transferred Epithet': 'the *silent bosom* of the clouds' = *le sein des nuages* silencieux; 'a *line* of *blue* far-off hills' = *une ligne* bleue *de collines éloignées*; 'the innumerable *white* threads of waterfalls' = *les innombrables filets de* blanches *cascades*.

(*d*) The rhythm and balance may be approximated more closely to what is described in the next paragraph as the normal French sentence.

§66. **The French sentence.** The French sentence tends to be shorter than the English—often occupying about 1½ lines. It usually gives the impression of being carefully written. The writer evidently considers terseness a virtue. He has taken the trouble to sort out his ideas and set them clearly before us, each idea in a separate clause. He is a man with a plan. The beginning is considered the best place for putting expressions of time; the movement is a crescendo leading up to something of importance, reserved for the end, which in normal French speech bears the chief stress. Care is taken not to overload the verb with adverbial phrases. When several occur, they are distributed in the sentence, those of place usually preceding those of manner.

There is no law against complex sentences, but simple ones are on the whole preferred. Within each sentence, or within each clause, every word is in its proper place—usually in the regulation order: subject, verb, then the direct or the indirect object, whichever be the shorter. Not: *Dieu | a donné | à toutes les créatures humaines | sa grâce*, but: *Dieu | a donné | sa grâce | à toutes les créatures humaines*. If the direct object *sa grâce* were lengthened by further qualification, then it would come after the indirect object: *Dieu | a donné | à toutes les créatures humaines | sa grâce divine et fortifiante, dont*, etc.

The aim is not only clarity, but rhythm and balance. The regulation order is followed, but not to the point of jerkiness or disproportion. As far as possible, the various elements of the sentence are placed in ascending order of length. In artistic writing the sentence falls into a certain number of rhythmical groups, short enough to be easily read in one breath, i.e. containing not more than seven or eight syllables, with the longer group at the end. Flaubert's prose in some of his works almost scans like verse, *e.g.* the beginning of *Salammbô*: '*C'était à Mégara*,(6) *| faubourg de Carthage*,(5) *| dans les jardins d'Hamilcar*(7); and the beginning of *Un Cœur Simple*: *Pendant un demi-siècle*(6) *| les bourgeoises de Pont-l'Évêque*(8) *| envièrent à Mme Aubain*(7) *| sa servante Félicité*(8).'

Terseness, clarity and rhythm are not of course French prerogatives. An English sentence may display these qualities just as admirably. But national taste differs and, as a rule, an English sentence, when put into French, seems longer, sometimes lengthy or long-winded. To a French reader it may appear to begin anyhow, ramble along with no very definite objective and end up with a remark which gives the impression of an afterthought. What in English was spontaneous, unstudied, natural, fresh, is apt to become in French haphazard and pointless. When translated, a French sentence may look *too* neat, an English one, untidy.

§67. Alteration of the English sentence: terseness. No chance should therefore be missed of making the expression terser. 'There is nothing more notable than...'=Rien *de plus* *remarquable* que.... 'There was no noise' = *Point de bruit.* 'He is cheerful, frank *and* witty' = *Il est gai, ouvert, spirituel.* A change to the active form is often an improvement: 'The moon was hidden from us by the clouds': *Des nuages nous cachaient la lune* is shorter, neater, more incisive than: *La lune était cachée à nos regards par des nuages.* So, 'I have frequently been puzzled by this exception' = *Cette exception m'a souvent intrigué'.* There is, however, one occasion for minor expansion which no French writer can resist—the possibility of slipping in *ne...que*: 'The world is toil and vanity' = *Le monde n'est* que *labeur et vanité;* 'affecting contempt for...' = n'*affectant* que *mépris pour....*

It is often advisable to break up the English sentence into two or more. For instance, instead of translating 'where' by *où* and continuing, somewhat wearily, in the same sentence, we may translate it by *là* and begin a new one: *Là,* or, yet more brightly, *C'était là que....* A simple expedient is to omit 'and'. The procession of 'and's' which in pseudo-archaic narrative has to go a long way before it reaches a full-stop becomes tedious if every 'and' is religiously rendered *et.* Indeed, in almost any circumstances the translator may well ask himself whether 'and' might not be better ignored. Occasionally *ainsi que* or *comme* can be substituted: 'He *and* his father' = *Lui,* ainsi que *son père;* 'In France *and* Germany' = *en France* comme *en Allemagne;*

or another part of speech: 'A well-dressed person came up *and* observing...' = *Survint un personnage bien mis,* qui, *voyant....* 'The sound ceased for a moment *and* began again...' = *Le bruit cessa un moment* pour *recommencer;* 'He left the room *and* returned in a few minutes, carrying', etc. = *Il quitta la pièce* pour *revenir quelques instants après, portant,* etc.

§ 68. **Complicated or involved** sentences are rare in French. A concatenation of *que*'s and *qui*'s is avoided, especially when each *que* or *qui* depends on the one which went before—a process ironically known as *une cascade.* Hence we should short-circuit a 'that' when we can: 'I did not know *that* you had that gift' = *Je ne vous connaissais pas ce talent.* 'I believe that...' = *A* mon avis.... 'He maintains *that* he saw' = *Il prétend* qu'*il a vu,* better: *Il prétend avoir vu.* 'She felt that she was forsaken by heaven' = *Elle sentit* qu'*elle était abandonnée du ciel,* better: *Elle se sentit abandonnée du ciel.* As for *qui*—when possible, leave it out without more ado; *ce passage* qui *est cité dans tel livre: ce* *passage cité dans tel livre*; or put a semi-colon and begin a fresh sentence.

Thus we could improve the translation of the following sentence (George Eliot, *Silas Marner*) by omitting the unnecessary *qui*'s and *que*'s: 'The prominent eyes *that* used to look trusting and dreamy now looked *as if they* had been made to see only one kind of thing, *that* was very small, like tiny grain, for which they hunted everywhere' = Les yeux proéminents, autrefois confiants et rêveurs, semblaient maintenant n'avoir été faits que pour regarder une seule espèce de chose très petite, un grain minuscule, qu'ils cherchaient partout à découvrir.

So also with *quand*, etc.: 'Anyone who does not work *when* he is young must work *when* he is old' = *Qui ne travaille pas* étant *jeune est obligé de travailler* étant *vieux*; and particularly the numerous conjunctions composed of *que*, such as *depuis que*: 'Since he was cured' = *Depuis* qu'*il est guéri*; neater: *Depuis sa guérison*. Chateaubriand wrote first: 'Lorsque *mon père était parti, et* que *ma mère était en prières, Lucile s'enfermait dans sa chambre*', and then 'corrected' his sentence to: *Mon père parti et ma mère en prières, Lucile*, etc.

A series of *de*'s is also to be avoided: 'the marble rocks of Genoa' = *les rochers* de *marbre* de *Gênes*; better, *les rochers* marmoréens *de Gênes*.

§ 69. **The rhythm of a sentence** depends largely on the proper placing of adverbial phrases. Here are three positions, given by M. Albalat: (1) not very good; (2) better; (3) best.

(1) *Comment oser croire*, après de pareilles menaces, *qu'il revienne*?

(2) *Comment oser croire qu'il revienne*, après de pareilles menaces?

(3) Après de pareilles menaces, *comment oser croire qu'il revienne*?

Usually, as here, the best effect is obtained by putting the adverbial phrase at the head of the sentence. When this is not possible, it should at least be placed near the beginning. So also in translation: 'The woods before and behind him seemed...'; say: *Devant et derrière lui les bois paraissaient....* 'Dragging a small and unwilling boy from the back of the room' = not: *Traînant un petit garçon qui résistait du fond de la salle*, but *Traînant du fond de la salle un petit garçon qui résistait*. 'We dismounted and watched *from the turf of the roadside* a pageant which', etc. = *Nous mîmes pied à terre* et, du bord gazonné de la route, *nous suivîmes du regard un spectacle que,* etc.

The essential thing is that such phrases should not be given one after another, all in a row. They should be separated and distributed so far as possible over the whole sentence. There is no objection to placing an adverbial phrase between a preposition and its noun: 'with clear fountains flowing beside it' = *avec,* auprès d'elle, *de claires fontaines*; 'with two white specks of huts in the distance' = *avec,* au loin, *ces deux points blancs qu'étaient les huttes.*

§70. **'Le travail du style.'** Flashes may occur *'dans le feu de la composition'*, but they are mostly to be expected during the subsequent patient work with file and hammer. Keats is said to have written, first, 'A thing of beauty is a constant joy'. Revision led to: 'A thing of beauty is a joy for ever.' Victor Hugo wrote, first, *Un souffle tiède était épars sur Galgala,* and then the perfect line: *Les souffles de la nuit flottaient sur Galgala.* In translation, style is largely a result of improvements on a first draft. 'First' is, of course, but a manner of speaking. There may have been several preliminary efforts, culminating in a version which, since its previous history concerns nobody but ourselves, may be fitly given the courtesy title of 'first draft'. It is an honest, a workmanlike, but not a finished, production. It seems correct, but we feel it is capable of improvement in two respects. The sense of the English could be rendered more closely; and the French could run more smoothly. We therefore proceed to reconsider the choice and order of our words, in the hope that the final draft will be a better translation and better French. But 'final draft', too, is only a manner of speaking. As Flaubert well says, 'La prose n'est jamais finie'.

The process will be best illustrated by a practical example, in the guise of a 'Model Lesson'.

CHAPTER V

MODEL LESSON

1. Once every people in the world believed that trees were divine, and could take a human or grotesque shape and dance among the shadows, and that deer, and ravens and foxes, and wolves and bears, and clouds and pools, almost all things under the sun and moon, and the sun and moon, were not less divine and changeable. **2.** They saw in the rainbow the still bent bow of a god thrown down in his negligence; they heard in the thunder the sound of his beaten war-jar, or the tumult of his chariot wheels; and when a sudden flight of wild duck, or of crows, passed over their heads, they thought they were gazing at the dead hastening to their rest, while they dreamed of so great a mystery in little things that they believed the waving of a hand, or of a sacred bough, enough to thrill far-off hearts or hood the moon with darkness. **3.** All old literatures are full of these or of like imaginations, and all the poets of races who have not lost this way of looking at things, could have said of themselves, as the poet of the *Kalevala* said of himself, 'I have learned my songs from the music of many birds, and from the music of many waters'.

W. B. YEATS, Ideas of Good and Evil.

1. Once every people in the world believed that trees were divine, and could take a human or grotesque shape and dance among the shadows, and that deer, and ravens and foxes, and wolves and bears, and clouds and pools, almost all things under the sun and moon, and the sun and moon, were not less divine and changeable.

First Draft. Jadis toutes les nations du monde croyaient que les arbres étaient divins et pouvaient prendre une forme humaine ou grotesque et danser parmi les ombres, et que les daims et les corbeaux et les renards et les loups et les ours, et les nuages et les mares, presque toutes les choses sous le soleil et la lune, et le soleil et la lune, n'étaient pas moins divins et variables.

When we sit back and re-read this version, it does not entirely satisfy us. We feel there is something amiss and suspect that the fault may be in certain words which, on revision, appear odd, and we underline these for re-consideration:

Jadis toutes les nations du monde croyaient que les arbres étaient divins et pouvaient prendre une forme humaine ou grotesque et danser parmi les ombres et que les daims et les corbeaux et les renards et les loups et les ours, et les nuages et les mares, presque toutes les choses sous le soleil et la lune, et le soleil et la lune, n'étaient pas moins divins et variables.

Jadis seemed a *trouvaille*, a word full of poetry and beauty, recalling Villon's '*Dames du temps jadis*'. But now it sounds abrupt as a beginning, and jars somehow with *nations*. Its delightful mediæval flavour recalls a time when (perhaps fortunately) there were as yet no 'nations' in the modern sense of the term, and we realize that we have made a false start. We had the choice between *Autrefois* and *Jadis*, between *nation* and *peuple*, and in both cases we have chosen the wrong word. There is nothing for it but to jettison the charming *Jadis*, and begin again: *Autrefois tous les peuples du monde*.... Whereupon the thought occurs that there is a yet better phrase available: *Il fut un temps où*....

We also notice that *et*'s are recurring with alarming frequency. Perhaps a few could be dropped. The first, for example? Is it really necessary? Does '*pouvaient prendre*', etc. add a new fact? Does it not rather amplify the word *divins*? But if this *et* were left out, the reader might wonder at first whether the subject of *pouvaient* is not *peuples*. For the second *et* we could put *pour*. *Daims* seemed good at first. But they are properly fallow-deer. They are associated with parks, with more peaceful scenes than those frequented by *les loups et les ours.* *Cerfs*, = red deer, is a 'nobler' term.

If we read the sentence over to ourselves, as we should always do, '*les corbeaux et les renards*' recalls La Fontaine rather too vividly. This *et* must therefore go. And now that it has gone, we are left with an easy choice between: (1) a long zoological list, without any *et* at all, except at the very end, or any *les*, except at the very beginning (les *cerfs, corbeaux, renards, loups* (*et*) *ours*); and (2) an altered grouping, *les cerfs et les corbeaux, les renards, les loups et les ours.*

Les mares are not necessarily artificial pools made by the hand of man. But they are small, they do sometimes mean 'duck-ponds' and they go less well with *nuages* than *étangs* would. Perhaps *presque* is rather abrupt; *qu'en somme presque* would make the progress of the thought clearer. The singular, *tout chose*, is a slight improvement. There is evidently some difficulty about '*et le soleil et la lune*'. Reflection on the matter suggests that *et* is being given an English stress which the French conjunction cannot stand; here 'and' is strongly emphasized, almost = '*nay*, the sun and moon *as well*'. We could carry on the construction with *que*, and give the full sense by adding *eux-mêmes*: *que le soleil et la lune eux-mêmes*, or simply say *voire même*.

Finally, *variables* was admittedly a stop-gap. For 'changeable', the English-French Dictionaries give only *changeant* and *variable*, and both often mean 'fickle'. Turning to Larousse with thoughts of 'transformation' in our minds, we are sent on to *métamorphose*, and, thence, to *se métamorphoser*, defined as *se changer en un être différent*. Littré, being consulted, gives *se transformer* = *changer de forme*. That suggests one possible ending to the sentence: *n'étaient pas moins divins et pouvaient changer de forme*. But 'not less' perhaps modifies 'changeable' as well as 'divine' and we continue our search for a single French adjective to balance *divins*. We find only *muable* and, with a better sound as the final word of a sentence, *transmuable*; but both are normally used of metals. We therefore fall back on *changeant* and say: *n'étaient pas moins divins ni d'apparence moins changeante.*

Making the above changes and a few trifling alterations, we arrive at a version which is better than the 'First Draft', because closer to the sense of the English, more characteristically French and, above all things, more harmonious:

Il fut un temps où tous les peuples du monde croyaient que les arbres étaient divins et pouvaient prendre une forme humaine ou grotesque pour danser parmi les ombres; que les cerfs et les corbeaux, les renards, les loups et les ours, les nuages et les étangs, qu'en somme presque toute chose sous le soleil et la lune, voire même le soleil et la lune, n'étaient pas moins divins ni d'apparence moins changeante.

2. They saw in the rainbow the still bent bow of a god thrown down in his negligence; they heard in the thunder the sound of his beaten war-jar, or the tumult of his chariot wheels; and when a sudden flight of wild duck, or of crows, passed over their heads, they thought they were gazing at the dead hastening to their rest, while they dreamed of so great a mystery in little things that they believed the waving of a hand, or of a sacred bough, enough to thrill far-off hearts, or hood the moon with darkness.

First Draft. Ils voyaient dans l'arc-en-ciel l'arc encore bandé qu'un dieu négligent avait laissé tomber; ils entendaient dans le tonnerre le roulement de son tambour de guerre, ou le fracas des roues de son char, et quand une volée soudaine de canards sauvages ou de corbeaux passait au-dessus de leur tête, ils croyaient voir les morts qui se hâtaient vers leur repos, tandis qu'ils rêvaient d'un si grand mystère dans les petites choses qu'ils croyaient qu'il suffirait d'agiter une main ou un rameau sacré pour faire frissonner des cœurs lointains ou voiler la lune d'obscurité.

The beginning seems satisfactory; '*l'arc-en-ciel l'arc*' is justifiable='rainbow...bow'; *avait* is defensible, but *aurait* (see p. 48, § 46) seems better, and leads us on to the poetical *choir* for *tomber*; *roulement* was arrived at after

vain efforts to work in both *bruit* and *battre*; *fracas* took
the place of *tumulte*; *le tumulte des armes* is normal, but *le
tumulte des roues* seemed too bold. Reading over the sentence for rhythm, we feel that after *ils voyaient dans* the
very similar *ils entendaient dans* falls rather flat. The insistence
on the same form of expression '*Ils...Ils*' suggests some
rhetorical intention, which fails to materialize. Our contrast
is between *voyaient* and *entendaient*, whereas in the English it
is between 'the rainbow' and 'the thunder'. Let us throw
the emphasis on to *dans le tonnerre* by transposing, and say:
dans le tonnerre ils entendaient.

We had hesitated between *un vol* and *une volée*, and now *une
volée soudaine* appears odd; *volée* suggests rather a large
number (cp. *une nuée*); it now seems inappropriate to
canards sauvages, which one tends to think of as distant and
aloof, and to *corbeaux*, of which *une volée* would blacken
the skies; besides, we recall 'un vol de noirs corbeaux' in
Leconte de Lisle. In short, *une volée soudaine* suggests a
sudden irruption rather than a flight suddenly noticed
overhead, possibly high overhead. [Cp. a remark by Yeats's
Irish fellow-countryman George Moore: 'Now and then
the sound of a falling leaf caught my ear, and I shall
always remember how a crow, flying high overhead towards the mountains, uttered an ominous "caw".'] We
therefore alter to *un vol soudain*. That correction made,
the thought occurs that *soudain* may just as well be an
adverb and will in fact be better as such: *quand un vol
de canards sauvages ou de corbeaux passait soudain au-
dessus de leur tête.* But *corbeaux*, short and abrupt, comes
in oddly after *canards sauvages*, with a slight suggestion of
anti-climax; it should go before. And, everything considered, *passait soudainement* or *subitement* gives better
rhythm than *passait soudain*: *quand un vol de corbeaux
ou de canards sauvages passait soudainement au-dessus de
leur tête.*

The remainder of the sentence presents a rather complicated network of subordinate clauses. By saying '*ils
croyaient voir*' we have indeed got rid of one *que* and escaped

the cacophony '*ils croyaient qu'ils voyaient*'. But further simplification seems possible and desirable; *se hâtant* is just as good as *qui se hâtaient*. As the sentence is quite long enough already, it is tempting to begin a new one by leaving out *tandis que*. In *qu'ils croyaient qu'il suffisait d'agiter*, one *que* can be omitted—by saying: *qu'ils croyaient* suffisant *d'agiter*.

Better words might be substituted here and there: *voir* appears rather crude when we think of the usual possible variants, *apercevoir* or *contempler*; *vers leur repos* might perhaps be better expanded—to *vers leur lieu de repos* or to *vers le lieu de leur repos*. On re-reading '*rêvaient d'un si grand mystère*', we are stopped for a moment by *rêvaient de*; it usually suggests dreaming of the future, e.g. *rêver d'un monde meilleur*; what is meant here is rather *imaginaient*. And *d'un grand mystère*, though correct enough, now sounds like an understatement; a more satisfying epithet to *mystère* might be *profond*: *imaginaient un mystère si profond dans les petites choses*. This, again, admits of improvement, for *les* plus *petites choses* would better balance *profond* and bring out more fully the force of 'great'. The rhythm of the sentence would gain by the obvious transposition: *imaginaient* dans les plus petites choses *un mystère si profond*.

On second thoughts, *pour faire frissonner des cœurs lointains* seems a defective phrase: 'hearts' may 'thrill', but hardly quite *frissonner*—better, *palpiter*; *des cœurs* is not *general* enough; what is meant is rather **les** *cœurs*. Perhaps also *cœurs lointains* is odd because of the *chœurs lointains*, the 'distant choirs', the 'far-off choruses', which the poets hear. Let us therefore remove all ambiguities and boldly say, with the inversion which the emotional tone of the English requires: *pour qu'au loin les cœurs palpitent, ou que la lune se voile de ténèbres*. And not only is *ténèbres* a more poetical word than *obscurité*; it is a better ending; it brings the sentence to a close not on the sharp, decisive *é* of *obscurité*, but on the lingering mysterious note of the *e* mute —on which see the illuminating quotation at the end of the next paragraph.

Ils voyaient dans l'arc-en-ciel l'arc encore bandé qu'un dieu négligent aurait laissé choir; dans le tonnerre ils entendaient le roulement de son tambour de guerre ou le fracas des roues de son char. Lorsqu'un vol de corbeaux ou de canards sauvages passait soudainement au-dessus de leur tête, ils croyaient contempler les morts se hâtant vers le lieu de leur repos; ils imaginaient dans les plus petites choses un mystère si profond qu'ils croyaient suffisant d'agiter une main ou un rameau sacré pour qu'au loin les cœurs palpitent, ou que la lune se voile de ténèbres.

3. All old literatures are full of these or of like imaginations, and all the poets of races who have not lost this way of looking at things, could have said of themselves, as the poet of the *Kalevala* said of himself, 'I have learned my songs from the music of many birds, and from the music of many waters'.

Toutes les vieilles littératures sont pleines de ces fantaisies ou de fantaisies pareilles et tous les poètes des races qui n'ont pas perdu cette façon de voir les choses auraient pu dire d'eux-mêmes ce que le poète du *Kalevala* disait de lui-même, 'J'ai appris mes chansons en écoutant la musique d'oiseaux sans nombre et la musique d'eaux innombrables'.

'*Toutes les vieilles littératures*' demands further consideration. Is *vieilles* better than *anciennes*? The sense of a word may be judged from its opposite. The opposite of *vieilles* is *jeunes* = youthful, fresh. The opposite of *anciennes* is *modernes* = belonging to the present era, sophisticated. Yeats probably means *anciennes*, since he says 'have not lost this way of looking at things' and mentions the old Finnish epic *Kalevala*.

Pleines is coldly correct: *remplies* is more sonorous, charged with more emotion. Cp. Félix Arvers, *Sonnet*: 'Elle dira, lisant ces vers tout *remplis* d'elle'. '*De ces fantaisies ou de fantaisies pareilles*' is not a good phrase, and would be no better if *imaginations* or *chimères* (not depreciatory in this context) were substituted for *fantaisies*. The repetition, hardly justified by the English, throws unnecessary emphasis on *fantaisies*; the second *fantaisies* is wrongly stressed, and it may be doubted whether *pareilles* is the right epithet; it has a slightly contemptuous ring about it. The choice seems to lie between *riches en fantaisies de cette nature* (or *de même nature*) and *remplies de semblables fantaisies*. Since both sentences are introduced by the same word *Toutes...et tous*, some rhetorical effect seems to be produced. It may be better to recognize this and make the rhetorical opposition definite—by suppressing *et*; *les poètes des races qui* seems ambiguous on a second reading; *de ces races qui* is clearer. Similarly, '*cette façon de voir les choses*' gives a translator pause when the thought of the English text has passed from his mind. It is a stock expression = 'this way of thinking'; cp. *Ce n'est pas ma façon de voir les choses* = 'That is not *my* conception'. The French phrase in fact is abstract, whereas 'this way of looking at things' is concrete. Consequently, *cette* manière *de* regarder *les choses* would be more exact: *manière* is more personal—more suggestive, for example, of an artist (cp. *la manière de Rubens*)—and *regarder* is more direct than *voir*. Although *auraient pu* is impeccable as a translation, it comes as a rather sudden assertion; *pourraient* runs more smoothly.

The repetition in the next few words is ponderous in French, which would rather say simply *comme le poète du Kalevala*; *chansons* is a slip for *chants*; it is apt to suggest minor poetical exercises, possibly flippant in tone, and the celebrated remark: *En France tout finit par des chansons!* For 'many...many' the prosaic *beaucoup de* or *bien des* is impossible; *sans nombre* gives the required emotional tone. Cp. Sully Prudhomme:

> *Bleus ou noirs, tous aimés, tous beaux.*
> *Des yeux sans nombre ont vu l'aurore.*

The repetition of '*la musique*', unlike that of 'music', jars slightly, but there is apparently no way of avoiding it. It must also be admitted that 'waters', a beautiful word, is

hardly quite rendered by *eaux*. But *innombrables*, which
sufficiently recalls *sans nombre* to balance 'many...many',
is a good 'last word'. It well accords with an important
principle set forth thus by a master in the art of French
Composition, Mr H. E. Berthon:

'Special care should be given to the end of each sentence,
especially the final sentence of a paragraph. Take a hint
from the practice of musicians. A piece of music is generally
brought to a close with a full chord whether *piano* or *forte*.
Choose a fairly substantial word, with long vowels, soft, full
consonants and if possible an *e* mute in the last syllable.
Remember that *e* mute is the only relief, the only flexible
ending, the only *rebound* in the French language, a fact
which explains its necessity in verse and makes it compulsory
for every alternate couplet. A final *e* mute lengthens the
preceding vowel and gives elasticity to the cadence of the
phrase, as when the hands of the pianist release the keys
after the final chord.'

Toutes les littératures anciennes sont remplies de
semblables fantaisies; tous les poètes de ces races qui
n'ont pas perdu cette manière de regarder les choses
pourraient dire d'eux-mêmes comme le poète du
Kalevala: J'ai appris mes chants en écoutant la
musique d'oiseaux sans nombre et la musique d'eaux
innombrables.

Suggested Rendering

Il fut un temps où tous les peuples du monde croyaient
que les arbres étaient divins et pouvaient prendre une forme
humaine ou grotesque pour danser parmi les ombres; que les
cerfs et les corbeaux, les renards, les loups et les ours, les
nuages et les étangs, qu'en somme presque toute chose sous
le soleil et la lune, voire même le soleil et la lune, n'étaient
pas moins divins ni d'apparence moins chargeante. Ils
voyaient dans l'arc-en-ciel l'arc encore bandé qu'un dieu
négligent aurait laissé choir; dans le tonnerre ils enten-

daient le roulement de son tambour de guerre ou le fracas des roues de son char. Lorsqu'un vol de corbeaux ou de canards sauvages passait soudainement au-dessus de leur tête, ils croyaient contempler les morts se hâtant vers le lieu de leur repos; ils imaginaient dans les plus petites choses un mystère si profond qu'ils croyaient suffisant d'agiter une main ou un rameau sacré pour qu'au loin les cœurs palpitent, ou que la lune se voile de ténèbres. Toutes les littératures anciennes sont remplies de semblables fantaisies; tous les poètes de ces races qui n'ont pas perdu cette manière de regarder les choses pourraient dire d'eux-mêmes comme le poète du *Kalevala*: J'ai appris mes chants en écoutant la musique d'oiseaux sans nombre et la musique d'eaux innombrables.

PASSAGES FOR TRANSLATION

* Easy. ** Moderately difficult. *** Difficult.
**** Very difficult.

I. DESCRIPTIVE

**1. SUNRISE

I must not close my letter without giving you one principal
event of my history, which was that—in the course of my
late tour—I set out one morning before five o'clock, the
moon shining through a dark and misty autumnal air, and
got to the sea-coast time enough to be at the sun's levee. I
saw the clouds and dark vapours open gradually to right and
left, rolling over one another in great smoky wreaths, and
the tide—as it flowed gently in upon the sands—first
whitening, then slightly tinged with gold and blue; and all
at once a little line of insufferable brightness that—before I
can write these five words—was grown to half an orb, and
now to a whole one, too glorious to be distinctly seen. It is
very odd it makes no figure on paper; yet I shall remember
it as long as the sun, or at least as long as I can endure. I
wonder whether anybody ever saw it before. I hardly believe
it.   THOMAS GRAY, *Letters.*

**2. DAWN OVER LONDON

Already the southern slopes[1] of London are in sight, shadowy
and indistinct in outline, yet with a clearness seldom seen,
and peculiar[2] only to the smokeless summer dawn.[3] Away
still on the horizon runs the inner rim of the London basin,[4]
the line along which rise the heights of Richmond...and
Blackheath. Not so long ago, and its southern limit was still
a wooded solitude; now the life of London has flowed far
over[5] its crest to the south, west and east. The rooks are
spreading out across the sky as they sail from their nests to[6]
the distant pastures. As the light ripens, the view enlarges

of greater London[7] stretching away to the north. Like the arms of a great octopus, its fringes strike far into the open land. Farther in, caught between them,[8] rises bravely many a pleasant grove; parks, open spaces, and even fields gleam a fitful green[9] among the bricks in the morning light—but surrounded[10] all; doomed, injected morsels[11] waiting to be digested at leisure, to serve the strenuous purposes[12] of another life.

BENJAMIN KIDD, *A Philosopher with Nature* (Methuen and the Executors of Benjamin Kidd).

1 See p. 91, § 4, SLOPES.　　2 *qui n'appartient qu'aux.*　　3 Translate as if: 'smokeless skies (see p. 7, § 9, SKY) of summer dawns'.　　4 Cp. *le bassin parisien.*　　5 *a débordé, bien au-dessus de.*　　6 Use *quitter... pour.*　　7 *la grande banlieue de Londres.*　　8 *pris dans leur étreinte.*　　9 *verdoient par instants.*　　10 Which seems preferable: *cerner* or *envelopper?*　　11 *comme des bouchées englouties déjà.*　　12 *pour se prêter aux vigoureuses exigences.*

***3. LA RICCIA

The noon-day sun came slanting down the rocky slopes of La Riccia; and their masses of entangled and tall foliage, whose autumnal tints were mixed with the wet verdure of a thousand evergreens, were penetrated with it as with rain. I cannot call it colour, it was conflagration. Purple, and crimson, and scarlet, like the curtains of God's tabernacle, the rejoicing trees sank into the valley in showers of light, every separate leaf quivering with buoyant and burning life; each, as it turned to reflect or to transmit the sunbeam, first a torch and then an emerald. Every glade of grass burned like the golden floor of heaven, opening in sudden gleams as the foliage broke and closed above it, as sheet-lightning opens in a cloud at sunset; the motionless masses of dark rock—dark though flushed with scarlet lichen, casting their quiet shadows across its restless radiance, the fountain underneath them filling its marble hollow with blue mist and fitful sound; and over all, the multitudinous bars of amber and rose, the sacred clouds that have no darkness, and only exist to illumine, were seen in fathomless intervals between the solemn and orbed repose of the stone pines, passing to lose themselves in the last, white, blinding lustre of the measureless line where the Campagna melted into the blaze of the sea. JOHN RUSKIN, *Modern Painters*, vol. I.

***4. A NOVEMBER AFTERNOON

A Saturday afternoon in November was approaching the time of twilight,[1] and the vast tract of unenclosed wild[2] known as Egdon Heath embrowned itself moment by moment. Overhead the hollow stretch of whitish cloud shutting out the sky was as a tent which had[3] the whole heath for its floor.

The heaven being spread with this pallid screen and the earth with the darkest vegetation, their meeting-line at the horizon was clearly marked. In such contrast the heath wore the appearance of an instalment[4] of night which had taken up its place[4] before its astronomical hour was come:[5] darkness had to a great extent arrived[4] hereon, while day stood distinct in the sky. Looking upwards, a furze-cutter would have been inclined to continue work; looking down, he would have decided to finish his faggot and go home. The distant rims of the world and of the firmament seemed to be a division in time no less than a division[6] in matter. The face of the heath by its mere complexion[7] added half an hour to evening; it could in like manner retard the dawn, sadden noon,[8] anticipate[9] the frowning of storms scarcely generated,[10] and intensify the opacity of a moonless midnight to a cause[11] of shaking and dread.

THOMAS HARDY, *The Return of the Native* (Macmillan and the Trustees of the Hardy estate).

1 *l'heure crépusculaire.* 2 *lande encore sans clôture.* 3 Tense (in a simile)? See p. 48, § 46. 4 The metaphors seem military: *une avant-garde… avait pris position…l'obscurité l'avait envahie.* 5 Turn by a noun; *en attendant l'arrivée de.* 6 Simplify: 'a division as well in time as in matter'. 7 *par sa seule couleur.* 8 *l'heure de midi* (to avoid confusion with *le midi* = 'south'). 9 *devancer.* 10 *à peine éclos.* Cp. La Fontaine, I, viii: *L'Hirondelle et les petits oiseaux*:
  Celle-ci prévoyait jusqu'aux moindres orages,
  Et, devant qu'ils fussent éclos…
11 Turn 'cause' by a verb and transpose, *e.g., rendre intense, à faire trembler d'effroi l'obscurité de,* etc.

**5. TWILIGHT

The day had drawn to its close. The stars had not yet come, nor the moon. Far to the west a red cloud poised on the horizon like a great whale and, moment by moment, it paled and faded until it was no more than a pink flush. On high, clouds of pearl and snow piled and fell and sailed away on easy voyages. It was the twilight—a twilight of such quietude that one could hear the soft voice of the world as it whispered through leaf and twig. There was no breeze to swing the branches of the trees or to creep among the rank grasses and set them dancing, and yet everywhere there was unceasing movement and a sound that never ceased. About them, for mile upon mile, there was no habitation of man; there was no movement anywhere except when a bird dipped and soared in a hasty flight homewards, or when a beetle went slugging by like a tired bullet.

JAMES STEPHENS, *The Demi-Gods* (Macmillan).

**6. A MIDSUMMER NIGHT

With every step upward[1] a greater mystery surrounded me. A few stars were out, and the brown night mist was creeping along the water below: but there was still light enough[2] to see the road, and even to distinguish the bracken in the deserted hollows. The highway became little better[3] than a lane: at the top of a hill[4] it plunged under the tall pines, and was vaulted over with darkness.[5] The kingdoms that have no walls, and are built up of shadows, began to oppress[6] me as the night hardened. Had I had companions, still we would only have spoken in a whisper, and in that dungeon of trees, even my own self[7] would[8] not raise its voice within me.

It was full night when I had[9] reached a vague clearing in the woods, right up on the height of that flat hill. This clearing was called 'The Fountain of Magdalen'. I was so far relieved by[10] the broader sky of the open field that I could⁹ wait and rest a little and there, at last, separate from men, I thought⁹ of a thousand things.

HILAIRE BELLOC, *The Path to Rome* (Allen and Unwin).

1 *A chaque pas que je faisais en montant la colline.* 2 See p. 9, § 12, LIGHT. 3 *n'était plus guère.* 4 *une colline* or *une côte?* See p. 4, § 4, SLOPES. 5 *se couvrait d'une voûte de ténèbres.* 6 See p. 24, § 18, OPPRESS. 7 *mon âme elle-même.* 8 Evidently not the Conditional tense; say e.g. *n'osait élever.* 9 Tense? These are consecutive events. 10 *soulagé devant.*

**7. A MIDSUMMER NIGHT (*continued*)

The air was full of midsummer, and its mixture of exaltation and fear cut me off from ordinary living. I now understood why our religion has made sacred this season of the year; why we have, a little later, the night of St John, the fires in the villages, and the old perception of fairies dancing in the rings of the summer grass. A general communion of all things conspires at this crisis of summer against us reasoning men that should live in the daylight, and something fantastic possesses those who are foolish enough to watch upon such nights.

So I, watching, was cut off. There were huge, vague summits, all wooded, peering above the field I sat in, but they merged into a confused horizon. I was on a high plateau, yet I felt myself to be alone with the immensity that properly belongs to plains alone. I saw the stars, and remembered how I had looked up at them on just such a night when I was close to the Pacific, bereft of friends and possessed with solitude. There was no noise; it was full darkness. The woods before and behind me made a square frame of silence, and I was enchased here in the clearing, thinking of all things.

HILAIRE BELLOC, *The Path to Rome* (Allen and Unwin).

*8. NIGHT SILENCE

Leaving the inn, the chattering crowd, we passed down the narrow street, under the high shuttered¹ windows and flowery balconies, and emerged² on the lake front. The

promenade was silent and deserted and we looked upon[3] a
scene of incredible[3] beauty. The moonlight fell on the dark
water, the[4] dim outlines of the mountains, the[4] distant
Borromean Islands terraced with lights,[5] and the lake shore
fringed with white villas. On our way back to Baveno, the
grass was jewelled with glowworms, the trees faintly stirred
in the hot air, and the wind sang in the tall cypress, standing
like a Noah's Ark tree, the black sentinel[6] of a garden or
harbour walk. Across the lake Pallanza glittered, but not so
brightly[7] as the clear stars overhead. As we walked in the
night silence, broken only by the chirp of the grasshopper,
we reflected that the drama we had seen[8] was a part of this
land of beauty and romance.[9]

CECIL ROBERTS, *Half Way* (Hutchinson).

1 *aux volets clos.*   2 *pour déboucher sur.*   3 See p. 4, § 3 (*a*).   4 It is
clearer to repeat *sur.*   5 *aux lumières étagées.*   6 Expand, *e.g.* 'sentinel posted in'.   7 *avec moins d'éclat.*   8 Use *assister à.*   9 *ce beau
pays de roman.* Or *ce paysage plein de beauté et de merveilleux.*

**9. IN THE MOONLIGHT

It was one hour after midnight, and the prospect around was
lovely. The grey old towers of the ruin, partly entire, partly
broken—here bearing the rusty weather stains of ages, and
there partially mantled with ivy—stretched along the verge
of the dark rock which rose on Mannering's right hand. In
his front was the quiet bay, whose little waves, crisping and
sparkling to the moonbeams, rolled successively along its
surface, and dashed with a soft and murmuring ripple
against the silvery beach. To the left, the woods advanced
far into the ocean, waving in the moonlight along ground of
an undulating and varied form, and presenting these
varieties of light and shade, and that interesting combination
of glade and thicket, upon which the eye delights to rest,
charmed with what it sees, yet curious to pierce still deeper
into the intricacies of the woodland scenery. Above rolled
the planets, each, by its own liquid orbit of light, distinguished from the inferior or more distant stars. So strangely

can imagination deceive even those by whose volition it has been excited, that Mannering, while gazing upon these brilliant bodies, was half inclined to believe in the influence ascribed to them by superstition over human events.

SIR WALTER SCOTT, *Guy Mannering.*

***10. A TRANSFORMATION SCENE[1]

The dancing was at last over[2] and the radiant company had left the room. A long and weary night it had been for the two players,[3] though a stimulated interest[4] had hindered physical exhaustion in one of them for a while. With tingling fingers and aching arms they came out of the alcove into the long and deserted apartment, now pervaded by a dry haze. The lights had burnt low,[5] and Faith and her brother were waiting by request[6] till the wagonette was ready to take them home, a breakfast being in course of preparation for them meanwhile.

Christopher had crossed the room to relieve[7] his cramped limbs, and now peeping through a crevice in the window curtains, he said suddenly: 'Who's for a transformation scene? Faith, look here!'

He touched the blind, up it flew and a gorgeous scene presented itself to her[8] eyes. A huge inflamed sun was breaking the horizon of a wide sheet of sea which, to her surprise, the mansion overlooked. The brilliant disk fired all the waves that lay between it and the shore at the bottom of the grounds, where the water tossed the ruddy light from one undulation to another in glares as large and clear as mirrors, incessantly altering them, destroying them and creating them again; while further off they multiplied, thickened and ran into one another like struggling armies, till they met the fiery source of them all.[9]

'O, how wonderful it is,' said Faith, putting her hand on Christopher's arm. 'Who knew[10] that while we were all shut in here with our puny illumination, such an exhibition as this was going on outside? How sorry and mean the stately room looks now!'

Christopher turned his back on the window, and there were the hitherto beaming candle-flames shining no more radiantly than tarnished javelin heads,[11] while the snow-white lengths of wax showed themselves clammy and cadaverous as the fingers of a corpse. The leaves and flowers which had appeared so very green and blooming by the artificial light were now seen to be faded and dusty. Only the gilding of the room in some degree brought itself into keeping with the splendours outside.

THOMAS HARDY, *The Hand of Ethelberta* (Macmillan and the Trustees of the Hardy estate).

1 *Changement de décor.* 2 *On avait enfin fini de danser.* 3 *musiciens.*
4 *l'intérêt renouvelé du spectacle.* 5 *Les bougies s'étaient consumées.*
6 *ainsi qu'on les en avait priés.* 7 *détendre.* 8 '*ses*' would be ambiguous: *aux yeux de la jeune fille.* 9 *leur commune source embrasée.*
10 *Qui se doutait que...?* + Indicative. 11 *pointes* (f.).

**11. IN A LONDON GARDEN

One shower I remember that wrought magic in a London garden. A kind of judicious neglect by the owner had made the garden a kindly party to any unusual trick of the elements. On the lawn was a sundial that made Time an alluring toy. At the bottom of the garden, beyond the lawn, was an enclosed space of warm rank grasses, and, rising over them, a vapour of cow-parsley flowers. A white steam from the soil faintly misted the grass to the level of the tallest buttercups. Rain was falling, and the grasses and overhanging elm-trees seemed to be suffering for their quietness and loneliness, to be longing for something, as perhaps Eden also dropped 'some natural tears' when left a void. A hot, not quite soothing perfume crept over the lawn. All night I was haunted by those elms which appeared as grey women in cloaks of that strange mist. For the time, that garden was the loneliest place on earth, and I loved and feared its loneliness.

EDWARD THOMAS, *Rosacre Papers* (Duckworth).

**12. A Strange Sensation

The rain was now steady; from every tree a fountain
poured. So cool and easy had his mind become[1] that he was
speculating on what kind of shelter the birds could[2] find,
and how the butterflies and moths[3] saved their coloured
wings from washing. Folded close they might hang under[4]
a leaf, he thought. Lovingly he looked into the dripping
darkness of the coverts on each side, as one of their children.[5]
Then he was musing on a strange sensation he experienced.
It ran up one arm with an indescribable thrill, but communicated nothing to his heart.[6] It was purely physical,
ceased for a time, and recommenced, till he had it all
through his blood, wonderfully thrilling. He grew aware
that the tiny leveret he carried in[7] his breast was licking his
hand there. The small rough tongue going over and over the
palm of his hand produced this strange sensation he felt.
Now that he knew the cause, the marvel ended; but now
that he knew the cause, his heart was touched and made
more of it.[8]

GEORGE MEREDITH, *The Ordeal of Richard Feverel*
(Chapman and Hall).

1 Beware of Inversion; see p. 49, § 50.   2 Does 'could' here mean 'were
able to'=*pouvaient* or 'would be able to'=*pourraient*?   3 Use *phalène*
(f.).   4 *peut-être se suspendaient-ils à.*   5 *comme s'il eût été de leur
nichée.*   6 *mais sans rien éveiller en son cœur.*   7 *qu'il portait serré
contre sa poitrine.*   8 *y attachait plus de prix.*

**13. Birds in the Morning

In the garden the birds that had sung erratically and
spasmodically in the dawn on that tree, on that bush, now
sang together in chorus, shrill and sharp; now together, as
if conscious of companionship, now alone as if to the pale
blue sky. They swerved, all in one flight, when the black
cat moved among the bushes, when the cook threw cinders
on the ash heap and startled them. Fear was in their song,

and apprehension of pain, and joy to be snatched quickly now at this instant. Also they sang emulously in the clear morning air, swerving high over the elm tree, singing together as they chased each other, escaping, pursuing, pecking each other as they turned high in the air. And then tiring of pursuit and flight, lovelily they came descending, delicately declining, dropped down and sat silent on the tree, on the wall, with their bright eyes glancing, and their heads turned this way, that way; aware, awake; intensely conscious of one thing, one object in particular.

VIRGINIA WOOLF, *The Waves* (Hogarth Press).

***14. THE BEGINNING OF A STORM

The hours passed dismally. Thickened by huge black clouds, the twilight came on in a sultry and expectant silence,[1] and it was prematurely night. The reflections of distant lightnings, flashing far away[2] below the horizon, illuminated the eastern sky. The peaks and ridges of the Apennines stood out black against the momentary pale expanses of silvered vapour[3] and disappeared again in silence; the attentive hush was still unbroken.[4] With a kind of sinking apprehension— for she was terrified of storms—Moira sat at her window, watching[5] the black hills leap out[6] against the silver and die again, leap out and die. The flashes brightened; and then, for the first time, she heard the approaching thunder, far off and faint like the whisper of the sea in a shell. Moira shuddered. The clock in the hall struck nine, and, as though the sound were a signal prearranged,[7] a gust of wind suddenly shook the magnolia tree that stood at the crossing of the paths in the garden below. Its long stiff leaves rattled together[8] like scales of horn. There was another flash. In the brief white glare she could see[9] the two funereal cypresses writhing and tossing as though in the desperate agitation[10] of pain. And then all at once the storm burst catastrophically, it seemed directly overhead. At the savage violence of that icy downpour Moira shrank back and shut the window.

ALDOUS HUXLEY, *Brief Candles* (Chatto and Windus).

1 *dans un silence lourd d'attente.*   2 *lointain...loin* at so close an interval should be avoided. How? See p. 8, § 2.   8 Transpose: e.g. *sur la pâleur momentanée du vaste écran de vapeurs,* etc.   4 Say: nothing came to break, etc. (see p. 16, § 18, BREAK).   5 For 'sat...watching' see p. 54, § 51, To SIT. • 6 *surgir.*   7 *comme si c'eût été là le signal convenu.* 8 *raclaient les unes contre les autres.*   9 Is 'could' to be translated? See p. 50, § 51, COULD. If not, is this *elle vit* or *elle voyait*?   10 *convulsions* (f.).

***15. THE EAST COAST OF SCOTLAND

Nothing is wilder than the long stretch of sandy coast which runs from the East Neuk of Fife right up to Aberdeen.

Inland, the wind-swept fields, with their rough walls, without a kindly feal upon the top, as in the west, look grim and uninviting in their well-farmed ugliness.

The trees are low and stunted, and grow twisted by the prevailing fierce east winds, all to one side, just like the trees so often painted by the Japanese upon a fan.

The fields run down, until they lose themselves in sandy links, clothed with a growth of bent.

After the links, there intervenes a shingly beach, protected here and there by a low reef of rocks, all honeycombed and limpet-ridden, from which streamers of dulse float in the ceaseless surge.

Then comes the sea, grey, sullen, always on the watch to swallow up the fishermen, whose little brown-sailed boats seem to be scudding ceaselessly before the easterly haar towards some harbour's mouth.

Grey towns, with houses roofed with slabs of stone, cluster round little churches built so strongly that they have weathered reformations and the storms of centuries.

Grey sky, grey sullen sea, grey rocks, and a keen whistling wind that blows from the North Sea, which seems to turn the very air a steely grey, have given to the land a look of hardness not to be equalled upon earth.

R. B. CUNNINGHAME GRAHAM, *Scottish Stories: A Princess* (Duckworth).

*16. A LONELY BOAT

In returning from a cruise to[1] the English coast, you see often enough a fisherman's humble boat far away from all shores, with an ugly black sky above, and an angry sea beneath; you watch the grisly old man at the helm carrying his craft[2] with strange skill through the turmoil of waters, and the boy, supple-limbed, yet weather-worn already, and with steady eyes that look through the blast;[3] you see him understanding commandments from[4] the jerk of his father's white eyebrow....Stale enough is the sight, and yet when I see it I always stare anew, because that a poor boat, with the brain[5] of a man and the hands[5] of a boy on board, can match herself so bravely against black Heaven and Ocean.

Well, so[6] when you have travelled for days and days over an Eastern Desert without meeting the likeness of a human being,[7] and then at last see an Englishman and his servant come listlessly slouching along from out the forward horizon,[8] you stare at the wide unproportion between this slender company and the boundless plains of sand through which they are keeping their way.   A. W. KINGLAKE, *Eothen.*

1 Expand to, *e.g., quand vous cinglez vers.*   2 *qui tient la barre, dirigeant sa barque,* etc.   3 See p. 52, § 51, LOOK.   4 'from' after *comprendre* is *à* (cp. *reconnaître...à,* p. 64, § 57, BY): *rien qu'au mouvement nerveux.* 5 Use less concrete terms; see p. 70, § 60.   6 *il en est de même.*   7 *sans rencontrer âme qui vive.*   8 *qui s'avancent nonchalamment du fond de l'horizon.*

**17. WOLF'S CRAG

The roar of the sea had long announced their approach to the cliffs, on the summit of which, like the nest of some sea-eagle, the founder of the fortalice had perched his eyry. The pale moon, which had hitherto been contending with flitting clouds, now shone out, and gave them a view of the solitary and naked tower, situated on a projecting cliff that beetled on the German Ocean.

On three sides the rock was precipitous; on the fourth, which was that towards the land, it had been originally

fenced by an artificial ditch and drawbridge, but the latter
was broken down and ruinous, and the former had been in
part filled up, so as to allow passage for a horseman into the
narrow courtyard, encircled on two sides with low offices
and stables, partly ruinous, and closed on the landward
front by a low embattled wall, while the remaining side of the
quadrangle was occupied by the tower itself, which, tall and
narrow, and built of a greyish stone, stood glimmering in the
moonlight, like the sheeted spectre of some huge giant.

A wilder or more disconsolate dwelling, it was perhaps
difficult to conceive. The sombrous and heavy sound of the
billows, successively dashing against the rocky beach at a
profound distance beneath, was to the ear what the landscape was to the eye—a symbol of unvaried and monotonous
melancholy, not unmingled with horror.

SIR WALTER SCOTT, *The Bride of Lammermoor.*

***18. THE 'MERRY MEN'

The night, though we were so little past midsummer, was as
dark as January. Intervals of a groping twilight[1] alternated
with spells of utter blackness; and it was impossible to
trace[2] the reason of these changes in the flying horror of the
sky.[3] The wind blew the breath out of a man's nostrils; all
heaven seemed to thunder overhead like one huge sail; and
when there fell a momentary lull[4] on Aros, we could hear the
gusts dismally sweeping in the distance.

Over all the lowlands of the Ross, the wind must have
blown as fierce as on the open sea; and God only knows the
uproar that was raging around the head of Ben Kyaw.
Sheets of mingled spray and rain[5] were driven in our faces.
All round the isle of Aros the surf, with an incessant,
hammering thunder, beat upon the reefs and beaches. Now
louder in one place,[6] now lower in another,[6] like the combina-
tions of orchestral music, the constant mass of sound was
hardly varied for a moment. And loud above all this hurly-
burly I could hear the changeful voices of the Roost and the
intermittent roaring of the Merry Men.

At that hour, there flashed into my mind the reason of the name that they were called. For the noise of them[7] seemed almost mirthful, as it out-topped the other noises of the night; or if not mirthful, yet instinct with a portentous joviality. Nay, and it seemed even human. As[8] when savage men have drunk away their reason,[9] and, discarding speech,[10] bawl together in their madness by the hour; so,[8] to my ears, these deadly breakers shouted by Aros in the night.

R. L. STEVENSON, *The Merry Men* (Chatto and Windus).

1 *de vague crépuscule.* 2 *découvrir.* 3 *dans l'horreur qui volait par le ciel.* 4 *lorsque, par moments, une accalmie descendait.* 5 *Des gerbes d'embrun mêlé de pluie.* 6 *à tel endroit...à tel autre.* 7 *le bruit qu'ils faisaient.* 8 *De même que...de même.* 9 *ont bu à perdre leur raison.* 10 *renonçant aux paroles.*

***19. Sails

On deck, to Oliver's eyes, the spectacle was overwhelming. Some untapped reservoir of emotion seemed suddenly to burst within him and flood his whole being. But why? A ship under full sail in halcyon weather, how often has it been praised, and painted and photographed? Beautiful, certainly, but hackneyed, like the daisy and the rose and the lark and the nightingale, and all the other commonplaces of popular poetry. And Oliver cared little for poetry; to his adolescent mind raptures over the beautiful were simply silly. Had he never, perhaps, felt the beautiful until now? The spread of canvas, unexpectedly enormous, at first alarmed his instinct by its aerial incalculable boldness: if the gods suddenly blew a little harder what would become of all these vast gossamer wings? Yet at once the sense of security was restored and heightened into a sense of power, by the evident steadiness and friendliness of that harnessed force. The gods had made a covenant, a conditional covenant, with man, and promised, if he obeyed, to carry him on their shoulders. Everything trembled and everything held; each part was alive and self-propelling, yet all moved together slightly swaying and justly balanced in a firm advance. The wildness of a topsail or a flying jib was like the treble voices of choir boys in a glorious anthem; while the taut sheets and halyards, the yards and booms, were like manly baritones and basses, holding the ground note and sustaining the harmony.

GEORGE SANTAYANA, *The Last Puritan* (Constable).

**20. AMYAS ON THE ISLAND

Once on the island, Amyas felt sure enough[1] that if its wild tenant had not seen them approach, he certainly had not heard them, so deafening was the noise[2] which filled his brain, and seemed to make the very leaves upon the bushes quiver, and the solid stone beneath his feet to reel and ring. For[3] two hundred yards and more above[4] the fall, nothing met his eye but one white waste of raging foam, with here and there a transverse dyke of rock,[5] which hurled columns of spray and surges of beaded water[6] high into the air, strangely contrasting with the still and silent cliffs of green leaves which walled[7] the river right and left, and more strangely still with the knots[8] of enormous palms upon the islets, which reared their polished shafts a hundred feet into the air, straight and upright as masts, while their broad plumes and golden clustered fruit[9] slept in the sunshine far aloft, the[10] image of the stateliest repose amid the wildest wrath of Nature. Gradually his ear became accustomed to the roar, and, above its mighty undertone,[11] he could hear the whisper of the wind among the shrubs, and the hum of myriad insects.　　CHARLES KINGSLEY, *Westward Ho!*

1 *eut la quasi-certitude.*　2 How can the English order of words be retained? See p. 74, § 64.　3 *Sur.*　4 *en amont de.*　5 *une barrière transversale de rochers.*　6 *des masses d'eau perlée.*　7 *les murailles de verdure qui bordaient*, etc.　8 *les bouquets.*　9 *leurs grappes de fruits dorés.*　10 Omit the article in apposition.　11 *sa basse puissante.*

***21. THE MARQUESAS

These Marquesas did not capture his imagination, they stunned it, so that afterwards, when they had shaken themselves over the horizon and he found himself once again in the green-blue bowl of sky and ocean, he could hardly believe that he had really seen them. . . . They did not compete with other places, and it was absurd to begin comparing them with other places. These were the landscapes of dark and splendid dreams, of *Macbeth* and Beethoven's *Fifth Symphony*. Black crags, pinnacles and tortured promontories had been flung out of the water and piled up in wild confusion; there were jagged peaks lost in cloud, and high smoky valleys; forests were hanging in the air, dripping and glittering; and rising sheer from the green depths were immense dark walls where innumerable white threads of waterfall were swaying and a hundred thousand white birds went circling. Every island seemed to have just been plucked from the very heart of the sea, so that it still dripped with salt water. They were black mountains and dark green woods for ever seen through a mist of spray. They were the Gothic castles of the deep Pacific. . . . They were terrifying, beautiful, and incredible. And the *Rose Marie*, now a toy boat, moved cautiously from one to the other of these incredibilities, carrying with her, for their delight, a good selection of cheap tobacco, tinned meat, cotton goods, imitation jewellery, patent medicines, household utensils, fishing tackle, soap, scent, and a few discreet cases of gin and Tahiti rum.   J. B. PRIESTLEY, *Faraway* (Heinemann).

**22. TROPICAL FISH

It seemed as if[1] nothing moved, yet fish and ship swept on[2] through the tropical ocean. And the fish moved, they changed places all the time. They moved in a little cloud, and with the most wonderful sport they were above, they were below, they were to the fore,[3] yet all the time the same one speed, the same one[4] speed, and the last fish just touching with his tail-flukes the iron cut-water of the ship. Some would be[5] down in the blue, shadowy, but horizontally motionless in[6] the same speed. Then with[7] a strange revolution, these would be up in pale green water, and others would be down. Even the toucher,[8] who touched the ship, would in a twinkling be changed. And ever, ever the same pure horizontal speed, sometimes a dark back skimming the water's surface light,[9] from beneath, but never the surface broken....All the time, so swift, they seemed to be laughing.   D. H. LAWRENCE, *Phoenix* (Heinemann).

1 See p. 54, § 51, IT SEEMS.   2 *filaient toujours.*   3 *à l'avant du navire.*
4 *uniforme.*   5 Tense?   6 *à.*   7 *par.*   8 Say, *e.g.* *le poisson de queue, celui qui touchait,* etc.   9 *la surface lumineuse de l'eau.*

***23. SPRING IN HOLLAND**

There was blue sky above the Castle, and, between the great tree trunks of the avenue, the wheeling sections of the lake held streaks of blue in their grey ripple. This is how spring comes in England, Lewis thought, when spring has been delayed; at night you go to bed remembering the winter and in the morning summer is come. The grass at the foot of the trees was bright and fresh; yellow and white flowers had sprung up among it; and where the sun fell on the barrel of the tower, the dark masonry and the creeper mounting it threw out a radiance of gold and green by which the water was enriched, the water and, it seemed, the air above the water, for the atmosphere of that morning, particularly in its contact with the surface of the pools, was charged with a golden opalescence; the windows of the Castle shone with it and the plumage of birds was washed in its brilliance as they passed through the air. Soon it will be May! Lewis began to count the April days, and, thinking that the war must certainly be decided before the third winter, he imagined the tranquillity of his own summer spread out before him. Even the summer would end. He looked at the trees, the Castle, the flickering water, seeing them all as part of a vanishing interlude in the reality of his own life; and that they might not escape him he halted in the avenue, listening to the rustle of an unseen bird in the foliage but hearing time drumming in his ears.

CHARLES MORGAN, *The Fountain* (Macmillan).

***24. A Sunday in Spring

On this particular Sunday,[1] there was no doubt but that[2] the spring had come at last. It was warm, with a latent shiver in the air that made the warmth only the more welcome. The shallows of the stream glittered and tinkled among bunches of primrose. Vagrant scents of the earth[3] arrested Archie by the way[4] with[5] moments of ethereal intoxication. The grey, Quakerish[6] dale was still only awakened in places and patches from the sobriety of its winter colouring; and he[7] wondered at its beauty; an essential beauty of the old earth it seemed to him, not resident in particulars but breathing to him from the whole. He surprised himself by a sudden impulse to write poetry— he did so sometimes, loose, galloping octosyllabics in the vein of Scott—and when he had taken his place[8] on a boulder, near some fairy falls and shaded by a whip of a tree[9] that was already radiant with new leaves, it still more surprised him that he should find nothing to write.[10]

R. L. STEVENSON, *Weir of Hermiston* (Chatto and Windus).

1 *Ce dimanche-là surtout.*   2 Construction after *douter?* See p. 51, § 51, To DOUBT.   3 *Les senteurs vagabondes de la terre.*   4 *au passage.* 5 Expand: *e.g., lui procuraient.*   6 Give the sense: *e.g., quelque peu austère.*   7 *il* would refer to *vallon*; repeat *Archie.*   8 Use *s'installer.* 9 *à l'ombre du rameau d'un arbre.*   10 Use *manquer d'inspiration.*

*25. Summer in Portugal

The day was intensely hot, notwithstanding the coldness of the preceding nights, and the brilliant sun of Portugal now illumined a landscape of entrancing beauty. Groves of cork trees covered the farther side of the valley and the distant acclivities, exhibiting here and there charming vistas, where various flocks of cattle were feeding; the soft murmur of the stream, which was at intervals chafed and broken by huge stones, ascended to my ears and filled my mind with delicious feelings. I sat down on the broken wall and remained gazing and listening and shedding tears of rapture;

for of all the pleasures which a bountiful God permitteth his children to enjoy, none are so dear to some hearts as the music of forests and streams, and the view of the beauties of his glorious creation.

GEORGE BORROW, *The Bible in Spain.*

***26. A BATHE IN THE TYRRHENIAN SEA

Old gentlemen in clubs[1] were not more luxuriously cradled than I along the warm Tyrrhenian. Arms outstretched, like a live cross, I floated face upwards[2] on that blue and tepid sea. The sun beat down on me, turning the drops on my face and chest to salt. My head was pillowed[3] in the unruffled water; my limbs and body dimpled the surface of a pellucid mattress[4] thirty feet thick and cherishingly resilient[5] through all its thickness, down to the sandy bed on which it was spread....

The sky above me was filmy with the noonday heat. The mountains, when I turned towards the land to look for them, had almost vanished behind a veil of gauze. But the Grand Hotel, on the other hand, though not perhaps quite so grand as it appeared in[6] its illustrated prospectus...made no attempt to conceal itself; the white villas glared out unashamedly[7] from their groves of pines; and in front of them, along the tawny beach, I could see the bathing huts, the striped umbrellas, the digging children, the bathers splashing and wallowing in the hot shallows—half-naked men like statues of copper,[8] girls in bright tunics, little boiled shrimps instead of little boys, and sleek ponderous walruses with red heads, who[9] were the matrons in their rubber caps and their wet black bathing garments.... Sometimes, at the head of its white wake, a motor boat would pass, and suddenly my transparent mattress would[10] rock beneath me, as the waves of its passage lifted me and let me drop[11] and lifted me up again, more and ever more languidly, till[12] all was once more smooth.

ALDOUS HUXLEY, *Those Barren Leaves* (Chatto and Windus).

1 A literal translation raises too many difficulties. Turn freely, *e.g.*, *Le repos où s'enfoncent les vieux messieurs...n'est pas plus voluptueux que le mien sur*, etc. 2 *le visage tourné vers le ciel.* 8 *enfonçait* (see p. 46, § 41) *mollement dans.* 4 *un matelas* is too specific: *une couche.* 5 Turn, *e.g.*, *qui me soulevait amoureusement.* 6 *sur.* 7 *brillaient d'un éclat indiscret dans.* 8 *semblables à des statues cuivrées.* 9 Is this *qu'étaient* or *qui étaient?* See p. 44, § 89. 10 *se mettait à.* 11 *tomber?* Or *retomber?* See p. 58, § 54, AGAIN. 12 *jusqu'au moment où.*

**27. THE COMING OF WINTER AT ENKENDAAL

The days were fast shortening, and Lewis, who had been accustomed to spend one or two afternoons in each week riding with van Leyden over his estates, heard him grumble that the summer was over. 'I hate the winter,' he said, 'it ties me to my desk and makes a clerk of me.' The foliage of the avenue was the first to change its colour, but autumn spread to the little hills surrounding the lakes, and one day, while Lewis and Julie were standing near the boat-house, a fierce gust brought down a torrent of leaves and the surface of the water was lively with a golden fleet. The gold vanished, the sodden leaves drifted on for a little while, a mottle of black on steel.

As though even the seasons were in haste, storms blew through the sunshine of that autumn, and soon the pattern of branches stood everywhere naked against the sky. Nothing remained but the dark glitter of evergreens which clacked and hissed as the breeze jostled them. At last the winds ceased. The lakes were grey and dull and motionless, speckled with a sleety rain. In the early weeks of December the earth was saturated by snow and thaw, the sky, whether dark or pale, was unluminous, and all the interior of the Castle—the rugs, the polished tables, the gilt frames, the silver—seemed to have sunk into a lethargy. Colour itself had fallen asleep. Shape was emptied of its vitality.

CHARLES MORGAN, *The Fountain* (Macmillan).

***28. A Winter Landscape in Amsterdam

I call to mind a winter landscape in Amsterdam—a flat foreground[1] of waste land, with here and there stacks of timber, like the huts of a camp of some very miserable tribe; the long stretch of the Handelskade; cold, stone-faced[2] quays, with the snow-sprinkled ground and the hard frozen water of the canal, in which were set[3] ships one behind another with[4] their frosty[5] mooring-ropes hanging slack[5] and[4] their decks idle and deserted, because, as the master stevedore (a gentle, pale person, with a few golden hairs on his chin[6] and a reddened nose) informed[7] me, their cargoes were frozen-in up-country on barges and schuyts. In the distance,[8] beyond the waste ground, and running parallel with the line of ships, a line of brown, warm-toned houses[9] seemed bowed under snow-laden roofs. From afar at the end of Tsar Peter Straat, issued in the frosty air the tinkle of bells[10] of the horse tramcars, appearing and disappearing in the opening between the buildings, like little toy carriages[11] harnessed with toy horses and played with by people that appeared no bigger than children.

JOSEPH CONRAD, *The Mirror of the Sea* (Methuen).

1 *au premier plan une étendue plate.*   2 *avec leur revêtement de pierre.*
3 'set'=caught in the ice=*pris.*   4 'with...and': *dont...pendaient...et dont...étaient* will make a better sentence.   5 Transfer the epithet: 'hanging slack and frosty' (*givré*).   6 *au menton.*   7 The French verb should come much earlier in the sentence; *e.g., comme me l'apprit le chef arrimeur.*   8 *Au fond* (as opposed to *au premier plan* in l. 1).   9 *maisons d'un brun chaud.*   10 The choice of the French word depends (see p. 15, § 18, BELL) on whether they are small bells attached to the harness or large clanging bells which in the distance only 'tinkled'.   11 Not *voitures d'enfant*=perambulators; say, *e.g., des jouets d'enfant, voitures minuscules,* etc.

**29. Dieppe to Paris

There is no such journey in the world as the journey from Dieppe to Paris on a fine May morning. Nobody forgets his first glimpse of Rouen Cathedral in the diamond air, the branching river and the tall ships anchored in the deep current. We are dreaming of the cathedral long after we have left Rouen behind us, and when we awake from our dream we are in the midst of a flat green country, the river winding about islands and through fields in which stand solitary poplar-trees, formerly haunts of Corot and Daubigny. We can see the spots where they set their easels—that slight rise with the solitary poplar for Corot, that rich river bank and shady backwater for Daubigny. Soon after comes into sight the first weir, and then the first hay-boat; and at every moment the river grows more serene, more gracious; it passed its arms about a flat, green-wooded island, on which there is a rookery; and sometimes we see it ahead of us, looping up the verdant landscape as if it were a gown, running through it like a white silk ribbon, and over there the green gown disappearing in fine muslin vapours, drawn about the low horizon.

GEORGE MOORE, *Memoirs of my dead Life* (Heinemann).

**30. DORLCOTE MILL

Just by the red-roofed town the tributary Ripple flows with a lively current[1] into the Floss. How lovely the little river is, with its dark changing wavelets! It seems to me like[2] a living companion while I wander along the bank and listen to its low placid voice, as to[3] the voice of one who is deaf and loving. I remember those large dipping[4] willows. I remember the stone bridge.

And this is Dorlcote Mill. I must stand[5] a minute or two here on the bridge and look at it, though the clouds are threatening, and it is far on in the afternoon. Even in this leafless time of departing February[6] it is pleasant to look at —perhaps the chill damp season adds a charm to the trimly-kept comfortable dwelling-house, as old as the elms and chestnuts that shelter it from the northern blast. The stream is brimful now, and lies high in this little withy plantation, and half drowns the grassy fringe of the croft in front of the house. As I look at the full stream, the vivid grass, the delicate bright-green[7] powder softening the outline of the great trunks and branches that gleam from under the bare purple[8] boughs, I am in love with[9] moistness, and envy the white ducks that are dipping their heads far into the water[10] here among the withes, unmindful of the awkward appearance they make in the drier world above.

GEORGE ELIOT, *The Mill on the Floss.*

1 Turn differently, *e.g.*, 'the rapid waters of...flow (see p. 6, § 7, To FLOW) into'.   2 *Elle me donne l'impression de....*   3 = 'as I should listen', etc. The ellipse should be completed in French.   4 Use, *e.g.*, *baigner* (see p. 45, § 41).   5 See p. 55, § 51, To STAND.   6 Say, *e.g.*, *en ces jours de février finissant, tout dépouillé de feuilles.*   7 See p. 10, § 18 (c). 8 'purple' here probably *la pourpre des rameaux.*   9 Say *je me prends à aimer.*   10 *plongent la tête profondément sous l'eau.*

***31. THE MILL ON THE FLOSS

The rush of the water, and the booming of the mill, bring a dreamy deafness, which seems to heighten the peacefulness of the scene. They are like a great curtain of sound, shutting one out from the world beyond. And now there is the thunder of the huge covered waggon coming home with sacks of grain. That honest waggoner is thinking of his dinner, getting sadly dry in the oven at this late hour; but he will not touch it till he has fed his horses,—the strong, submissive, meek-eyed beasts, who, I fancy, are looking mild reproach at him from between their blinkers, that he should crack his whip at them in that awful manner as if they needed that hint! See how they stretch their shoulders up the slope towards the bridge, with all the more energy because they are so near home. Look at their grand shaggy feet that seem to grasp the firm earth, at the patient strength of their necks, bowed under the heavy collar, at the mighty muscles of their struggling haunches! I should like well to hear them neigh over their hardly-earned feed of corn, and see them, with their moist necks freed from the harness, dipping their eager nostrils into the muddy pond. Now they are on the bridge, and down they go again at a swifter pace, and the arch of the covered waggon disappears at the turning behind the trees.   GEORGE ELIOT, *The Mill on the Floss.*

**32. MOUNTAIN RANGES

The country was the grandest that can be imagined. How often have I sat[1] on the mountain side and watched the waving downs, with the two white specks of[2] huts in the distance, and the little square of garden behind them; the paddock with a patch of bright green oats above the huts, and the yards and wool-sheds down on the flat below;[3] all seen as through the wrong end[4] of a telescope, so clear and brilliant was the air, or as upon a colossal model or map spread out beneath me.

Beyond the downs was a plain, going down to[5] a river of great size, on the farther side of which there were other high mountains, with[6] the winter's snow still not quite melted; up the river, which ran winding in many streams[7] over a bed some two miles broad, I looked upon the second great chain, and could see a narrow gorge where the river retired and was lost. I knew that there was a range still farther back; but except from one place near the very top of my own mountain, no part of it was visible: from this point, however, I saw, whenever there were no clouds, a single snow-clad peak, many miles away, and I should think[8] about as high as any mountain in the world.

SAMUEL BUTLER, *Erewhon* (Cape).

1 'sat...and watched': turn by the past participle; see p. 54, § 51, To SIT.
2 Say *qu'étaient* or *qui étaient*; see p. 45, § 39.   3 *en bas sur le terrain plat.*
4 *comme par le gros bout.*   5 *qui s'abaissait jusqu'à.*   6 Use *où*; see
p. 66, § 57, WITH.   7 Say: *dont les bras nombreux serpentaient.*   8 Render the sense; turn 'I should think' by *à mon idée.*

**33. COLOUR IN LANDSCAPE

The sun came out as I left the shelter of a pine-wood, and I beheld suddenly a fine wild landscape to the south. High rocky hills, as blue as sapphire, closed the view, and between these lay ridge upon ridge, heathery, craggy, the sun glittering on veins of rock, the underwood clambering in the hollows, as rude as God made them at the first. There was not a sign of man's hand in all the prospect; and indeed not a trace of his passage, save where generation after generation had walked in twisted footpaths, in and out among the beeches, and up and down upon the channelled slopes. The mists, which had hitherto beset me, were now broken into clouds, and fled swiftly and shone brightly in the sun. I drew a long breath. It was grateful to come, after so long, upon a scene of some attraction for the human heart. I own I like definite form in what my eyes are to rest upon; and if landscapes were sold, like the sheets of characters of my boyhood, one penny plain and twopence coloured, I should go the length of twopence every day of my life.

R. L. STEVENSON, *Travels with a Donkey* (Chatto and Windus).

***34. MOUNTAIN SCENERY

The road at this point was terraced out[1] of one of the sides of a deep valley. The ground rose steeply, in places almost precipitously,[2] above it. Below it the green mountain meadows,[3] brilliant in the sunshine and dotted here and there with clumps of chestnut trees, fell away into[4] the depths of the valley, which the afternoon sun had left already in a vaporous smoky shadow. Profoundly shadowed, too, were the hills on the farther side of the narrow cleft. Huge black masses, smoky[5] with the same vapour as that which floated at the bottom of the valley, they rose up almost in silhouette against the bright light beyond. The sun looked down, over their clouded summit, across the intervening gulf, touching the green hillside, on the slope of which Calamy was standing, with a radiance that, in contrast[6] to the dark hills opposite, seemed almost unearthly. To the right, at the head[7] of the valley, a great pinnacle[8] of naked rock, pale brown and streaked here and there with snow-white veins of marble, reached up into the clouds[9] and above them, so that the summit shone like a precious stone in the sunlight, against the blue of the sky. A band of white vapour hung round the shoulders[10] of the mountain. Beneath it appeared the lower buttresses of rock and the long slopes of hanging wood and meadowland falling away into the valley, all shadowy under the clouds, shadowy and dead, save where, here and there,[11] a great golden beam broke through, touching some chosen tract of woodland or rock with[12] an intense and precarious life.

ALDOUS HUXLEY, *Those Barren Leaves* (Chatto and Windus).

1 *s'avançait en terrasse sur.*   2 See p. 5, § 4, STEEP.   3 *prairies* (f.) *en pente.*   4 *allaient s'enfoncer jusque dans.*   5 *embuées de.*   6 *par contraste avec.*   7 *à l'entrée.*   8 *un pinacle* will hardly do (see p. 25, § 18, PINNACLE), but *en forme de pinacle* could be worked in.   9 *se dressait jusqu'aux nues.*   10 *s'accrochait à l'épaule.*   11 *sauf, çà et là, les endroits où.*   12 Say, e.g., *qui, touchant...rocher, lui prêtait une vie*, etc.

*35. THE VIEW FROM THE BATTLEMENTS

It was upon the evening of a sultry summer's day, when the sun was half-sunk behind the distant western mountains of Liddesdale, that the lady took her solitary walk on the battlements of a range of buildings, which formed the front of the castle, where a flat roof of flagstones presented a broad and convenient promenade. The level surface of the lake, undisturbed except by the occasional dipping of a teal-duck or coot, was gilded with the beams of the setting luminary, and reflected, as if in a golden mirror, the hills amongst which it lay embosomed. The scene, otherwise so lonely, was occasionally enlivened by the voices of the children in the village, which, softened by distance, reached the ear of the lady in her solitary walk, or by the distant call of the herdsman, as he guided his cattle from the glen in which they had pastured all day, to place them in greater security for the night, in the immediate vicinity of the village. The deep lowing of the cows seemed to demand the attendance of the milk-maidens, who, singing shrilly and merrily, strolled forth, each with her pail on her head, to attend to the duty of the evening. The Lady of Avenel looked and listened; the sounds which she heard reminded her of former days, when her most important employment, as well as her greatest delight, was to assist Dame Glendinning and Tibb Tacket in milking the cows at Glendearg. The thought was fraught with melancholy.   SIR WALTER SCOTT, *The Abbot.*

*36. Church Island

Church Island lies in a bay under a rocky shore, and the farmer who cuts the grass there[1] in the summertime has[2] a boat to bring away the hay. It was delightful to step into it, and as the oars chimed I said to myself, 'I have Marban's poem in my pocket—and will[3] read it walking up the little path leading from his cell[4] to his church.' The lake was like a sheet of blue glass, and the island lay yellow and red in it. As we rowed, seeking a landing-place under the tall trees that grow along the shores, the smell of autumn leaves mingled with the freshness of the water. We rowed up[5] a beautiful little inlet overhung with bushes. The quay is at the end of it, and, on getting out of the boat, I asked the boatman to point out to me what remained of Marban's Church. He led me across the island—a large one,[6] the largest in the lake— not less than seven acres or nine, and[7] no doubt some parts of it[7] were once cultivated by Marban. Of his church, however, very little remains—only one piece of wall, and we had great difficulty in seeing it, for it is now surrounded by a dense thicket. The little pathway leading from his cell to the church still exists; it is almost the same as[8] he left it—a little overgrown, that is all.

GEORGE MOORE, *The Lake* (Heinemann).

1 Omit.   2 *se sert de.*   3 refers to the immediate future: see p. 45, § 45.   4 *grotte* (f.); *cellule* (f.) would suggest one of many cells in a monastery.   5 Use simply *pénétrer dans.*   6 Translate as if: 'which is large, the largest.'   7 'and...it'='which'.   8 *presque dans l'état où.*

*37. The Lake

We did not think it possible to see the lake in any new aspect, yet there it lay as we had never seen it before, so still, so soft, so grey, like a white muslin scarf flowing out, winding past island and headland. The silence was so intense that one thought of the fairy books of long ago, of sleeping woods and haunted castles; there were the castles on islands lying in misted water, faint as dreams. Now and then a chaffinch uttered a piercing little chatter from the branches of the tall larches, ending defiantly, and ducks talked in the reeds, but their talk was only a soft murmur, hardly louder than the rustle of the reeds now in full leaf. Everything was spellbound that day; the shadows of reed and island seemed fixed for ever as in a magic mirror—a mirror that somebody had breathed upon, and, listening to the little gurgle of the water about the limestone shingle, one seemed to hear eternity murmuring its sad monotony.

GEORGE MOORE, *Memories of my dead Life* (Heinemann).

***38. SWEET BELLS

On the other side of the valley a group of red roofs and a belfry showed among the foliage. Thence some inspired bell-ringer made the afternoon musical[1] on a chime of bells. There was something very sweet and taking in the air he played; and we thought we had never heard bells speak so intelligibly or sing so melodiously as these. It must have been to some such measure[2] that the spinners and the young maids sang, 'Come away, Death,[3]' in the Shakespearian Illyria. There is so often a threatening note, something blatant and metallic, in the voice of bells, that I believe[4] we have[5] fully more pain than pleasure from hearing them; but these, as they sounded abroad,[6] now high, now low, now with a plaintive cadence that caught the ear like the burthen of a popular song, were always moderate and tunable, and seemed to fall in[7] with the spirit of still, rustic places, like the noise of a waterfall or the babble of a rookery in spring.

I could have asked the bell-ringer for his blessing, good, sedate old man, who swung the rope so gently to the time[8] of his meditations.

R. L. STEVENSON, *An Inland Voyage* (Chatto and Windus).

1 Simplify: *e.g.*, 'filled the afternoon with the music of his chime'. 2 *C'est sur une cadence semblable que...devaient chanter.* 3 *Viens, ô Mort: Twelfth Night (Soir des rois)* II, iv. 4 How could the number of *que*'s be reduced? See p. 77, § 68. 5 Use *éprouver.* 6 *dans les airs.* 7 *s'harmoniser avec.* 8 *au rythme de.*

***39. The Fair Singer

In the middle of the wood there was a sandy mound, rising half the height of the lesser firs, bounded by a green-grown vallum, where once an old woman, hopelessly a witch, had squatted, and defied the authorities to make her budge: nor could they accomplish the task before her witch-soul had taken flight in the form of a black night-bird, often to be heard jarring above the spot. Lank dry weeds and nettles, and great lumps of green and grey moss, now stood on the poor old creature's place of habitation, and the moon, slanting through the fir-clumps, was scattered on the blossoms of twisted orchard-trees, gone wild again. Amid this desolation, a dwarfed pine, whose roots were partially bared as they grasped the broken bank that was its perch, threw far out a cedar-like hand. In the shadow of it sat the fair singer. A musing touch of her harp-strings drew the intruders to the charmed circle, though they could discern nothing save the glimmer of the instrument and one set of fingers caressing it. How she viewed their rather impertinent advance toward her, till they had ranged in a half-circle nearer and nearer, could not be guessed. She did not seem abashed in any way, for, having preluded, she threw herself into another song.

GEORGE MEREDITH, *Sandra Belloni* (Constable).

***40. The Bonfire

While the men and lads were building the pile, a change took place in the mass of shade which denoted[1] the distant landscape. Red suns and tufts of fire one by one began to arise, flecking[2] the whole country round. They were the bonfires of other parishes and hamlets that were engaged in the same sort of commemoration.[3] Some were distant, and stood[4] in a dense atmosphere, so that bundles of pale strawlike beams radiated around them in the[5] shape of a[5] fan. Some were large and near,[6] glowing scarlet-red from the shade, like wounds in[7] a black hide. Some were Maenades, with winy faces and blown hair. These[8] tinctured the silent bosom of the clouds above them and lit up their ephemeral caves, which seemed thenceforth to become scalding cauldrons.

Perhaps as many as[9] thirty bonfires could be counted within[10] the whole bounds of the district; and as the hour may be told on a clock-face when the figures themselves are invisible, so did the men recognize the locality of each fire by its angle and direction, though nothing of the scenery could be viewed.

THOMAS HARDY, *The Return of the Native* (Macmillan and the Trustees of the Hardy estate).

1 Say *tenait lieu du paysage lointain.*   2 Use *étoiler.*   3 *occupés à célébrer la même fête commémorative.*   4 'stood'=*brûlaient.*   5 Is the article required? See p. 33, § 19 (*c*), and p. 33, § 20 (*b*).   6 Say, *e.g., D'autres, plus rapprochés, paraissaient plus grands.*   7 *sur.*   8 Expand, *e.g., Leurs reflets.*   9 *jusqu'à.*   10 Say, *e.g., dans les limites de toute la région.*

**41. THE VIEW FROM THE TERRACE

The terrace in front of the house was a long narrow strip of turf, bounded along its outer edge by a graceful stone balustrade. Two little summer-houses of brick stood at either end. Below the house the ground sloped very steeply away, and the terrace was a remarkably high one; from the balusters to the sloping lawn beneath was a drop of thirty feet. Seen from below, the high unbroken terrace wall, built like the house itself of brick, had the almost menacing aspect of a fortification—a castle bastion, from whose parapet one looked out across airy depths to distances level with the eye. Below, in the foreground, hedged in by solid masses of sculptured yew trees, lay the stone-brimmed swimming-pool. Beyond it stretched the park, with its massive elms, its green expanses of grass, and, at the bottom of the valley, the gleam of the narrow river. On the farther side of the stream the land rose again in a long slope, chequered with cultivation. Looking up the valley, to the right, one saw a line of blue, far-off hills.

ALDOUS HUXLEY, *Crome Yellow* (Chatto and Windus).

***42. Two Cottages

No contrast can be more painful than that between the dwelling of any well-conducted English cottager, and that of the equally honest Savoyard.

The one, set in the midst of its dull flat fields and un-interesting hedgerows, shows[1] in itself the love of brightness and beauty; its daisy-studded garden-beds, its smoothly swept brick path to the threshold, its freshly sanded floor and orderly shelves of household furniture,[2] all testify[3] to energy of heart, and happiness in the simple course and simple possessions of daily life.

The other cottage, in the midst of an inconceivable, in-expressible beauty, set on some sloping bank of golden sward, with clear fountains flowing beside it, and wild-flowers, and noble trees, and goodly rocks gathered round into a perfection as of Paradise, is itself a dark and plague-like stain in the midst of the gentle landscape. Within a certain distance of its threshold the ground is foul and cattle-trampled; its timbers are black with smoke, its garden choked with weeds and nameless refuse,[4] its chambers empty and joyless, the light[5] and wind gleaming and filtering through the crannies of their stones.

All testifies that to its inhabitant the world is labour[6] and vanity,[6] that for him neither[7] flowers bloom, nor birds sing, nor fountains glisten; and that his soul hardly differs from the grey cloud that coils[8] and dies upon his hills, except in having no fold of it touched[9] by the sunbeams.

JOHN RUSKIN, *Modern Painters*, vol. IV.

1 *porte.*   2 *ustensiles de ménage rangés avec ordre sur les étagères.*   3 *tout cela atteste.*   4 Use *un indescriptible rebut.*   5 *tandis que la lumière luit et que le vent passe à travers.*   6 Should the Partitive Article be used? See p. 84, § 22 (*a*).   7 Some emphasis is required; *e.g.*, *ce n'est pas pour lui que s'épanouissent les fleurs, que*, etc.   8 Use *s'enrouler.*   9 Turn by the active form: *si ce n'est que les rayons du soleil n'atteignent aucun de ses plis.*

***43. Scrooge's Counting-House

Once upon a time—of all the good days in the year, on Christmas Eve—old Scrooge sat busy in his counting-house. It was cold, bleak, biting weather: foggy withal: and he could hear the people in the court outside go wheezing up and down, beating their hands upon their breasts, and stamping their feet upon the pavement-stones to warm them. The City clocks had only just gone three, but it was quite dark already: it had not been light all day: and candles were flaring in the windows of the neighbouring offices, like ruddy smears upon the palpable brown air. The fog came pouring in at every chink and keyhole, and was so dense without, that although the court was of the narrowest the houses opposite were mere phantoms. To see the dingy cloud come drooping down, obscuring everything, one might have thought that Nature lived hard by, and was brewing on a large scale.

The door of Scrooge's counting-house was open that he might keep his eye upon his clerk, who, in a dismal little cell beyond, was copying letters. Scrooge had a very small fire, but the clerk's fire was so very much smaller that it looked like one coal. But he couldn't replenish it, for Scrooge kept the coal-box in his own room; and so surely as the clerk came in with the shovel, the master predicted that it would be necessary for them to part. Wherefore the clerk put on his white comforter, and tried to warm himself at the candle; in which effort, not being a man of strong imagination, he failed. CHARLES DICKENS, *A Christmas Carol.*

***44. The Black Country

A dense cloud of pestilential smoke hangs over it[1] for ever, blackening even the grain that grows upon it; and at night the whole region burns like a volcano spitting fire from[2] a thousand tubes of brick.

But, oh, the wretched hundred and fifty thousand mortals that grind out[3] their destiny there! In the coal mines they are literally naked, many of them, all but trousers;[4] black as ravens, plashing about among dripping caverns, or scrambling among heaps of broken mineral; and thirsting unquestionably for beer.

In the iron mills it was little better;[5] blast furnaces were roaring like the voice of[6] many whirlwinds all around; the fiery metal was hissing through[7] its moulds or sparkling and spitting under hammers of a monstrous size, which fell like so many little earthquakes. Here they were wheeling charred coals, breaking their iron-stone and tumbling all into their fiery pit; there they were turning and boring cannon with a hideous shrieking noise such as the earth could hardly parallel; and through the whole,[8] half-naked demons pouring with sweat and besmeared with soot were hurrying to and fro in their red nightcaps and sheet-iron breeches,[9] rolling or hammering or squeezing their glowing metal as if it had been wax or dough.

They also had a thirst for ale. Yet on the whole I am told they are very happy; they make forty shillings or more per week, and few of them will[10] work on Mondays.

THOMAS CARLYLE, *Correspondence*.

1 Expand, *e.g., plane à jamais sur le pays.*   2 *par.*   3 *y tournent la meule de leur destinée.*   4 *sauf le pantalon.*   5 *ce n'était guère mieux.* 6 *avec une clameur pareille à celle de,* etc.   7 For translation of verb and preposition, see p. 57, § 52 (*b*). Say, *e.g., coulait en sifflant dans.*   8 *au milieu de tout cela.*   9 *jambières* (f.).   10 Meaning? *consentent à travailler,* or *travailleront,* or *veulent travailler?*

****45. AMERICAN LANDSCAPE

Twelve hours later, he was in the train to Chicago, still tired, and rather hot and short of breath. A large and untidy landscape, powdered with snow, went jolting past; he sat and stared and tried to read jumping print among a strange people, mostly with loud confident voices, dried cheeks, and anxious eyes; black men, easy and jovial fellows who seemed to have retained some secret of a rich luscious life that their masters had lost, set before him unfamiliar dishes, admirable to the eye but queerly disappointing to the palate and digestive system; he undressed and slept behind green curtains.... Chicago came, roared and rattled at him, showed him a bright glimpse of an icy lake, darkened above him, then finally sped away, before the windows of another train, into the double shadow of night and fading illusion. It was not long before the landscape became larger and untidier than ever, and gradually men began to disappear from it. Dusty plains followed the cultivated fields, only to be followed in their turn by sheer desert, leagues of fantastic rock, and hills as uncompromisingly barren and as wrinkled in the sun as an old man's brown gums. The train stopped at stations with names that seemed the very syllables of outlandish romance, but the places themselves were rarely more than a dull huddle of boxes along the track. Somehow, little or nothing came to light up his sense of wonder. The landscape, the look of the skies, and the very climate, these changed as the miles, hundreds and hundreds and hundreds of them, were run off; but there was something alternately maddening and depressing about the way in which the lives of these people refused to change, as if God had ordained that they should carry with them into these wildernesses an Ark of the Covenant containing specimens of Chesterfield and Lucky Strike cigarettes, the universal Life-savers, chewing gum, and Coco Cola, and a model of a Ford car.

J. B. PRIESTLEY, *Faraway* (Heinemann).

***46. CHICAGO

Suddenly the meaning and significance of it all dawned upon Laura. The Great Grey City, brooking no rival, imposed its dominion upon a reach of country larger than many a kingdom of the Old World.

For[1] thousands of miles beyond its confines was[2] its influence felt.[2] Out, far out, far away in the snow and shadow of Northern Wisconsin forests, axes and saws bit the bark of century-old trees, stimulated by[3] this city's energy. Just as far to the southward pick and drill leaped to the assault of veins of anthracite, moved by her central power. Her force turned[4] the wheels of harvester and seeder a thousand miles distant in Iowa and Kansas. Her force spun the screws and propellers of innumerable squadrons of lake steamers crowding[5] the Sault Sainte Marie. For her and because of her all the Central States,[6] all the Great Northwest roared[7] with traffic and industry; saw-mills screamed; factories, their smoke blackening the sky, clashed and flamed; wheels[8] turned, pistons leaped in their cylinders, cog gripped cog, beltings clasped the drums of mammoth wheels, and converters of forges belched into the clouded air their tempest-breath of molten steel.

It was Empire, the[9] resistless subjugation of all this central world of the lakes and the prairies. Here, midmost in the land, beat the Heart of the Nation, whence inevitably must come its immeasurable power, its infinite, inexhaustible vitality. Here, of[10] all her cities, throbbed the true life— the true power and spirit of America; gigantic, crude with the crudity of youth, disdaining rivalry; sane and healthy and vigorous; brutal in its ambition, arrogant in the new-found knowledge of its giant strength, prodigal of its wealth, infinite in its desires.[11]

FRANK NORRIS, The Pit (Alexander Moring).

1 *Jusqu'à.*   2 Avoid the passive; see p. 46, § 42 (b).   3 *réagissant à.*
4 *C'était sa force qui faisait tourner.*   5 Use *encombrer.*   6 *les États du Centre.*   7 Use *retentir de.*   8 = 'flywheels' = *volants.*   9 Can the English order of words be kept? See p. 74, § 64.   10 *entre.* See OF, p. 65, § 57.   11 *pleine de désirs infinis.*

*47. THE CÔTE D'OR

Every traveller who has gone by railway from Dijon to Chalon will remember how the great plain of Burgundy is bounded on the west by a steep and lofty bank of land, precipitous here and there, and almost interminably long, covered with vineyards, and with many rich villages at its base. That steep long bank of stony ground is the famous *Côte d'Or....* It is a region where the perennial flow of grape-juice, always easily transmuted into money, has made all but the imprudent rich....The inhabitants are manly, frank, hospitable, and good tempered, though rather hasty; and as for intelligence, it is not easy to find a region in all Europe where men's wits are so keen and lively. But, notwithstanding all these recommendations, the *Côte d'Or* is not a land where I should care to live....There is no water, with its pleasant life and changefulness; no hills are visible but the steep *Côte*, except on a very clear day, when you get a sight of the distant Jura, like a pale mist far away; there are no trees, or hardly any, so precious is the land for the wealth-producing vines; and your only refuge from the wearisome monotony of the scenery is to go up one of the dry narrow rocky gorges which penetrate at intervals into the elevated land.

PHILIP GILBERT HAMERTON, *Round my House* (Macmillan).

**48. THE APPROACH TO VENICE

In the olden days of travelling, there were few moments of which the recollection was more fondly cherished by the traveller than that which brought[1] him within sight of Venice, as his gondola shot into the open lagoon from[2] the canal of Mestre.

Not but[3] that the aspect of the city itself was generally the source of some slight disappointment, for, seen in this direction, its buildings are far less characteristic than those of the other great towns of Italy; but this inferiority was partly disguised by distance, and more than atoned for by the strange rising[4] of its walls and towers out of the midst, as it seemed, of the deep sea, for it was impossible that the mind[5] or the eye could at once comprehend the shallowness of the vast sheet of water which stretched away in leagues[6] of rippling lustre to the north and south, or trace the narrow line of islets bounding it to the east.

The salt breeze, the white moaning sea-birds, the masses of black weed separating and disappearing gradually, in knots of heaving shoal,[7] under the advance of the steady tide, all proclaimed it to be indeed the ocean on whose bosom⁸ the great city rested so calmly; not such blue, soft, lake-like ocean as bathes the Neapolitan promontories, or sleeps beneath the marble rocks of Genoa, but a sea with the bleak power of our own northern waves, yet subdued into a strange spacious rest, and changed⁹ from its angry pallor into a field of burnished gold, as the sun declined behind the belfry of the lonely island church, fitly named 'St George of the Sea-weed'.

JOHN RUSKIN, *The Stones of Venice.*

1 *que celui où il arrivait en vue de Venise.* 2 *sortant du canal.* 8 *Non pas que l'aspect...ne laissât point de causer,* etc. 4 *par l'étrange spectacle de...tours surgissant.* 5 *il était impossible à l'esprit...de comprendre d'emblée.* 6 *pendant des lieues en ondulations étincelantes.* 7 *en bancs enchevêtrés et onduleux.* 8 Simplify the expression: e.g., *que c'était bien sur l'océan que reposait.* 9 The transition from 'pallor' to 'field' will seem bold in French. Use, e.g., *surface: et dont la surface...avait fait place à une nappe.*

**49. THE ARICIAN GROVE

Who does not know Turner's picture of the Golden Bough? The scene, suffused with the golden glow of imagination in which the divine mind of Turner steeped and transfigured even the fairest natural landscape, is a dream-like vision of the little woodland lake of Nemi, 'Diana's Mirror', as it was called by the ancients. No one who has seen that calm water, lapped in a green hollow of the Alban Hills, can ever forget it. The two characteristic Italian villages which slumber on its banks, and the equally Italian palace whose terraced gardens descend steeply to the lake, hardly break the stillness, and even the solitariness, of the scene. Diana herself might still linger by this lonely shore, still haunt these woodlands wild.

In antiquity this sylvan landscape was the scene of a strange and recurring tragedy. On the northern shore of the lake, right under the precipitous cliffs on which the modern village of Nemi is perched, stood the sacred grove and sanctuary of Diana Nemorensis, or Diana of the Wood. The lake and the grove were sometimes known as the lake and grove of Aricia. But the town of Aricia (the modern La Riccia) was situated about three miles off, at the foot of the Alban Mount, and separated by a steep descent from the lake, which lies in a small crater-like hollow on the mountain side.

In this sacred grove there grew a certain tree round which at any time of the day, and probably far into the night, a grim figure might be seen to prowl. In his hand he carried a drawn sword, and he kept peering warily about him as if every instant he expected to be set upon by an enemy. He was a priest and a murderer; and the man for whom he looked was sooner or later to murder him and hold the priesthood in his stead. Such was the rule of the sanctuary. A candidate for the priesthood could only succeed to office by slaying the priest, and having slain him, he retained office till he was himself slain by a stronger or a craftier.

SIR JAMES G. FRAZER, *The Golden Bough* (Macmillan).

**50. THE ARICIAN GROVE (*continued*)

The post which he held[1] by this precarious tenure carried with it[2] the title of king; but surely no crowned head ever lay uneasier,[3] or was visited by more evil dreams, than his.[4] For year in year out, in summer and winter, in fair weather and in foul, he had to keep his lonely watch, and whenever he snatched a troubled slumber[5] it was at the peril of his life. The least relaxation of his vigilance, the smallest abatement of his strength of limb or skill of fence,[6] put him in jeopardy; gray hairs might seal[7] his death-warrant.

To gentle and pious pilgrims at[8] the shrine the sight of him[9] may well have appeared[10] to darken the fair landscape, as when[11] a cloud suddenly blots the sun on a bright day. The dreamy blue of Italian skies, the dappled shade of summer woods, and the sparkle of waves in the sun can have accorded but ill with that stern and sinister figure. Rather we picture to ourselves the scene as it may have been witnessed[12] by a belated wayfarer on one of those wild autumn nights when the dead leaves are falling thick, and the winds seem to sing the dirge of the dying year.

It is a sombre picture set[13] to melancholy music—the background[14] of forest showing black and jagged against a lowering and stormy sky, the sighing of the wind in the branches, the rustle of the withered leaves under foot, the lapping of the cold water on the shore, and in the foreground, pacing to and fro, now in twilight[15] and now in gloom, a dark figure with a glitter as of steel at the shoulder[16] whenever the pale moon, riding clear of the cloud-rack, peers down at him through the matted boughs.

SIR JAMES G. FRAZER, *The Golden Bough* (Macmillan).

1 *La charge qu'il occupait en vertu de ce droit précaire.*   2 Is there a single verb expressing 'carried with it'? See p. 56, § 52.   3 *jamais tête couronnée ne connut sommeil plus....*   4 Omit 'than his'.   5 *s'il lui arrivait de goûter quelques moments d'un sommeil,* etc.   6 *son habileté à manier l'épée.*   7 Say, *e.g., signifier.*   8 Expand.   9 *sa vue.*   10 *pouvait bien paraître.*   11 Omit 'when'.   12 Use *en être le témoin.*   13 *accompagné d'accents mélancoliques.*   14 *au fond, la forêt.*   15 *le crépuscule?* Or *la pénombre?* See p. 9, § 12, SHADOW.   16 *luisant à son épaule.*

*51. THE PASS OF GLENCOE

In the Gaelic tongue, Glencoe signifies the Glen of Weeping: and in truth that pass is the most dreary and melancholy of all the Scottish passes, the very Valley of the Shadow of Death. Mists and storms brood over it through the greater part of the finest summer; and even on those rare days when the sun is bright, and when there is no cloud in the sky, the impression made by the landscape is sad and awful.

The path lies along a stream which issues from the most sullen and gloomy of mountain pools. Huge precipices of naked stone frown on both sides. Even in July the streaks of snow may often be discerned in the rifts near the summits. All down the sides of the crags heaps of ruin mark the headlong paths of the torrents. Mile after mile the traveller looks in vain for the smoke of one hut, or for one human form wrapped in a plaid, and listens in vain for the bark of a shepherd's dog, or the bleat of a lamb. Mile after mile the only sound that indicates life is the faint cry of a bird of prey from some storm-beaten pinnacle of rock.

The progress of civilisation, which has turned so many wastes into fields yellow with harvests or gay with apple blossoms, has only made Glencoe more desolate. All the science and industry of a peaceful age can extract nothing valuable from that wilderness: but, in an age of violence and rapine, the wilderness itself was valued on account of the shelter which it afforded to the plunderer and his plunder.

LORD MACAULAY, *History of England.*

*52. YARROW

In such manner[1] did life pass by in the grey stone dwelling which crowned the Yarrow braes, with[2] Yarrow crooning in the nooks below. It was but yesterday I passed[3] the place,[4] which no lapse of years can change. The vale of long green hills which falls eastward from the lochs is treeless and desert for miles, with a wan stream sweeping[5] 'neath barren hill-shoulders and the grey-green bent lending[5] melancholy to all. But of a sudden it changes to a defile; the hills huddle together till[6] the waters can scarce find passage; and a forest of wildwood chokes the gorge. Brown heather and green hazels crest[7] every scarred rock and fringe[8] the foot of Birkenshaw Tower, which looks steeply[9] down on its woodland valley. Soft meadow-grass is shaded by a tangle of ashes, and in every dell the burn's trickle slips through a wild flower-garden; while in broad pools and shining stretches Yarrow goes singing her ageless song for evermore.

JOHN BUCHAN (LORD TWEEDSMUIR), *A Lost Lady of Old Years* (Nelson).

1 Say, *e.g., C'est ainsi que les jours s'écoulaient.*   2 *tandis que*+verb. 3 Use *passer par.*   4 *ce pays*; see p. 11, § 15.   5 Form new sentences, *e.g., ...y poursuit son cours rapide.*   6 Use *au point que.* See p. 68, § 59, TILL.   7 *font une crête à.*   8 *mettent une frange à.*   9 Say, *e.g., qui, du haut d'un escarpement, domine,* etc.

**53. TRINITY COLLEGE, CAMBRIDGE

The windows of my study look on the tranquil court of an ancient college, where the sundial marks the silent passage of the hours and in the long summer days the fountain plashes drowsily amid flowers and grass; where, as the evening shadows deepen, the lights come out in the blazoned windows of the Elizabethan hall and from the chapel the sweet voices of the choir, blent with the pealing music of the organ, float on the peaceful air, telling of man's eternal aspirations after truth and goodness and immortality.

Here, if anywhere, remote from the tumult and bustle of the world with its pomps and vanities and ambitions, the student may hope to hear the still voice of truth, to penetrate through the little transitory questions of the hour to the realities which abide, or rather which we fondly think must abide, while the generations come and go. I cannot be too thankful that I have been allowed to spend so many quiet and happy years in such a scene, and when I quit my old college rooms as I soon shall do, for another home in Cambridge, I shall hope to carry forward to new work in a new scene the love of study and labour which has been not indeed implanted, but fostered and cherished in this ancient home of learning and peace.

SIR JAMES G. FRAZER, *Pausanias* (Macmillan).

****54. KING'S COLLEGE, ABERDEEN

Memory is a musician with whom you cannot call the tune. Ask for a true tale of the past, and you get nothing but snatches of irrelevant lyric.[1] So, when I try to remember[2] what the days were like when the long tradition was broken and women first came[3] to King's, I become lost in a reverie[4] of beautiful inconsequent images. The irregular black houses of the descending Spital, made[5] miraculously strange and solemn by a fresh fall of snow, a flight of birds pulsing across the great virginal-blue sky above the Aulton turrets on a mild Saint Valentine's morning, a shaft of jewelled light[6]

striking through the carved places of the Chapel, the dissolving[7] groups of the quadrangle, and the proud poise[8] of
some bright head that moves no longer among the living,
the joy of hearing for the first time the rushing cadence of
Swinburne, thrown out[9] like a golden libation in the quiet
class-room, the sense of spiritual adventure in the air, the
setting of the untired falcon of the will[10] at impossible
quarry—all the irresponsible gaiety and exaggerated pessi-
mism, the bright audacities, the not ignoble follies[11] of
youth, ebbing and flowing under that dreaming Crown-
tower so compassionately used[12] to the ways of youth—
these are the treasures of remembrance. And, brooding on
these, one hardly cares to think if one were with the men or
with the women.[13]

MRS RACHEL ANNAND TAYLOR, *The Coming of the Women*
Students.

1 Say, *e.g.*, *des bribes de poèmes absolument hors de propos.* 2 *me repré-
sente en mémoire les jours où*, etc. 3 *furent admises à King's College.*
4 *tissée de.* 5 Turn by a relative clause: *qu'une récente tombée de neige
avait*, etc. 6 *une flèche de lumière irisée filtrant.* 7 *se formant et se
dispersant.* 8 *le port altier.* 9 *répandue.* 10 Say, *e.g.*, *la volonté,
telle un faucon à son premier vol, lancée à la poursuite de*, etc. 11 *les
juvéniles folies qui ne déshonorent point.* 12 *habitués à regarder avec tant
d'indulgence.* 13 *étudiants...étudiantes.*

***55. THE INTERIOR OF ST MARK'S

Through the heavy door, whose bronze network closes the
tomb, let us enter the church itself. It is lost in still deeper
twilight, to which the eye must be accustomed for some
moments before the form of the building can be traced; and
then there opens before us a vast cave, hewn out into the
form of a Cross, and divided into shadowy aisles by many
pillars.

Round the domes of its roof the light enters only through
narrow apertures like large stars; and here and there a ray
or two from some far-away casement wanders into the
darkness, and casts a narrow phosphoric stream upon the
waves of marble that heave and fall in a thousand colours

along the floor. What else there is of light is from torches or
silver lamps, burning ceaselessly in the recesses of the
chapels; the roof sheeted with gold, and the polished walls
covered with alabaster give back, at every curve and angle,
some feeble gleaming to the flames; and the glories round
the heads of the sculptured saints flash out upon us as we
pass them, and sink again into the gloom.

JOHN RUSKIN, *The Stones of Venice.*

**56. TINTERN ABBEY

Almost precisely midway between Monmouth and the
juncture with the Severn Tintern Abbey is the gem,[1] the
heart of hearts, of all this region. It could hardly have a[2]
more enchanting site than here on the broad meadow half
encircled by the Wye where it sweeps round[3] in one of its
characteristic curves. On all sides rise the hills. Of the
lesser buildings which made up the old monastic establishment, only hummocks, foundations, jutting stub-ends[4] of
massive masonry and low bits of wall remain. .Above all
these, out of the green meadow, the great church rises,
roofless, but as to its shell[5] almost complete. In[6] the
perfection of its form, the mellowed richness of its colouring,
the grace of its clustered pillars and aspiring[7] arches,
lifting[7] to a height of 70 ft., and the tracery which yet
remains in its noble west window, it stands, by common
consent, unique among the ecclesiastical ruins of the
country. And if it is lovely to us, what must it have been
to the people of this valley when it first arose?

We can in a measure picture the groping lives they lived,
the darkness of their homes, the lack[8] of music, of light and
colour in their days, the blackness of their nights. How
beautiful upon the mountains[9] to them must have been the
swell and throb of the Abbey bells; how profound the spell
as they entered the stately fane, and, with the glory cf its
coloured windows, the splendour of its music, rolling up[10]
into the shadows of that lofty roof, the solemn ritual, the
vestments, and the incense. We, nowadays, go from

Cathedral to Cathedral. We think one choir[11] is not so good as some other[11]. We do not admire that window. We like such and such a preacher only moderately. Spoiled, critical, surrendering ourselves only with reservations,[12] how can we imagine the emotions excited in[13] that simple people who had no reading, saw no pictures, travelled not at all, by such a church as Tintern when it was in all its beauty?[14] What remains to us in these grey walls, glowing so warmly[15] in the afternoon sun against the green of the river meadow, is but a memory, an echo, a faint fragrance of something more wonderful than we in these days can ever know.[16] We have lost the very capability of ever knowing.[16]

The Times, 30 Sept. 1925.

1 *bijou* or *joyau?* See p. 22, § 18, JEWEL. 2 Is 'a' to be translated? See p. 33, § 19 (c). 3 Say, *e.g.*, *qui la contourne*. 4 *tronçons*. 5 *mais l'armature presque intacte*. 6 *Par*. 7 *élancées, s'élevant à*. 8 *la désolation de leurs jours sans musique, sans*, etc. 9 *Quelle beauté a dû verser sur les montagnes la...voix des cloches*, etc. 10 Use *monter* and expand. 11 *tel chœur...tel autre*. 12 *ne nous abandonnant jamais complètement à l'admiration*. 13 *provoquées chez*. 14 *alors dans l'éclat de toute sa beauté*. 15 *dont les teintes si chaudes...tranchent sur*. 16 *savoir* will hardly do; use *se faire une idée de*.

*57. THE GLASS AT CHARTRES

How true it is that in order to know a place you must see it often! First impressions can be vivid, and their impact of suddenness and freshness is, of course, irrecoverable; but they can be very misleading too. I first saw Chartres Cathedral twenty years ago, and ever since then I have had in my mind's eye stained glass of glorious purple richness. But when I saw it again I found that the glass of reality was not equal to the glass of defective recollection. Nothing else was a disappointment. And the formation of the windows that held the glass was even more beautiful than I had thought; indeed, the famous rose window over the Portail Royal—la Rose Occidentale—must be one of the loveliest pieces of delicate stone-work in the world: you must go to York to excel it; which leads to the reflection that in our pleasure in coloured glass we are too apt not to give enough credit to the masons who devised these lace-like frameworks.   E. V. LUCAS, *Zigzags in France* (Methuen).

*58. A MOSQUE

He had always liked this mosque. It was gracious, and the arrangement pleased him. The courtyard—entered through[1] a ruined gate—contained an ablution tank of fresh clear water, which[2] was always in motion, being indeed part of a conduit that supplied the city. The courtyard was paved with broken slabs. The covered part of the mosque was deeper than is usual; its effect was that of an English parish church whose side had been[3] taken out. Where he sat, he looked into three arcades whose darkness was illuminated by a small hanging[4] lamp and by the moon. The front—in full moonlight—had the appearance of marble, and the ninety-nine names of God on the frieze stood out black, as the frieze stood out white against the sky. The contest[5] between this dualism and the contention of shadows within pleased[6] Aziz, and he tried[6] to symbolize[7] the whole into some truth of religion or love. A mosque by winning his approval let loose his imagination. The temple of another creed, Hindu, Christian, or Greek, would have bored him and failed[8] to awaken his sense of beauty. Here was Islam,[9] his own country, more than a Faith, more than a battle-cry, more, much more....Islam, an attitude towards life both exquisite and durable, where[10] his body and his thoughts found their home.[11]

E. M. FORSTER, *A Passage to India* (Arnold).

1 *à laquelle on accédait par.*   2 *où une eau...circulait sans cesse, étant en effet branchée sur un conduit,* etc.   3 Tense in similes? See p. 48, § 46. 4 *suspendue au plafond.*   5 *Le conflit entre ce dualisme et la lutte d'ombres à l'intérieur.*   6 Tense? Is 'pleased' = 'was pleasing to' Aziz. Or = 'gave Aziz a shock of pleasure'?   7 *se représenter le tout comme symbolique d'une vérité.*   8 = 'would have been unable to'. Use *pouvoir.*   9 *Ici c'était l'Islam.*   10 For clearness repeat the noun: *l'Islam, où.*   11 *leur refuge naturel.*

**59. CHRISTMAS

Fine old Christmas, with the snowy hair and ruddy face, had done his duty that year in the noblest fashion, and had set off his rich gifts of warmth and colour with all the heightening contrast of frost and snow.

Snow lay on the croft and river-bank in undulations softer than the limbs of infancy; it lay with the neatliest finished border on every sloping roof, making the dark-red gables stand out with a new depth of colour; it weighed heavily on the laurels and fir-trees, till it fell from them with a shuddering sound; it clothed the rough turnip-field with whiteness, and made the sheep look like dark blotches; the gates were all blocked up with the sloping drifts, and here and there a disregarded four-footed beast stood as if petrified 'in unrecumbent sadness'; there was no gleam, no shadow, for the heavens, too, were one still, pale cloud—no sound or motion in anything but the dark river that flowed and moaned like an unresting sorrow.

GEORGE ELIOT, *The Mill on the Floss.*

*60. EN PROVINCE

The long warm summers and the pleasant surroundings of a rural French town have aided in the formation[1] of these habits. There are the avenues to walk under[2]—fine avenues of elm, or linden, or oriental plane-tree,[3] the green seats to rest upon and talk,[4] the *cafés* close by, with their tables and chairs outside on the broad *trottoir*, the club-rooms upstairs,[5] with their open windows and balconies, from which you have perhaps a view[6] of hill or wood, or winding river.

Then there is nothing particularly[7] disagreeable in the little town itself—no coal-smoke, no rows of especially ugly houses, but the old streets are quaintly picturesque, and the new boulevard is bright and gay, so that one can walk pleasantly anywhere.

And the country is so near all round! In a quarter of an

hour you have passed[8] the old walls, and are in it, amongst the gardens.

There are gardens, too, in the heart of the little city itself; the doctor walks in his garden,[9] and plucks a peach, between the visits[10] of two patients; the banker's counting-house is in his garden, and he walks about amongst his flowers, which refresh[11] his mind with other thoughts than[12] that eternal money.   PHILIP GILBERT HAMERTON, *Round My House.*

1 ='have helped to form' (*établir*).   2 *où l'on peut se promener.*   3 *sycomores* (note the spelling).   4 *s'entretenir.*   5 *au premier.*   6 *d'où on peut découvrir des collines.*   7 *par trop.*   8 Use *dépasser.*   9 To avoid undue repetition of *jardin*, say *dans le sien.*   10 *entre deux visites de clients.*   11 *reposer.*   12 *des pensées autres que.*

*61. IN THE TRENCHES

'Mind yer nut', said Trotter, as Raleigh followed him up the steep, earthy steps to his first duty in the trenches. 'These tin 'ats 'ave saved many a skull from being cracked on low roofs.'

They stood together in the trench while Trotter wheezily regained his breath. The crisp, cool air and the grey darkness of the night were startling in contrast to the stuffy, candle-lit dugout. There had been a dense, solid stillness down there, a stillness which had made voices hollow and unreal. Up here in the trenches it was different, a vague awe-inspiring *something* lay over them. There were sounds—sounds which Raleigh did not understand. Sometimes there was the dull, far-off rumble that he had heard before. It came now, it seemed, with each light rustle of the breeze. Shadows crept slowly here and there with the rise and fall of Very lights. Now and then machine-guns rapped out vigorously and single rifles cracked. The sounds of the bullets passing overhead were like long-drawn-out sighs. Then there were intervals of silence, broken by the low drone of talking men, and once a big shell passed high above the clouds, bringing to them the quiet sound of a rippling stream.

R. C. SHERRIFF and VERNON BARTLETT, *Journey's End*
(Gollancz).

*62. THE SHAP GRADIENT

They passed by Lancaster, skirting the sea on which the
moon shone bright, setting the fishing-boats in silver[1] as
they lay scarcely moving[2] on the waves. Then, so to speak,
the train set its face up against[3] Shap Fell, and, puffing
heavily, drew up into the hills, the scattered grey stone
houses of the north, flanked by their gnarled and twisted ash
trees, hanging upon the edge of the streams, as lonely, and
as cut off from the world (except the passing train) as they
had been in Central Africa. The moorland roads, winding
amongst the heather, showed that the feet[4] of generations
had marked them out, and not the line, spade and theodo-
lite, with all the circumstance of modern road makers.[5]
They, too, looked white and unearthly in the moonlight, and
now and then a sheep, aroused by the snorting of the train,
moved from the heather into the middle of the road, and
stood there motionless, its shadow filling[6] the narrow track,
and flickering on the heather at the edge.

R. B. CUNNINGHAME GRAHAM, *Scottish Stories: Beattock
for Moffat* (Duckworth).

1 *encadrant d'argent.*   2 *qui remuaient à peine.*   3 Use simply
s'attaquer à; 'so to speak' and 'face' could then be left untranslated.
4 *les pas.*   5 *tout l'appareil de nos ingénieurs modernes.*   6 = 'filling...
with its shadow which flickered.'

***63. A SCOTTISH FUNERAL

Four stalwart neighbours, holding their hats, which tapped
upon their legs, hoisted the coffin to their shoulders and
shuffled to the door. They stooped to let their burden pass
beneath the eaves which overhung the entrance, and then
emerging, dazed, into the light, their black clothes dusted
over with the white ashes from the fire, set down the coffin
on the cart. Once more the men gathered into a circle and
listened to a prayer, some with their heads bare to the rain,
and others with their hats held on the slant to fend it off as
it came swirling down the blast.

A workman in his ordinary clothes took the tall, white-faced horse close by the bit, and, with a jolt which made the coffin shift up against the backboard, the cart set out, swaying amongst the ruts, with now and then a wheel running up high upon one side and now and then a jerk upon the trace-hooks, when the horse, cold with his long wait, strained wildly on the chains.

The rain had blotted out the hills, the distant village with its rival kirks had disappeared, and the grey sky appeared to touch the surface of the moor. A whitish dew hung on the grass and made the seeded plants appear gigantic in the gloom. Nothing was to be heard except the roaring of the burn and the sharp ringing of the high caulkins of the horse as he struck fire amongst the stones on the steep, rocky road.

Leaning against the doorpost, the widow stood and gazed after the vanishing procession till it had disappeared into the mist, her tears, which she had fought so bravely to keep back, now running down her face.

When the last sound of the cart-wheels and of the horse's feet amongst the stones had vanished into the thick air, she turned away, and, sitting down before the fire, began mechanically to smoor the peats and tidy up the hearth.

R. B. CUNNINGHAME GRAHAM, *Scottish Stories*: *At Dalmary*
(Duckworth).

***64. RAISING THE 'KEEN'

Outside the church door, when benediction ended[1] and no one was left in the building[2] but the schoolmaster teaching children their catechism in Irish, a ritual more distinctive still was enacted.[3]

Perhaps fifty out of that immense congregation made their way into the churchyard, and stood[4] for the most part chatting in a group round the monument to[5] a departed priest. But a few women there[6] detached themselves from the rest, and, each of them picking her way through the grass to a gravestone or the little cross that marked a tomb still simpler, knelt down, and, bending forward, pressed her face close to the ground. Then—from the very earth it seemed—there rose a faint crying, hardly louder at first than a cricket's noise—swelling, dying down, swelling again, yet always so faint that out there in the open it was hardly audible ten yards off, unless one strained[7] to hear it.

But then a woman raised the chant[8] from a grave just beside us; and, as one listened to her cry near at hand, and the other faint wailings, all chanted to[9] the same heart-rending little tune, they[10] seemed to fill all earth and heaven. It was like the cry, not of this or that wife or mother, but of the land itself—a voice issuing here from among the graves —the wailing of Ireland after her scattered sons.

STEPHEN GWYNN, *For Second Reading: A Sunday in Donegal.*

1 Turn as if 'after benediction, when'.   2 *à l'intérieur.*   3 Use *se dérouler.*   4 *demeurer* +à+ Infinitive.   5 Something must be supplied (see p. 62, § 55), *e.g.*, *élevé.*   6 Expand; see p. 39, § 30, SOME, FEW. 7 *à moins de tendre l'oreille.*   8 *fit entendre cette psalmodie sur une tombe.* 9 Use *moduler sur.*   10 *elles* would be ambiguous; say *ces voix.*

II. PORTRAITS

*65. JOHN MILTON

He had abroun* hayre. His complexion exceeding faire—he was so faire that they called him *the lady of Christ's College.* Ovall face. His eie a darke gray.

He had a delicate tuneable voice, and had good skill. His father instructed him. He had an organ in his howse; he played on that most.

Of a very cheerfull humour.—He would be chearfull even in his gowle-fitts, and sing. . . .

He had a very good memorie; but I beleeve that his excellent method of thinking and disposing did much to helpe his memorie. . . .

His exercise was chiefly walking.

He was an early riser (scil. at 4 a clock manè); yea, after he lost his sight. He had a man read to him. The first thing he read was the Hebrew Bible, and that was at 4 h. manè ½h. +. Then he contemplated.

At 7 his man came to him again, and then read to him again, and wrote till dinner: the writing was as much as the reading. His (2) daughter, Deborah, could read to him Latin, Italian and French, and Greeke. Maried in Dublin to one Mr Clarke (sells silke, etc.); very like her father. The other sister is (1) Mary, more like her mother.

After dinner he used to walke 3 or foure houres at a time (he always had a garden where he lived); went to bed about 9.

Temperate man, rarely dranke between meales. Extreme pleasant in his conversation, and at dinner, supper, etc.; but satyricall.   JOHN AUBREY, *Brief Lives*, 1669–1696.

* *abroun* = auburn.

***66. WATTEAU'S 'GILLES'

Gilles is standing[1] immediately in front of us, on purpose, as if he has been told to stand[1] still. His arms hang straight down at his sides.[2] He has shoes tied with ribbons, a white ruff, and a wide hat.[3] Underneath[4] this he wears a nightcap, or perhaps it is[5] the white cap[6] of a pierrot, for his hat is too big for him. So are his clothes. They hang loosely upon him, and look as if they had been borrowed. As for his face, he has dark eyebrows and a full mouth.[7] And his expression tells[8] us he is not certain if[9] he can make us laugh. Mezzetin, il Dottore, and the rest of the company are chattering noisily in the background, low down, at the level[10] of his knees, while a garden term[11] smiles cynically at them from underneath the boughs.

But the figure[12] of Gilles holds all the attention. He does not look[13] as if he knew what to do next. He is playing the peasant.[14] This is apparent in his doltish attitude, and in the fact that his trousers are cut short in order to exaggerate the length of his body. This is an attitude of the peasant; but the legs of Gilles are not really short, for his hands, though they hang down straight before him, do not reach below his coat. He is a tall, thin young man, posing as[15] a peasant. His arms should hang down nearly to the ground, so that he need not stoop to[16] the soil; but, all the time, the waist of Gilles is somewhere high up, hidden above the pockets of his tubular coat. This is white as moonlight; while his sleeves, so as to add to the lie[17] that he is a little man posing in clothes that are too big for him, have so many folds above the elbows that, in effect, they are pulled up and arranged there, or else,[18] pierrot-like, his sleeves would cover up his hands. As for his ruff, it is for Sunday best.

SACHEVERELL SITWELL, *Dance of the Quick and Dead*
(Faber and Faber).

1 See p. 55, § 51, To STAND.   2 *le long du corps.*   3 *un grand chapeau?* Or *un chapeau à grands bords?* Or *à larges bords?* Which seems best? 4 Continue: *Là dessous?* Or, continuing the sentence, *sous lequel?*   5 *à moins que ce ne soit?* Or *ou peut-être est-ce?* Which seems the better?   6 *ca-lotte* (f.).   7 *il a...les lèvres fortes.*   8 *nous apprend?* Or *nous dit?* Or *nous prévient?*   9 *sûr de pouvoir.*   10 *à la hauteur de?* Or *au niveau de?*   11 *un dieu terme de jardin.*   12 *la personne.*   13 *Il ne semble pas très bien savoir.*   14 *il joue un rôle de paysan.*   15 *posant au paysan.*   16 *pour qu'il n'ait pas à se courber vers.*   17 *pour ajouter à l'illusion.*   18 *sans quoi.*

***67. FREDERICK THE GREAT

He is a King every inch of him, though without the trappings of a King. Presents himself in a Spartan simplicity of vesture: no crown but an old military cocked hat generally old, or trampled and kneaded into absolute *softness* if new; no sceptre but one like Agamemnon's, a walking-stick cut from the woods, which serves also as a riding stick (with which he hits the horse 'between the ears', say authors) and for royal robes, a mere soldier's blue coat with red facings, coat likely to be old, and sure to have a good deal of Spanish snuff on the breast of it; rest of the apparel dim, unobtrusive in colour or cut, ending in high over-knee military boots, which may be brushed (and, I hope, kept soft with an underhand suspicion of oil), but are not permitted to be blackened or varnished: Day and Martin with their soot-pots forbidden to approach.

The man is not of godlike physiognomy, any more than of imposing stature or costume: close-shut mouth with thin lips, prominent jaws and nose, receding brow, by no means of Olympian height; head, however, is of long form, and has superlative gray eyes in it. Not what is called a beautiful man; nor yet, by all appearance, what is called a happy. On the contrary, the face bears the evidence of many sorrows, as they are termed, of much hard labour done in this world; and seems to anticipate nothing but more still coming. Quiet stoicism, capable enough of what joys there were, but not expecting any worth mention; great unconscious and some conscious pride, well tempered with a cheery mockery of humour—are written on that old face; which carries its chin well forward, in spite of the slight stoop about the neck; snuffy nose rather flung into the air, under its old cocked hat—like an old snuffy lion on the watch; and such a pair of eyes as no man or lion or lynx of that century bore elsewhere, according to all the testimony we have. 'Those eyes', says Mirabeau, 'which, at the bidding of his great soul, fascinated you with seduction or with terror.'

THOMAS CARLYLE, *Frederick the Great.*

***68. SWINBURNE

Swinburne's entry was[1] for me a great moment. Here, suddenly visible in the flesh, was the legendary being and divine singer. Here he was, shutting the door behind him, as might anyone else, and advancing—a strange small figure in grey, having an air at once noble and roguish, proud and skittish. My name was roared to him. In shaking his hand, I bowed low, of course—a bow *de cœur*; and he,[2] in the old aristocratic manner, bowed equally low, but with such swiftness that we narrowly escaped concussion.

You do not usually associate[3] a man of genius, when you see one, with any social class; and, Swinburne being of an aspect so unrelated as it was to any species of human kind,

I wondered the more that almost the first impression he made on me, or would make on anyone, was that of a very great gentleman indeed. Not of an *old* gentleman, either. Sparse and straggling though the grey hair was that fringed the immense pale dome of his head, and venerably haloed though he was for me by his greatness, there was yet about him something—boyish? girlish? childish, rather; something of a beautifully well-bred child. But he had the eyes of a god, and the smile of an elf.

In figure,[4] at first glance, he seemed almost fat; but this was merely because of the way he carried himself, with his long neck strained so tightly back that he all receded from the waist upwards. I noticed afterwards that this deportment made the back[5] of his jacket hang quite far away from his legs;[6] and so small and sloping[7] were his shoulders that the jacket seemed ever so likely to slip right off. I became aware, too, that when he bowed he did not unbend his back, but only his neck—the length of the neck accounting for the depth of the bow. His hands were tiny, even for his size, and they fluttered[8] helplessly, touchingly, unceasingly.   MAX BEERBOHM, *And Even Now* (Heinemann).

1 *était* or *fut?*   2 *lui*; see p. 41, § 34 (*b*).   3 Transpose: *En voyant un homme de génie...on ne le rattache*, etc.   4 *de sa personne.*   5 *les basques.*   6 *hanches.* Use *tombant.*   8 *s'agitaient.*

**69. MRS POYSER

Do not suppose, however, that Mrs Poyser was elderly or shrewish in her appearance; she was a good-looking woman, not more than eight-and-thirty, of fair complexion and sandy hair, well-shapen, light-footed: the most conspicuous article in her attire was an ample checkered linen apron, which almost covered her skirt; and nothing could be plainer or less noticeable than her cap and gown, for there was no weakness of which she was less tolerant than feminine vanity, and the preference of ornament to utility.

The family likeness between her and her niece Dinah Morris, with the contrast between her keenness and Dinah's

seraphic gentleness of expression, might have served a
painter as an excellent suggestion for Martha and Mary.
Their eyes were just of the same colour, but a striking test
of the difference in their operation was seen in the demeanour of Trip, the black-and-tan terrier, whenever that
much-suspected dog unwarily exposed himself to the
freezing arctic ray of Mrs Poyser's glances. Her tongue was
not less keen than her eye, and whenever a damsel came
within earshot, seemed to take up an unfinished lecture, as a
barrel-organ takes up a tune, precisely at the point where it
had left off.   GEORGE ELIOT, *Adam Bede*.

****70. CLARA MIDDLETON

She had the mouth that smiles[1] in repose. The lips[2] met full
on the centre of the bow and thinned along to a lifting
dimple;[2] the eyelids also lifted slightly at the outer corners
and seemed, like the lip into the limpid cheek, quickening
up the temples, as with a run of light. Her features were
playfellows of one another, none of them pretending to rigid
correctness, nor the nose to the ordinary dignity of governess
among merry girls,[3] despite which the nose was of a fair
design, not acutely interrogative or inviting to gambols.
    Aspens imaged in water, waiting for the breeze, would
offer a susceptible lover[4] some suggestion of her face: a pure
smooth-white face, tenderly flushed in the cheeks, where the
gentle dints were faintly intermelting even during quietness.
Her eyes were brown, set well[5] between mild lids, often
shadowed, not unwakeful. Her hair of lighter brown,
swelling above her temples on the sweep to the knot,
imposed[6] the triangle of the fabulous wild woodland visage
from brow to mouth and chin, evidently in agreement with
her taste; and the triangle suited her; but her face was not
significant of a tameless wildness or of weakness; her
equable shut mouth[7] threw its long curve to guard the small
round chin from that effect; her eyes wavered only in
humour, they were steady when thoughtfulness was
awakened; and at such seasons the build of her winter-

beechwood hair lost the touch of nymph-like and whimsical, and strangely, by mere outline,[8] added to her appearance of studious concentration.

GEORGE MEREDITH, *The Egoist* (Chapman & Hall).

1 *Sa bouche était de celles* (see p. 44, § 37 (*d*)) *qui sourient.*   2 Work in, e.g., *l'arc des lèvres, s'amincir, se relever.*   3 *fillettes.*   4 *un amoureux sensitif.*   5 *bien enchâssés dans.*   6 *donnaient à son visage...une forme triangulaire.*   7 *ses lèvres projetaient leur longue courbe, préservant contre cette expression, etc.*   8 *par son seul contour.*

**71. SCROOGE

Oh! But he was a tight-fisted hand at the grindstone, Scrooge! a squeezing, wrenching, grasping, scraping, clutching, covetous, old sinner! Hard and sharp as flint, from which no steel had ever struck out generous fire; secret and self-contained, and solitary as an oyster. The cold within him froze his old features, nipped his pointed nose, shrivelled his cheek, stiffened his gait; made his eyes red, his thin lips blue; and spoke out shrewdly in his grating voice. A frosty rime was on his head, and on his eyebrows, and his wiry chin. He carried his own low temperature always about with him; he iced his office in the dog-days, and didn't thaw it one degree at Christmas.

External heat and cold had little influence on Scrooge. No warmth could warm, nor wintry weather chill him. No wind that blew was bitterer than he, no falling snow was more intent upon its purpose, no pelting rain less open to entreaty. Foul weather didn't know where to have him. The heaviest rain, and snow, and hail and sleet, could boast of the advantage over him in only one respect. They often 'came down' handsomely, and Scrooge never did.

CHARLES DICKENS, *A Christmas Carol.*

**72. MR SLOPE

Mr Slope is tall, and not ill made. His[1] feet and hands are large, as has ever been the case with all his family, but he has a broad chest and wide shoulders, and on the whole his figure is good. His countenance, however, is not specially prepossessing. His hair is lank, and of a dull pale reddish hue.[2] It is always formed into[3] three straight lumpy masses, each brushed with admirable precision, and cemented with much grease;[4] two of them adhere closely to the sides of his face[5] and the other lies at right angles above them. He wears no whiskers, and is always punctiliously shaven. His face is nearly of the same colour as his hair, though perhaps a little redder; it is not unlike beef—beef, however, one would say, of a bad quality. His forehead is capacious and high, but square and heavy, and unpleasantly shining. His mouth is large, though his lips are thin and bloodless; and his big, prominent, pale brown[6] eyes inspire anything but[7] confidence. His nose, however, is his redeeming feature: it is pronounced, straight and well-formed.

ANTHONY TROLLOPE, *Barchester Towers.*

1 The usual construction would be awkward here because of the agreement of the adjective; say *il a de grands pieds et de grandes mains.* 2 For 'of a reddish hue' *d'un roux* will suffice. 3 Use *disposé en.* 4 *à grand renfort de cosmétique.* 5 *les tempes* (f.). 6 See p. 10, § 13 (c). 7 *ne ...rien moins que.*

**73. An English Stage-Coachman

Wherever an English stage-coachman may be seen, he cannot be mistaken for any other craft or mystery.

He has commonly a broad, full face, curiously mottled with red, as if the blood had been forced by hard feeding into every vessel of the skin; he is swelled into jolly dimensions by frequent potations of malt liquors, and his bulk is still further increased by a multiplicity of coats, in which he is buried like a cauliflower, the upper one reaching to his heels. He wears a broad-brimmed, low-crowned hat; a huge roll of coloured handkerchief about his neck, knowingly knotted and tucked in at the bosom; and has in summertime a large bouquet of flowers in his buttonhole; the present, most probably, of some enamoured country lass. His waistcoat is commonly of some bright colour, striped, and his small-clothes extend far below the knees, to meet a pair of jockey-boots which reach about half-way up his legs.

All this costume is maintained with much precision; he has a pride in having his clothes of excellent materials; and, notwithstanding the seeming grossness of his appearance, there is still discernible that neatness and propriety of person which is almost inherent in an Englishman.

WASHINGTON IRVING, *The Sketch Book* (Macmillan).

*74. THE KOOKABURRA

You find him nearly all over Australia; for he likes[1] mankind, he enjoys[1] society, he loves[1] a joke, and shyness is a vice he is commendably free from.[2] He is a species of kingfisher: a jovial broad-shouldered person in a badly crumpled morning coat, obviously ready-made. His wife ought to brush it for him, but she is just as happy-go-lucky as he is. 'Bust appearances!' she says (for her tongue[3] is as free as her husband's): 'our job is to kill snakes. Observe our bill. Could anything be better[4] to grab them with? Could anything (you will forgive the slight touch of swagger? —it runs in the family!) be more imposing?' You have to admit that nothing could.[5]

This gigantic dagger of[6] a bill is the first bit of kookaburra you see. He sits hunched up on an old stump, his big domed head sunk on his chest,[7] and his brown coat-tails drooping behind him. Now and again he chuckles to himself[8] in Rabelaisian reminiscence. You approach cautiously, forgetting that you have on an old frayed school tie, a relic of dressier[9] days. Kookaburra spies it: jerks himself to life, and throws back his head to bawl the good news to a friend.

'Hi! Jack! 'Ere's a bloke wi' red'n black feathers rahnd 'is neck! Tell Bill. Hoo-kukka-kukka-*ray*!'

Jack does. The bush rings with the riotous tidings as they are shouted from tree to tree.

'...bloke wi' red'n black feathers rahnd 'is neck!'... They laugh and laugh...and all you can do, helplessly, is to sit down on the ground and laugh with them.

THOMAS WOOD, *Cobbers* (Oxford University Press).

1 For all three words the stock translation is *lui plaît*. Use it for 'enjoys' and say, for the other two, *e.g., est à son goût* and *il aime*.   2 Say, *e.g., et, louable particularité, la timidité est son moindre défaut.*   3 *son langage.*
4 *Pourrait-on rien imaginer de mieux pour*, etc.   5 *avouer que non.*
6 Translate as if 'which this bill is' and use *qu'est* as in the examples, p. 44, § 39.   7 *lui tombant sur la poitrine.*   8 *des souvenirs rabelaisiens lui arrachent un petit rire étouffé.*   9 *relique de vos élégances de naguère.*

****75. Mr Chester Coote**

There comes a gentlemanly figure into these events, and for a space takes a leading part therein, a Good Influence, a refined and amiable figure, Mr Chester Coote. You must figure him as about to enter our story, walking with a curious rectitude of bearing through the evening dusk towards the Public Library, erect, large-headed—he had a great big head, full of the suggestion of a powerful mind well under control—with a large official-looking envelope in his white and knuckly hand. In the other he carries a gold-handled cane. He wears a silken gray jacket suit, buttoned up, and anon he coughs behind the official envelope. He has a prominent nose, slaty gray eyes, and a certain heaviness about the mouth. His mouth hangs breathing open, with a slight protrusion of the lower jaw. His straw hat is pulled down a little in front, and he looks each person he passes in the eye, and, directly his look is answered, looks away.

Thus Mr Chester Coote, as he was on the evening when he came upon Kipps. He was a local house-agent, and a most active and gentlemanly person, a conscious gentleman, equally aware of society and the serious side of life. From amateur theatricals of a nice refined sort to science classes, few things were able to get along without him. He supplied a fine full bass, a little flat and quavery perhaps, but very abundant, to the St Stylites's choir....

He goes on towards the Public Library, lifts the envelope in salutation to a passing curate, smiles, and enters....

H. G. WELLS, Kipps (Macmillan).

***76. LEWIS ALISON

Lewis Alison, a dark, craggy[1] man of more than common height, gave no sign of sharing in the general curiosity. He stayed in his place, seeming to have wrapped himself in a composure not easily to be disturbed.[2] Thirty years[3] had left upon him more than their accustomed mark—not upon his physical appearance only, but upon his manner, delaying his smile and giving an air of deliberateness to his speech and movement. Vigour and eagerness lay in[4] his eyes, and his hair,[5] full and black, had the glisten of youth upon it;[6] his body was pliant and his cheeks could darken with colour when whipped by excitement,[7] but his good looks were of[8] maturity, and owed so much to something austere and self-disciplined in his expression that it was hard for one who had[9] not known him in the past to imagine him as a very young man, sanguine and impetuous. But while he sat in this train, which the early twilight of winter was already filling with shadow, even his boyhood might have been guessed at by one[10] who watched him closely. When he spoke, there was in his voice a mingling[11] of quietness and animation which made him master of his company. Throughout the morning and the afternoon he had spoken little. A book on[12] his knee had occupied him, and the turn of his fingers as he lifted[13] a page suggested a loving reader.

CHARLES MORGAN, *The Fountain* (Macmillan).

1 *anguleux.* 2 *difficile à + active* Infinitive. 3 *La trentaine.* 4 *se lisaient dans.* 5 *chevelure* (f.)? Or *cheveux?* See p. 21, § 18, HAIR. 6 Omit 'upon it'. 7 *sous le coup de l'émotion.* 8 Expand to 'those of'. 9 Tense? See p. 48, § 46. 10 *on eût pu, à l'observer attentivement, deviner jusqu'à* (see p. 59, § 54, EVEN). 11 Use *se mêler.* 12 Expand (see p. 62, § 55); *e.g., qu'il tenait sur.* 13 *quand il tournait la page.*

III. NARRATIVE

**77. DEATH OF MR VALIANT

After this it was noised abroad that Mr Valiant-for-truth
was taken with a summons by the same post as the other,
and had this as a token that the summons was true, 'That
his pitcher was broken at the fountain'. When he understood
it he called for his friends, and told them of it. Then said he,
I am going to my Father's, and though with great difficulty
I am got hither, yet now I do not repent me of all the
Trouble I have been at to arrive where I am. My Sword, I
give to him that shall succeed me in my Pilgrimage, and my
Courage and Skill, to him that can get it. My Marks and
Scars I carry with me, to be a Witness for me, that I have
fought his Battles who now will be my Rewarder. When the
Day that he must go hence was come, many accompanied
him to the River side, into which as he went, he said,
'Death, where is thy Sting?' And as he went down deeper,
he said, 'Grave, where is thy Victory?' So he passed over,
and all the Trumpets sounded for him on the other side.

JOHN BUNYAN, The Pilgrim's Progress.

*78. THE DEATH OF SHELLEY

I trust that the first news[1] of the dreadful calamity which has
befallen us here will have been broken to you by report,[1]
otherwise I shall come on you with a most painful abrupt-
ness; but[2] Shelley, my divine-minded friend, your friend,
the friend of the universe, he has perished at sea.

He was going in a boat with his friend Captain Williams,
going from Leghorn to Lerici, when a storm arose, and it is
supposed the boat must have foundered. It was on the 8th
instant, about four or five in the evening, they guess.[3] A
fisherman says he saw[4] the boat a few minutes before it
went down;[5] he looked again and it was gone. He saw the
boy[6] they had with them aloft furling one of the sails.

We hope his story is true, as their passage from life to
death will then have been short; and what adds to the hope[7]

is, that in S.'s pocket (for the bodies were both thrown on shore[8] some days afterwards,—conceive our horrible certainty, after trying all we could to hope!) a copy[9] of Keats's last volume, which he had borrowed of me to read on his passage, was found *open* and doubled back as if it had been thrust in, in the hurry of a surprise.[9]

I cannot help thinking of him as if he were alive as much as ever, so[10] unearthly[11] he always appeared to me, and so[10] seraphical a thing[12] of the elements; and this is what all his friends say.

LEIGH HUNT, *Letter to Horace Smith*, Pisa, 25 July 1822.

1 Turn transitively: *le bruit qui court vous aura préparé aux premières nouvelles.* 2 Omit. 3 Put earlier in the sentence: *croit-on.* 4 The Infinitive (see p. 77, § 68) is neater than *que.* 5 Mood? See p. 66, § 59, BEFORE. 6 Meaning of 'boy' here? See p. 15, § 18, BOY. 7 *cet espoir.* 8 Use *rejeter sur la côte.* 9 It seems justifiable here to alter the English order of words: *on a trouvé...plié en deux comme...surprise un exemplaire ...pour lire pendant la traversée.* 10 *tant.* Its position in the sentence? See p. 61, § 54, So. 11 *étranger à ce monde.* 12 *une créature.*

*79. SOBIESKI'S FAREWELL

At the great gate his horse stopped and neighed with a strange sound.

'Poor Saladin!' cried Thaddeus, stroking his neck, 'are you so sorry at leaving Warsaw that, like your unhappy master, you linger to take a last look?'

His tears redoubled, and the warder, as he closed the gate after him, implored permission to kiss the hand of the noble Count Sobieski, ere he should turn his back on Poland, never to return. Thaddeus looked kindly around, and shaking hands with the honest man, after saying a few friendly words to him, rode on with a loitering pace till he reached that part of the river which divides Poland from the Prussian dominions.

Here he flung himself off his horse, and standing for a moment on the hill that rises near the bridge, retraced, with his almost blinded sight, the long and desolated lands through which he had passed; then, involuntarily dropping on his knees, he plucked a tuft of grass, and pressing it to his lips, exclaimed, 'Farewell, Poland! Farewell, all my earthly happiness!'

Almost stifled by emotion, he put this poor relic of his country into his bosom, and remounting his noble animal, crossed the bridge.

JANE PORTER, *Thaddeus of Warsaw* (Routledge).

**80. JULIE DE LESPINASSE

She died on the 22nd of May, 1776, in the forty-fourth year of her life.[1] She was buried quietly[2] in the cemetery of Saint-Sulpice, d'Alembert and Condorcet performing the final rites.[3] For d'Alembert, however, there was one more duty. She had named him her executor; it was his task[4] to examine her papers; and, when he did so,[5] he made a discovery which cut him to the heart. Not a single letter of his own[6] had been preserved among all the multitude; instead, it was Mora, Mora, Mora, and nothing else. He had fondly imagined that, among her[7] friends, his own place had been the first. In his distress, he rushed to Guibert, pouring out[8] his disappointment, his cruel disillusionment: 'Oh! we were all of us mistaken; it was Mora that she loved!' Guibert was silent. The tragic irony was complete. A thousand memories besieged him, a thousand thoughts of past delights[9] of vanished conversations, of delicious annihilated hours; he was stifled[10] by regrets, by remorse, by vain possibilities; he was blinded[10] by endless visions of a pearl richer than all his tribe; a dreadful mist of tears, of desecration, of horror, rose up and clouded[11] him for ever from his agonised and deluded friend.

LYTTON STRACHEY, *Characters and Commentaries*
(Chatto and Windus).

1 Omit 'of her life'. Say: 'in her forty-fourth year'.   2 *simplement.*
3 *où d'Alembert...lui rendirent les derniers devoirs.*   4 *il avait la charge de.*   5 *en s'acquittant.*   6 See p. 40, § 32.   7 *ses,* meaning 'his' as well as 'hers', might be ambiguous; *les amis de la défunte.*   8 *courut vite trouver Guibert pour épancher,* etc.   9 *transports passés.*   10 French prefers the active form (see p. 46, § 42 (a)): *les regrets...l'étouffaient...les visions...l'aveuglaient.*   11 Use *séparer.*

**81. A Story in Boccaccio

The clear waves seemed to invite her; she wished she could lie down to sleep on them and pass from sleep into death. But Romola could not directly seek death; the fullness of young life in her forbade that. She could only wish that death would come.

At the spot where she had paused there was a deep bend in the shore, and a small boat with a sail was moored there. In her longing to glide over the waters that were getting golden with the level sun-rays, she thought of a story which had been one of the things she had loved to dwell on in Boccaccio, when her father fell asleep and she glided from her stool to sit on the floor and read the 'Decamerone'. It was the story of that fair Gostanza who in her love-lornness desired to live no longer, but not having the courage to attack her young life, had put herself into a boat and pushed off to sea; then, lying down in the boat, had wrapt her mantle round her head, hoping to be wrecked, so that her fear would be helpless to flee from death.

GEORGE ELIOT, *Romola* (Blackwood).

**82. On the Window-sill

At the side of the room were high windows[1] of Ham-hill stone, upon either sill[2] of which she could sit by first mounting a desk and using it[3] as a footstool. As the evening advanced, here[4] she perched herself, as was her custom on such wet and gloomy occasions,[5] put on a light shawl and bonnet, opened the window, and looked out at the rain.

The window overlooked a field called the Grove, and it was the position[6] from which she used to survey the crown of Dick's passing hat[7] in the early days of their acquaintance and meetings. Not a living soul was now visible anywhere; the rain kept all people indoors who were not forced abroad by necessity,[8] and necessity[8] was less importunate on Sundays than during the week.

Sitting here and thinking again—of her lover, or of the

sensation she had created at church that day?—well, it is
unknown[9]—thinking[10] and thinking,[10] she saw a dark
masculine figure arising into distinctness[11] at the further
end of the Grove—a man without an umbrella. Nearer[12]
and nearer he came, and she perceived that he was in deep
mourning, and then that it was Dick.

THOMAS HARDY, Under the Greenwood Tree (Macmillan and
the Trustees of the Hardy estate).

1 *D'un côté la pièce était percée de deux hautes fenêtres.*   2 Simplify: *e.g.*,
'She could sit on the sill of either'.   3 *qu'elle utilisait.*   4 *là.* How is
the emphasis on 'here' to be shown? See p. 59, § 54, HERE.   5 *lorsque
le temps était pareillement,* etc.   6 *c'était de ce poste que.*   7 Say, *e.g.*,
elle examinait au passage la calotte de, etc.   8 *contraints de sortir...le
besoin de sortir.*   9 *qui sait?*   10 *poursuivant le fil de ses pensées.*
11 *se préciser.*   12 *Comme il s'approchait toujours, elle,* etc.

**83. SHY CAROL-SINGERS

When I woke the next morning, it seemed as if all the events
of the preceding evening had been a dream, and nothing but
the identity of the ancient chamber convinced me of their
reality. While I lay musing on my pillow, I heard the sound
of little feet pattering outside of the door, and a whispering
consultation. Presently a choir of small voices chanted
forth an old Christmas carol, the burden of which was:

> *Rejoice, our Saviour he was born*
> *On Christmas day in the morning.*

I rose softly, slipped on my clothes, opened the door
suddenly, and beheld one of the most beautiful little fairy
groups that a painter could imagine. It consisted of a boy
and two girls, the eldest not more than six, and lovely as
seraphs. They were going the rounds of the house, and
singing at every chamber door; but my sudden appearance
frightened them into mute bashfulness. They remained for
a moment playing on their lips with their fingers, and now
and then stealing a shy glance, from under their eyebrows,
until, as if by one impulse, they scampered away, and as
they turned an angle of the gallery, I heard them laughing
in triumph at their escape.

WASHINGTON IRVING, The Sketch Book.

**84. Some One Expected

On the 1st of September, in[1] the[2] memorable year 1832, some one was expected at Transome Court. As early as two o'clock in[1] the afternoon the aged lodge-keeper had opened the heavy gate, green as[3] the tree-trunks were green with Nature's powdery paint, deposited year after year. Already in the village of Little Treby, which lay on the side of a steep hill not far off from the lodge gates, the elder matrons sat in their best gowns at the few cottage doors bordering the road, that they might be ready to get up and make their curtsy when a travelling carriage should come in sight;[4] and beyond the village several small boys were stationed on the look-out,[5] intending to run a race to the barn-like old church, where the sexton waited in the belfry to set the one bell[6] in joyful agitation just at the right moment. The old lodge-keeper had opened the gate and left it in the charge[7] of his lame wife, because he was wanted at the Court to sweep away the leaves, and perhaps to help in the stables. For though Transome Court was a large mansion, built in the fashion of Queen Anne's time, with a park and grounds as fine as any to be seen in Loamshire, there were very few servants about it.[8]

GEORGE ELIOT, *Felix Holt.*

1 *de.* 2 Say 'this'. 3 Say, *e.g., verte du vert des troncs d'arbre que la nature recouvre,* etc. 4 *quand on apercevrait.* 5 *s'étaient postés en sentinelle.* 6 *l'unique cloche.* 7 *en avait confié la surveillance à.* 8 *sur le domaine.*

**85. An Unwilling Guide

There were beds to be had some ten minutes' walk from where we were at a place called Pont. We stowed the canoes in a granary and asked among the children for a guide. The circle at once widened round us, and our offers of reward were received in dispiriting silence. We were plainly a pair of Bluebeards to the children; they might speak to us in public places, and where they had the advantage of numbers;

but it was another thing to venture off alone with two un-
couth and legendary characters, who had dropped from the
clouds upon their hamlet this quiet afternoon, sashed and
be-knived, and with a flavour of great voyages. The owner
of the granary came to our assistance, singled out one little
fellow and threatened him with corporalities; or I suspect
we should have had to find the way for ourselves. As it was,
he was more frightened at the granary man than the
strangers, having perhaps had some experience of the former.
But I fancy his little heart must have been going at a fine
rate; for he kept trotting at a respectful distance in front,
and looking back at us with scared eyes. Not otherwise
may the children of the young world have guided Jove or one
of his Olympian compeers on an adventure.

R. L. STEVENSON, *An Inland Voyage* (Chatto and Windus).

**86. A POOR WELCOME

We could not sufficiently congratulate each other on the
prospect, for we had been told there was a capital inn at
La Fère. Such a dinner[1] as we were going to eat! such beds
as we were to sleep in!—and all the while the rain raining[2]
on houseless folk over all[3] the poplared countryside! It
made our mouths water. The inn bore the name of some
woodland animal, stag, or hart, or hind, I forget which. But
I shall never forget how spacious and how eminently
habitable it looked as we drew near. The carriage entry was
lighted up, not by intention, but from the mere superfluity[4]
of fire and candle in the house. A rattle of many dishes
came to our ears; we sighted a great field of table-cloth; the
kitchen glowed like a forge and smelt like a garden of things
to eat.

Into this, the inmost shrine[5] and physiological heart of a
hostelry, with all its furnaces in action and all its dressers
charged with viands,[6] you are now to suppose us making our
triumphal entry, a pair of damp rag-and-bone men, each
with[7] a limp india-rubber bag upon his arm. I do not believe
I have a sound view[8] of that kitchen; I saw it through a sort

of glory: but it seemed to me crowded with the snowy caps of cookmen, who all turned round from their saucepans and looked at us with surprise. There was no doubt about the landlady, however: there she was, heading[9] her army, a[10] flushed, angry woman,[10] full of affairs. Her[11] I asked politely...if we could have beds: she surveying us coldly from head to foot.

'You will find beds in the suburb', she remarked. 'We are too busy for the like of you.'

R. L. STEVENSON, *An Inland Voyage* (Chatto and Windus).

1 *Quel dîner nous allions faire!* Or, *Le dîner que nous allions manger!*
2 *qui tombait.* 3 *partout dans ce pays de peupliers.* 4 *par la surabon-dance même.* 5 *le sanctuaire le plus secret.* 6 *mets.* 7 *portant...suspendu au bras.* 8 *une vision bien nette.* 9 *à la tête de.* 10 Omit.
11 The emphasis on 'Her' can be shown by using *C'est à elle que.*

*87. THERE WAS TROUBLE AFOOT

As the day drew on and nobody came near, I began to be aware of an uneasiness that I could scarce explain. It seemed there was trouble afoot; the sails of the windmill, as they came up and went down over the hill, were like persons spying; and, outside of all fancy, it was surely a strange neighbourhood and house for a young lady to be brought to dwell in.

At breakfast, which we took late, it was manifest that James More was in some danger or perplexity; manifest that Alan was alive to the same, and watched him close; and this appearance of duplicity upon the one side, and vigilance upon the other, held me on live coals. The meal was no sooner over than James seemed to come to a resolve, and began to make apologies. He had an appointment of a private nature in the town (it was with the French nobleman, he told me), and we would please excuse him till about noon.

R. L. STEVENSON, *Catriona* (Chatto & Windus).

*88. The Spy

The corrie[1] behind me was lit up with the westering sun and the bald cliffs were flushed with pink and gold. On each side of the stream was[2] turf like a lawn, perhaps[3] a hundred yards wide, and then[4] a tangle of long[5] heather and boulders right up to the edge of the great rocks. I had never seen a[6] more delectable evening, but I could not enjoy[7] its peace because of my anxiety about the Portuguese Jew. He had not been there more than half an hour, just about long enough for a man to travel to the first ridge across[8] the burn and back.[9] Yet he had found time to do his business.[10] He might have left a letter in some pre-arranged place—in which case I would stay there till the man it was meant[11] for turned up.[12] Or he might have[13] met someone, though I didn't think that possible....It was too dark to track his steps. That must be left for the morning, and I prayed that there would[14] be no rain in the night.

JOHN BUCHAN (LORD TWEEDSMUIR), *Mr Standfast*
(Hodder and Stoughton).

1 *la gorge.*　2 *il y avait?* Or *poussait?* See p. 55, § 51, THERE ARE (*c*). 3 Is this quite *peut-être?* See p. 61, § 54, PERHAPS.　4 *puis c'était.* See p. 55, § 51, THERE ARE, (*d*).　5 Use *haut.*　6 Must 'a' be translated? See p. 33, § 19 (*c*).　7 *goûter?* Or *jouir de?* See p. 73, § 63. 8 *après.*　9 Translate 'and come back', not forgetting *en.*　10 *pour s'acquitter de sa besogne.*　11 The construction after *destiner* is *à.*　12 A noun is simpler, *e.g., l'arrivée.*　13 *peut-être avait-il.*　14 *je priai le ciel qu'il ne plût pas pendant,* etc.

*89. Trapped

The unfortunate guardsman had now entirely recovered his senses, and found himself with a strap round his ankles, and another round his wrists, a captive inside a moving prison which lumbered heavily along the country road. He had been stunned by the shock of his fall, and his leg was badly bruised by the weight of his horse; but the cut on his forehead was a mere trifle, and the bleeding had already ceased. His mind, however, pained him more than his body. He sank his head into his pinioned hands, and stamped madly with his feet, rocking himself to and fro in his despair. What a fool, a treble fool, he had been! He, an old soldier, who had seen something of war, to walk with open eyes into such a trap! The King had chosen him, of all men, as a trusty messenger, and yet he had failed him—and failed him so ignominiously, without shot fired or sword drawn.

SIR ARTHUR CONAN DOYLE, *The Refugees* (Longmans and the Executors of Sir Arthur Conan Doyle).

**90. A DANGEROUS EXPEDITION

The gorge was narrow and precipitous; the river was now only a few yards wide, and roared[1] and thundered[1] against rocks of many tons in weight; the sound was deafening, for there was a great volume of water. We were two hours in making less than a mile, and that with danger, sometimes in the river and sometimes on the rock. There was[2] that damp black smell of rocks covered with slimy vegetation, as[3] near some huge waterfall where spray is ever rising. The air was clammy and cold. I cannot conceive how our horses managed[4] to keep their footing, especially the one with the pack, and I dreaded the having[5] to return almost as much as going forward. I suppose this lasted three miles, but it was well midday when the gorge got a little wider, and[6] a small stream came into it from a tributary valley. Farther progress up the main river was impossible, for the cliffs descended like walls; so we went up the side stream, Chowbok seeming to think that here must be the pass[7] of which reports existed among his people.

SAMUEL BUTLER, *Erewhon* (Cape).

1 Say, *e.g.*, *venait* (see p. 16, § 18, TO BREAK), *avec un grondement de tonnerre, se heurter à.* 2 *Il régnait* (see p. 55, § 51, THERE ARE) *là.* 3 *comme au voisinage d'une grande cascade.* 4 *firent pour ne pas trébucher.* 5 *redoutais autant d'avoir à revenir sur mes pas que de pousser plus avant.* 6 Some expansion seems necessary. 7 *le défilé au sujet duquel.*

*91. MYSTERIOUS LIGHT

He threw a casement open. The moon was hidden from us by clouds, but, a long way off, over the distant sea, there was an irregular patch of silver light, against which the chimneys of the opposite houses were silhouetted. The church clock began muffledly to chime the quarters behind us; then the hour struck—ten strokes.

Rangsley set one of his lanthorns on the window and twisted the top. He sent beams of yellow light shooting out to seawards. His hands quivered, and he was mumbling to himself under the influence of ungovernable excitement. His stakes were very large, and all depended on the flicker of those lanthorns out towards the men on the luggers that were hidden in the black expanse of the sea. Then he waited, and against the light of the window I could see him mopping his forehead with the sleeve of his coat; my heart began to beat softly and insistently—out of sympathy.

Suddenly, from the deep shadow of the cloud above the sea, a yellow light flashed silently out—very small, very distant, very short-lived. Rangsley heaved a deep sigh and slapped me heavily on the shoulder.

'All serene, my buck,' he said; 'now let's see after you. I've half an hour. What's the ship?'

I was at a loss, but Carlos said out of the darkness, 'The ship's the *Thames*. My friend, Señor Ortiz of the Minories, said you would know.'

'Oh, I know, I know,' Rangsley said softly; and, indeed, he did know all that was to be known about smuggling out of the southern counties of people who could no longer inhabit them.   JOSEPH CONRAD, *Romance* (Heinemann).

*92. A False Alarm

A great bell had begun to ring in[1] the château, and there was[2] a loud buzz of voices and a clatter of feet upon the stones. Hoarse orders were shouted, and there was[2] the sound of turning keys. All this coming suddenly in the midst of the stillness of the night showed only too certainly that the alarm had been given. Amos Green threw himself down in the straw, with his hands in his pockets, and De Catinat leaned sulkily[3] against the wall, waiting for[4] whatever might come to him. Five minutes passed, however, and yet another five minutes, without anyone appearing. The hubbub in the court-yard continued, but there was[2] no sound in the corridor which led to their cell.

'Well, I'll have that bar out, after all,' said the American at last, rising and stepping over[5] to the window. 'Anyhow, we'll see what all this caterwauling is about.' He climbed up as he spoke, and peeped out.[6]

'Come up!' he cried excitedly to his comrade. 'They've got some other game going on here, and they are all a deal too busy to bother their heads about us.'

De Catinat clambered up beside him, and the two stood staring down into the court-yard. A brazier had been lit at each corner, and the place was thronged with men, many of whom carried torches. The yellow glare played fitfully over[7] the grim gray walls, flickering up sometimes until[8] the highest turrets shone golden against the black sky, and then, as the wind caught them,[9] dying away until they scarce threw a glow upon the cheek of their bearer.

SIR ARTHUR CONAN DOYLE, *The Refugees* (Longmans).

1 = 'inside'; see p. 64, § 57, IN.   2 Tense? See p. 55, § 51, THERE ARE.
3 Turn the adverb by an adjective, *e.g., morose.*   4 *prêt à tout ce qui.*
5 *s'approchant de.*   6 *glissa un regard dans la cour.*   7 Turn freely, *e.g., éclairait d'un reflet capricieux.*   8 *de sorte que* + Indicative.   9 The difficulty caused by the substitution of a plural pronoun 'them' (= 'torches') for a singular noun subject ('glare') can be met, *e.g.,* by using a vague expression *sous le souffle du vent* and continuing with an Infinitive construction: *au point de rougir à peine la joue de.*

*93. SHOTS ON THE BANK

I looked at the carabinieri. They were looking at the newcomers. The others were looking at the colonel. I ducked down, pushed between two men, and ran for the river, my head down. I tripped at the edge and went in with a splash. The water was very cold and I stayed under as long as I could. I could feel the current swirl me and I stayed under until I thought I could never come up. The minute I came up I took a breath and went down again. It was easy to stay under with so much clothing and my boots. When I came up the second time I saw a piece of timber ahead of me and reached it and held on with one hand. I kept my head behind it and did not even look over it. I did not want to see the bank. There were shots when I ran and shots when I came up the first time. I heard them when I was almost above water. There were no shots now. The piece of timber swung in the current and I held it with one hand. I looked at the bank. It seemed to be going by very fast. There was much wood in the stream. The water was very cold. We passed the brush of an island above the water. I held on to the timber with both hands and let it take me along. The shore was out of sight now.

ERNEST HEMINGWAY, *A Farewell to Arms* (Cape).

***94. A Fire

The broad sky seemed on fire. Rising into the air with showers of sparks, and rolling one above the other, were sheets of flame, lighting the atmosphere for miles round,[1] and driving clouds of smoke in the direction where[2] he stood. The shouts grew louder as new voices swelled[3] the roar, and he could hear the cry of Fire! mingled with the ringing of an alarm-bell, the fall of heavy bodies, and the crackling of flames as they twined round some new obstacle, and shot aloft as though[4] refreshed by food. The noise increased as he looked. There were people there—men and women—light, bustle. It was like new life to him. He darted onward—straight, headlong[5]—dashing through brier and brake, and leaping gate and fence as madly as the dog, who careered with loud and sounding bark before him.

He came upon the spot. There were half-dressed figures tearing to and fro, some endeavouring to drag the frightened horses from the stables, others driving the cattle from the yard and out-houses, and others coming laden from the burning pile, amidst a shower of falling sparks, and the tumbling down[6] of redhot beams. The apertures, where doors and windows stood an hour ago, disclosed a mass of raging fire; walls rocked and crumbled into the burning well;

the molten lead and iron poured down, white hot, upon the ground. Women and children shrieked, and men encouraged each other with noisy shouts and cheers.

CHARLES DICKENS, *Oliver Twist.*

1 See p. 3, § 1, ROUND.   2 Is *où* alone sufficient? See p. 62, § 54, WHERE.   3 Say, *e.g.*, *se joignaient au tumulte.*   4 *comme ranimées par cet aliment.*   5 *à corps perdu.*   6 *un écroulement.*

***95. AN APPARITION

As he descended, the confronting heights grew mountainous before him, and the gleam of the western heaven sank rapidly from view. Halfway down, steep banks of wood rose up to meet him, and passing into their midst he heard on all sides the continuous dripping of soaked boughs like a sudden renewal of rain. Presently a sharp turn in the road which had hitherto led west gave an abrupt change to its character. In the place of wooded steep stood rifted rock,—precipitous walls through which, amid deepening gloom, the last stage of declivity was reached. Up this gully of darkness came a roar of waters; and across the far end, netted by branch and leaf, shot the dark hurrying skeins of a hill-born torrent.

A few paces more gave him full view of the flooded stream. Here to his dismay—for high underwood concealed a leftward turn—he saw the road abruptly cut short, on this side descending to an impassable gulf, on the other emerging all shorn of face, a rough hill-track furrowed and over-grown, deeply dinted by the tread of ponderous feet. He shrank as though a trap had suddenly opened before him, for the unaccustomed noise of waters disturbed and shook his brain. Yet before long fear turned to fascination; he slackened speed, and stood to watch.

Suddenly from the thicket below came the sharp crackle of trampled brushwood; from the soft bank of earth a heavy stone parted and plunged streamward, and he saw amid stems shaken and divided two monstrous antennae moving ominously towards him.

In another moment the apparition was explained: a man emerged bearing aloft a couple of fishing-rods. But the encounter was too sudden and unforeseen: the child quailed and turning started to run.

LAURENCE HOUSMAN, *Odd Pairs* (Cape).

***96. THE STORY OF A GOLD-HEADED CANE

I remember[1] reading a story of an old gentleman who used to walk out every afternoon, with a gold-headed[2] cane, in the fields opposite Baltimore House. He was frequently accosted by a beggar with a wooden leg, to whom[3] he gave money, which only[4] made him more importunate. One day, when he[5] was more troublesome than usual, a well-dressed person happening to come up, and observing how saucy the fellow was, said to the gentleman, 'Sir, if you will[6] lend me your cane for a moment, I'll give him a good thrashing for his impertinence'.

The old gentleman, smiling at the proposal, handed him his cane, which the other no sooner was going to apply to the shoulders of the culprit, than he[7] immediately whipped off his wooden leg, and scampered off with great alacrity, and his chastiser[8] after him as hard as he could go. The faster[9] the one ran, the faster[9] the other followed him, brandishing the cane, to the great astonishment of the gentleman who owned it,[10] till,[11] having fairly crossed the fields, they suddenly turned a corner, and nothing more was seen of either of them.   WILLIAM HAZLITT, *Wit and Humour*.

1 Construction. See p. 26, § 18, REMEMBER.   2 See p. 37, § 29. 8 Simplify, *e.g.*, 'to a beggar...whom his alms (*ses aumônes*) only made more importunate'.   4 See p. 61, § 54, ONLY.   5 For clarity, *cet individu*.   6 = simple future? Or = 'wish to'?   7 *ce dernier*.   8 *le judicier*.   9 Is *le* required? See p. 33, § 20 (*b*).   10 Say simply: *du propriétaire*.   11 *enfin*.

***97. HOW BECKY SHARP RECEIVED HER SITUATION

Worthy Miss Pinkerton, although she had a Roman nose and a turban, and was as tall as a grenadier, and had been up to this time an irresistible princess, had no will or strength like that of her little apprentice, and in vain did battle against her, and tried to overawe her. Attempting once to scold her in public, Rebecca hit upon the before-mentioned plan of answering her in French, which quite routed the old woman.

In order to maintain authority in her school, it became necessary to remove this rebel, this monster, this serpent, this firebrand; and hearing about this time that Sir Pitt Crawley's family was in want of a governess, she actually recommended Miss Sharp for the situation, firebrand and serpent as she was. 'I cannot, certainly,' she said, 'find fault with Miss Sharp's conduct, except to myself; and must allow that her talents and accomplishments are of a high order. As far as the head goes, at least, she does credit to the educational system pursued at my establishment.'

w. m. thackeray, *Vanity Fair.*

*98. The Eagle's Last Swoop

Like all true sportsmen, Struan Robertson was a naturalist, —studied[1] Nature's ongoings and all her children with a keen, unerring and loving[2] eye, from her lichens and moths (for which Rannoch is famous) to her eagles, red deer and *Salmo ferox*; and his stories, if recorded, would stand well[3] side by side with Mr St John's. One[4] we remember. He and his keeper were on a cloudless day in mid-winter walking across the head[5] of Loch Rannoch, which, being shallow,[6] was frozen over. The keeper stopped, and, looking straight up[7] into the clear sky, said to his master, 'Do you see that?' Keen as he was, Struan said, 'What?' 'An eagle'; and there, sure enough, was a mere speck in the far-off 'azure depths of air'. Duncan Roy flung a white hare he had shot along the ice, and instantly the speck darkened, and down came the mighty creature with a swoop, and not knowing of the ice, was 'made a round flat dish of,[8] with the head in the centre'.   DR JOHN BROWN.

1 *il observait.*   2 *plein d'affection.*   3 *soutiendraient bien la com-paraison avec celles de.*   4 Expand to 'Here is one which'.   5 *l'ex-trémité supérieure.*   6 Expand, *e.g., dont les eaux.*   7 *regardant droit au-dessus de lui dans,* etc.   8 '*une espèce de galette dont sa tête occupait le milieu.*'

****99. The Great Frost

The Great Frost was, historians tell us, the most severe that
has ever visited these islands. Birds froze in mid-air and
fell like stones to the ground. At Norwich a young country-
woman started to cross the road in her usual robust health
and was seen by the onlookers to turn visibly to powder and
be blown in a puff of dust over the roofs as the icy blast
struck her at the street corner. The mortality among sheep
and cattle was enormous. Corpses froze and could not be
drawn from the sheets. It was no uncommon sight to come
upon a whole herd of swine frozen immovable upon the
road. The fields were full of shepherds, ploughmen, teams of
horses, and little bird-scaring boys all struck stark in the
act of the moment, one with his hand to his nose, another
with the bottle to his lips, a third with a stone raised to
throw at the raven who sat, as if stuffed, upon the hedge
within a yard of him. The severity of the frost was so
extraordinary that a kind of petrifaction sometimes ensued;
and it was commonly supposed that the great increase of
rocks in some parts of Derbyshire was due to no eruption,
for there was none, but to the solidification of unfortunate
wayfarers who had been turned literally to stone where they
stood.   VIRGINIA WOOLF, *Orlando* (Hogarth Press).

*100. Rat Stories

I love to read tales about rats. They make my flesh creep so.[1]
I like that tale of Bishop Hatto and the rats. The wicked
bishop, you know, had ever so much[2] corn, stored in his
granaries, and would not let the starving people touch it,
but, when they prayed to him for[3] food, gathered them
together in his barn, and then shutting the doors on them,
set fire to the place and burned them all to death. But next
day there came thousands upon thousands of rats, sent to
do judgment on him. Then Bishop Hatto fled to his strong
tower that stood in the middle of the Rhine, and barred
himself in, and fancied that he was safe. But the rats, they

swam the river, they gnawed[4] their way through the thick stone walls, and ate him alive where[5] he sat....Oh, it's a lovely tale.

Then there is the story of the Pied Piper[6] of Hamelin, how first he piped the rats away, and afterwards, when the Mayor broke faith[7] with him, drew all the children along with him, and went into the mountain. What[8] a curious old legend that is! I wonder what it means, or has it a meaning at all?[9] There seems something strange and deep lying hid beneath the rippling rhyme. It haunts me, that picture of the quaint, mysterious old piper, piping through Hamelin's narrow streets, and the children following with dancing feet[10] and thoughtful, eager faces. The old folk[11] try to stay them, but the children pay no heed. They hear the weird, witched music, and must follow. The games are left unfinished, and the playthings drop from their careless hands. They know not whither[12] they are hastening. The mystic music calls to them, and they follow, heedless and unasking where. It stirs[13] and vibrates in their hearts, and other sounds grow faint. So they wander through Pied Piper Street away from Hamelin town.

JEROME K. JEROME, *Idle Thoughts of an Idle Fellow: On Cats and Dogs* (J. W. Arrowsmith).

1 *tellement.*   2 *des quantités.*   3 ='give them food': *leur donner à manger.*   4 Work in *à coups de dents.*   5 *où?* Or *là où?* See p. 62, § 54, WHERE.   6 *du joueur de flûte de Hamelin.*   7 *eut manqué à sa parole envers lui.*   8 Transpose: *Qu'elle est curieuse, cette vieille légende!* See p. 75, § 65.   9 *seulement.*   10 *d'un pas dansant.*   11 ='grown-ups'= *les grandes personnes.*   12 *vers quoi.*   13 Translate as if: 'stirs their hearts and vibrates in them'. See p. 75, § 65.

**101. LEVIATHAN AT BAY

Suddenly the three broad backs burst through the dancing water immediately ahead. The gunner swung his gun. There was a deafening crack and my ears sang. The black streak of the harpoon flying out. The coiling whip outwards of the line. And then a cataclysmic, hurtling, headlong rush down. Got him! Down went the line, rattling out, and down, down,

down. There was a sudden strange silence, a suspension of activity. The *Narval* wallowed, the waves flopping and flapping against her sides, and the harpoon-line no longer running out of the hold but hanging taut from the bows, straight up and down.

Then began a thrashing disturbance in the water a mile away to starboard. The terrible, lonely and titanic death struggle began. Dark against the lashed smother of foam there wheeled and thrashed now a forked tail, now a pointed head still grinning; now a ribbed belly showed, now a pointed flipper, raised on high, smacking down upon the water. Then a red fountain burst upwards, and another. He was spouting blood. It meant the end. 'Ah!' they said on the fore-deck. They were reloading the harpoon-gun. The smoking breech swung open and the empty cartridge was removed. The gunner turned to me.

'You got a picture—ja?'

'No', I admitted. The loud crack of the gun had made me pull the trigger too late. When you take photographs of a whale hunt you need to be as calm and collected as the gunner himself. 'No matter', said Jonassen. 'We will get some more, I think.'

Still the Leviathan fought for his life, his harmless, free and joyful life that had suddenly been struck from him at one dreadful blow. His comrades had disappeared and he fought his battle out, deserted and alone. He whirled in a fury of crimson foam. The winch rattled and the slack harpoon-line came in until it curved to him across the mile of water. Now it grew tight and pulled him. He drew towards us and suddenly he was still, his ribbed belly upwards, the crimson sea where he lay suddenly calm and a cloud of birds hovering above. In the distance a solitary iceberg, remote, forlorn and lonely, stood off and watched him die.   F. D. OMMANEY, *South Latitude* (Longmans).

***102. A CONCERT

The concert was much better after the interval. It began with[1] a longish thing in which[2] a piano played about one half, and most of the orchestra, for some of them never[3] touched[4] their instruments, played the other half. A little dark chap played the piano and there could be no doubt about it, he *could* play the piano. Terrum, ter-*rum*, terrum, terrum, trum, trum, trrrrr, the orchestra would go, and the little chap would lean[5] back, looking idly[6] at the conductor. But the second the orchestra stopped he would hurl himself[7] at the piano and crash out his own Terrum, ter-*rum*, terrum, terrum, trum trum trrr. Sometimes the violins would play very softly[8] and sadly,[8] and the piano would join in, scattering[9] silver[10] showers of notes or perhaps wandering up and down a ladder[11] of quiet chords, and then Mr Smeeth would feel himself very quiet and happy and sad all at the same time. In the end, they had[12] a pell-mell race, and the piano shouted to the orchestra and then went[13] scampering away, and the orchestra thundered at the piano and went charging after it, and they went up hill and down dale, shouting and thundering, scampering and charging, until one big bang, during which the little chap seemed to be almost sitting on the piano and the conductor appeared to be holding the whole orchestra up in his two arms, brought[14] it to an end.

This time Mr Smeeth clapped furiously, and so did the fierce man, and so did everybody else, even the violin players in the orchestra; and the little chap, now purple in the face, ran in[15] and out[15] a dozen times, bowing all the way. But he would[16] not play again, no matter[17] how long and loud they clapped, and Mr Smeeth, for his part, could not blame him. The little chap had done his share. My word, there was talent for you!

J. B. PRIESTLEY, Angel Pavement (Heinemann).

1 Use *par*.   2 *dont une moitié environ fut exécutée par un piano et l'autre par*, etc.   8 Not *jamais* here; *une fois*.   4 Tense?   5 Not *se pencher* =to lean forward; *se renverser*.   6 *sans rien faire*.   7 *se jetait sur son*

clavier.   8 The two adverbs would be clumsy; use *un   air*+adjectives.
See p. 57, § 53 (*b*).   9 Use *égrener.*   10 Is this *argenté* or *argentin*? See
p. 28, § 18, SILVERY.   11 *toute une gamme.*   12 Say, *e.g., Ce fut.* See
p. 55, § 51, THERE ARE, (*d*).   13 *Les voilà partis.*   14 Tense? Alter the
order of the words so as not to end on a very short verb.   15 See p. 57,
§ 52 (*b*).   16 Tense? See p. 56, § 51, WOULD.   17 Say, *e.g., quelque
nourris et répétés que fussent les rappels.*

*103. *FAUST* IN AN IRISH MARKET TOWN

The audience greeted him with enthusiasm; he smiled easily,
fumbled in his ample breast for Marguerita's token, and
began to sing.

My first feeling was one of disappointment. Never having
heard a great singer, I suppose that in my ignorance
I had expected something volcanic: and the voice in the
short recitative, though easy and full, seemed to me in no
way remarkable. The singer, too, seemed indifferent to his
work.

Then—suddenly—a change came over him. As the
piano sounded the introduction to the *aria*, he shut his
eyes. It might have been fancy, but I could swear a tremor
ran through him: he smiled to himself, and when he opened
his eyes again, their light was different. The look of bored
good humour had given place to a strange gleam, almost of
defiance. We were sitting right under him, and we could see
his smallest movement.

Then, once more, he closed his eyes, and sang. The great
notes rolled out pure and full, with an exaltation, an almost
savage power, that seemed to thrill through the very chairs
we sat on. When he came to the martial movement, he
opened his eyes and declaimed it with a volume and a fire
which was literally frightening. Then his voice sank magni-
ficently back upon the slow swell of the air. Inevitable as a
great wave sweeping to the shore, it rose towards the climax
of the music, gleamed there a moment in majesty, and rolled
out the final notes in rings and rings of sound.

There was a silence, then applause. It was frantic. We
clapped and stamped and shouted: I only stopped when my

hands hurt too much to go on. McCaragh himself seemed almost dazed: then his face lit up with an expression hard to analyse. Many times he had to come on, and bow again, and yet again, with a certain ironic dignity; yet it was obvious that he had been deeply moved.

L. A. G. STRONG, *The English Captain* (Gollancz).

***104. A STAGE ENTRY

Assuredly, by far the most tremendous stage entries[1] I ever saw were[2] those of Mr Wilson Barrett in his later days, the days when he had become his own dramatist. I remember particularly a first night[3] of his at which I happened to be sitting next to a clever but not very successful and rather sardonic old actor. I forgot just what great historic or mythic personage Mr Barrett was to represent, but I know that the earlier scenes of the play resounded with rumours of him[4]—accounts of the great deeds he had done, and of the yet greater deeds that were expected of him. And at length there was[5] a procession: white-bearded priests bearing wands; maidens playing upon the sackbut; guards in full armour; a pell-mell of unofficial citizens ever prancing[6] along the edge of the pageant, huzza-ing and hosanna-ing, mostly looking back over their shoulders and shading[7] their eyes; maidens strewing rose-leaves; and at last the orchestra crashing to a climax[8] in the nick of which my neighbour turned to me and, with an assumption[9] of innocent enthusiasm, whispered, 'I shouldn't *wonder* if this were Barrett'. I suppose (Mr Barrett at that instant amply appearing) I gave way to laughter; but this didn't matter; the applause would have drowned[10] a thunderstorm, and lasted for several minutes.

MAX BEERBOHM, *And Even Now* (Heinemann).

1 *les entrées en scène.*   2 *sont: étaient* would seem odd, and raise difficulties.   8 *une de ses 'premières'.*   4 *sa renommée.*   5 Tense? 6 *gambadant sans arrêt en bordure de,* etc.   7 *en se faisant une visière de leurs mains.*   8 *...un crescendo...au plus fort duquel.*   9 *simulant.* 10 *couvert.*

*105. A Station Incident

Some years ago I arrived at the Gare St Lazare at Paris two or three days before the August Bank Holiday about half an hour before the time of my train. I had sent my luggage an hour in advance, but when I got to the station it was still in the courtyard. There was a long queue of people waiting to have their luggage weighed and registered and I saw that I had no chance of catching the train at the rate at which things were moving. I went into the luggage-hall and saw that of four weighing-machines only one was being used, which accounted for the delay. I protested so vigorously that the station-master was sent for and immediately ordered all the four machines to be put in use. The other passengers were so grateful to me that they insisted on my luggage being weighed first, quite out of my turn. The strange thing was that, although some of them had been there for a couple of hours, not one had thought of doing what I did; but for my English impatience, three-fourths of them would have missed their trains, and then there would probably have been a small riot.

Now this incident is typical of the French attitude towards authority; the French will too often endure abuses for years without making any effective protest, and when at last the situation becomes absolutely unbearable they will break out and smash up everything. That is the reason why there have been so many revolutions in France; nobody thinks of making reforms until it is too late and a clean sweep has become inevitable.

ROBERT DELL, *My Second Country (France)*
(John Lane, The Bodley Head).

*106. A Nightmare

Parkins found that the picture which presented itself to him[1] was continuous. When he opened his eyes, of course, it went; but when he shut them once more[2] it framed itself afresh, and acted itself out again, neither quicker nor slower than before. What he saw was this:

A long stretch of shore—shingle edged by sand, and intersected at short intervals with black groynes[3] running down to the water—a scene, in fact, so like that of his afternoon's walk that, in the absence of any[4] landmark, it could not be distinguished therefrom.[5] The light was obscure, conveying an impression of gathering storm, late winter evening, and slight cold rain. On this bleak stage at first no actor was visible. Then, in the distance, a bobbing black object appeared; a moment more, and it was a man running, jumping, clambering over the groynes, and every few seconds looking eagerly back. The nearer[6] he came the more obvious it was that he was not only anxious, but even terribly frightened, though his face was not to be distinguished. He was, moreover, almost at the end of his strength.[7] On he came; each successive obstacle seemed to cause him more difficulty than the last.[8] 'Will he get over this next one?' thought Parkins; 'it seems a little higher than the others.' Yes; half climbing, half throwing himself, he did get over, and fell all in a heap on the other side (the side nearest to the spectator). There, as if really unable to get up again, he remained crouching under the groyne, looking up in an attitude of painful anxiety.

So far no cause whatever for the fear of the runner had been shown; but now there began to be seen, far up the shore, a little flicker[9] of something light-coloured moving to and fro with great swiftness and irregularity. Rapidly growing larger, it, too, declared itself as a figure in pale, fluttering draperies, ill-defined.

MONTAGU R. JAMES, *Ghost Stories of an Antiquary*
(Edward Arnold).

1 *à son esprit.* 2 Use *refermer.* 3 a groyne is *un épi.* 4 *du moindre.* 5 Use *distinguer l'un de l'autre.* 6 Is 'The' to be translated? See p. 33, § 20 (*b*). 7 *à bout de forces.* 8 *le précédent.* 9 Turn by a verb (*vaciller*).

***107. THE BELL

A rope tautened and scraped the hole in the oak floor through which it passed, communicating its movement to the mountings of the great bass bell whose inscription he had read last. There followed a groan of old wood in distress as the giant began to swing on its oak hanging, and then, as the clapper smote its concave bronze, a volume of sound so monstrous that it seemed as though their ear-drums must give way. In that small chamber there was no room for anything but these cruel vibrations. They broke forth angrily, then swooped, swerved, hovered, searching each corner of the belfry for some living thing whose senses they might over-power.

Claire and Ralph stood deafened among these stormy waves of sound. A ringing practice, she thought at first. She pictured Mr Hemus and his ringers below, each man standing to his woolly rope. If one bell were so monstrous, a practice would be hell let loose in that restricted space. But when the last pulsation had died down to a meditative hum, like that of a great tuning-fork, there was silence for a moment. Then, suddenly, the rasping and creaking began again. The bass bell swung. Once more the belfry was filled with a torment of sound.

'I can't stand this', Ralph shouted. 'Come along.' She saw his lips shape the words and followed him. The echoes pursued them malignantly down the spiral steps. He had been speaking and laughing all the time. Now of a sudden his voice became audible:

'It's a passing-bell', he was saying. 'I suppose some poor devil's dead.'

FRANCIS BRETT YOUNG, *Portrait of Claire* (Heinemann).

IV. HISTORICAL

**108. THE GOVERNMENT OF THE GERMANS

The government of the Germans, and that of all the northern nations, who established[1] themselves on the ruins of Rome, was always extremely free; and those fierce people, accustomed to independence and enured to arms, were more guided by persuasion than authority, in the submission[2] which they paid to their princes. The military despotism, which had taken place³ in the Roman empire, and which, previously to the irruption of those conquerors, had sunk⁴ the genius of men, and destroyed every noble principle of science and virtue, was¹ unable to resist the vigorous efforts of a free people; and Europe, as⁵ from⁶ a new epoch, rekindled her ancient spirit, and shook off⁷ the base servitude to arbitrary will and authority under which she had so long laboured.⁸ The free constitutions then established, however⁹ impaired¹⁰ by the encroachments of succeeding princes, still preserve an air of independence and legal¹¹ administration, which distinguish the European nations, and if that part of the globe maintain sentiments of liberty, honour, equity, and valour superior to the rest of mankind, it owes these advantages chiefly to the seeds implanted by those generous barbarians.

DAVID HUME, *History of England.*

1 Tense?   2 Use; *se soumettre à leurs princes.*   3 *avait prévalu.*
4 Use *rabaisser.*   5 Omit.   6 *au seuil d'une ère nouvelle.*   7 *secoua le joug d'une soumission avilissante.*   8 *subies depuis si longtemps.*
9 See p. 50, § 50, HOWEVER. What tense is required, when the verb of the main clause is in the present?   10 *entamées.*   11 *et de légalité dans l'administration.*

**109. THE BIRTH OF THE MODERN WORLD

For, indeed, a change was coming upon the world, the meaning and direction of which even still is hidden from us, a change from era to era. The paths trodden by the footsteps of ages were broken up; old things were passing away, and the faith and the life of ten centuries were dissolving like a dream. Chivalry was dying; the abbey and the castle were soon together to crumble into ruins; and all the forms, desires, beliefs, convictions of the old world were passing away never to return. A new continent had risen up beyond the western sea. The floor of heaven, inlaid with stars, had sunk back to an infinite abyss of immeasurable space; and the firm earth itself, unfixed from its foundations, was seen to be but a small atom in the awful vastness of the universe.

In the fabric of habit which they had so laboriously built for themselves, mankind were to remain no longer.

And now it is all gone—like an unsubstantial pageant faded; and between us and the old English there lies a gulf of mystery which the prose of the historian will never adequately bridge. They cannot come to us, and our imagination can but feebly penetrate to them. Only among the aisles of the cathedral, only as we gaze upon their silent figures sleeping on their tombs, some faint conceptions float before us of what these men were when they were alive; and perhaps in the sound of church bells, that peculiar creation of mediæval age, which falls upon the ear like the echo of a vanished world.   J. A. FROUDE, *History of England.*

***110. LOUIS XIV AT VERSAILLES

That life, with all it meant[1] to those who lived it, has long since vanished from the earth—preserved to us now only in the pages of its poets, or strangely shadowed forth to the traveller in the illimitable desolation of Versailles. That it has gone so utterly is no doubt, on the whole, a cause for rejoicing; but, as we look back upon it, we may still feel something of the old enchantment, and feel it, perhaps, the more keenly for its strangeness—its dissimilarity to the experiences of our own days.[2] We shall catch glimpses[3] of a world of pomp and brilliance, of ceremony and decoration, a small, vital, passionate world which has clothed itself in ordered beauty, learnt a fine way of easy, splendid living, and come under the spell of a devotion to what is, to us, no more than the gorgeous phantom of high imaginations[4]—the divinity of a king.

When the morning sun was up and the horn was sounding down the long avenues, who would not wish,[5] if only in fancy, to join the glittering cavalcade where the young Louis led the hunt in the days of his opening[6] glory? Later, we might linger on the endless terrace, to watch the great monarch, with his red heels and his golden snuff-box and his towering periwig, come out among his courtiers, or in some elaborate grotto applaud a ballet by Molière. When night fell there would be dancing and music in the gallery blazing with a thousand looking-glasses, or masquerades and feasting in the gardens, with the torches throwing[7] strange shadows among the trees trimmed into artificial figures, and gay lords and proud ladies conversing together under the stars.

LYTTON STRACHEY, *Landmarks of French Literature* (Chatto and Windus).

1 *signifiait pour.* 2 Say, *e.g., tout ce que nous connaissons de l'époque actuelle.* 3 *Ainsi se laisse entrevoir un monde,* etc. 4 *d'imaginations exaltées.* 5 *qui n'aurait souhaité, au moins par la pensée.* 6 *au temps de sa gloire naissante.* 7 *où les flambeaux projettent.*

***111. THE IDEAL OF VERSAILLES

The vast edifice is an image of irrevocable failure—of a failure, too, which, like everything else in that strange cemetery, is invested with a grandeur of its own. For Versailles was, in its essence, an attempt to create the superhuman; and its tragedy is the tragedy of an impossible ideal. When La Bruyère compared the attitude of the courtiers towards the king to that of the saints in heaven towards God, he was drawing no exaggerated figure: he was describing the fundamental fact underlying the ideal of Versailles. The king was, in truth, invested with the attributes of divinity; he assumed the God; he became, in that dazzling world of his creation, divine.

The features of Louis XIV, in the waxen portrait of Benoist, bear upon them the marks of this inordinate assumption, grown rigid in their obsession of an arrogance so immense as almost to be what it pretends to be—something more than human. It is easy now to point the obvious moral; it is easy to show, after the manner of Thackeray, the mortal creature beneath the robes of greatness, to preach a sermon over the deity who could not keep his temper, who was swayed by women and by priests, and who always ate too much. All this is easy, and it is also cheap. It is more

profitable to try to realise in some measure the thoughts and
feelings which enabled a great age to lend itself to so extraordinary an experiment; to think of Versailles, not as an
emblem of foolish and degraded snobbery, but as a splendid
piece of spiritual *tour de force*.

The spirit is departed, but the mortal part remains....
One must go to Versailles...to get a glimpse both of what
it was and of what it is. One must linger among the
fountains and the oranges, the bronzes and the marble gods;
one must look back upon the palace through the great trees
with their pale spring foliage; one must walk, in autumn,
down the melancholy avenues banked with fallen leaves;
one must sit in the summer shade within earshot of dropping
water, and dream of vanished glories and beauties, of
crowned and desecrated loves.

LYTTON STRACHEY, *Characters and Commentaries*
(Chatto and Windus).

**112. A SECRET TREATY

Colbert himself immediately took one original[1] to France,
the other was consigned,[2] perhaps, to Clifford's despatch-
box, where it now reposes, and on the 4th June Charles fixed
his secret seal to the ratification, carefully countersigned
'Arlington, by his Majesty's command'.

Ten days passed in feasting and ceremonial—one at
Canterbury, where the Garter knights attended the service
of the Church their master had promised[3] to destroy, a
second there[4] in ballets and archery, a third at Dover with
John Caryll's 'Cautious Coxcomb' as the command performance, and a fourth in the King's yacht on a visit to the
fleet. Madame was all sunshine and quicksilver, happy to
have reconciled Arlington and Buckingham, as to have won
Charles' promise to raise the Secretary and Clifford to new
honours.

On the 2nd June she crossed to France, more English-
hearted[5] than she had ever been, in expectation, no question,
of more work[6] for her cause, and on the 28th was singing an

English song and writing to Clifford her first English letter. Early[7] on the 30th she died, protesting to Ralph Montagu that she had done this work for her dear brother's good.

So was cut down and withered this brief flower of courtesy, wit, and ambition; tortured, bled, and dissected that frail body; 'Vanitas vanitatum' was the text of Bossuet's sermon that ushered it to the grave—Bossuet, to whom went her last word, that she loved God with all her heart. At London there were cold rumours of poison, voiced by Rupert and Trevor, Buckingham called for instant war, the mob demonstrated against Colbert.

But neither piety nor wit, anger nor evil report, could touch Madame further or cancel what was writ; somewhere, signed and sealed by four English names, whether at Whitehall or already in a deep valley of Dartmoor, the secret treaty was concealed which put England at the mercy of Louis XIV.

KEITH FEILING, *British Foreign Policy* (Macmillan).

1 *un des deux originaux.*   2 Use simply *mettre...dans.*   3 Use *s'engager à.*   4 *au même endroit.*   5 *Anglaise de cœur.*   6 *de se voir* (see p. 46, § 42 (c)) *confier d'autres tâches.*   7 *de bon matin.*

*113. FREE INSTITUTIONS

The supreme fact upon the Continent in the latter half of the seventeenth century was the might of France. Her civil wars were over. All internal divisions had been effaced, and Louis XIV reigned over a united nation of eighteen or nineteen million souls possessed of the fairest region on the globe. Feudalism, with its local warriors and their armed retainers, had at length been blown away by gunpowder, and as wars were frequent, standing armies had arisen in all the states of Europe. The possession of organized regular troops, paid, disciplined, trained by the central Government, was the aim of all the rulers, and in the main the measure of their power. This process had in the course of a few generations obliterated or reduced to mere archaic survivals the Parliamentary and municipal institutions of

France. In different ways similar effects had followed the same process in other Continental countries. Everywhere sovereignty had advanced with giant strides. The peoples of Europe passed out of a long confusion into an age of autocracies in full panoply against all foes from within or from without.

But for the storm-whipped seas which lapped the British islands, our fortunes would have followed the road upon which our neighbours had started. England had not, however, the same compulsive need for a standing army as the land Powers. She stood aloof, moving slowly and lagging behind the martial throng. In the happy nick of time her Parliament grew strong enough to curb the royal power and to control the armed forces, and she thus became the cradle, as she is still the citadel, of free institutions throughout the world.   WINSTON S. CHURCHILL, *Marlborough* (Harrap).

**114. MARLBOROUGH CAPTAIN-GENERAL

The death of Mary forced William to recall Anne, who became by this event his successor; and with Anne the Marlboroughs returned to court. The King could not bend himself to trust the Earl again;[1] but as death drew near he saw in him[2] the one man whose splendid talents fitted him, in spite of the baseness and treason of his life, to rule England and direct the Grand Alliance in his stead. He employed Marlborough therefore to negotiate the treaty of alliance with the Emperor, and put him at the head of the army in Flanders. But the Earl had only[3] just taken the command when a fall from his horse proved fatal to the broken frame[4] of the King. 'There was a time[5] when I should have been glad to have been delivered out of my troubles,' the dying man whispered to Portland, 'but I own I see another scene and could wish to live a little longer.' He knew, however, that the wish was vain, and commended Marlborough to Anne as the fittest person to lead[6] her armies and guide her counsels.

Anne's zeal needed no quickening. Three days after her

accession the Earl was named Captain-General[7] of the English forces at home and abroad, and entrusted with the entire direction of the war.

JOHN RICHARD GREEN, *A Short History of the English People* (Macmillan).

1 *rendre sa confiance au Comte.* 2 *reconnut en lui.* 3 *à peine.* 4 *la constitution usée.* 5 *Il fut un temps où.* 6 *commander.* 7 *Commandant-en-Chef.*

***115. THE ROMANCE OF EDINBURGH

Down in the palace John Knox reproved his queen in the accents of modern democracy. In the town, in one of those little shops plastered like so many swallows' nests among the buttresses of the old Cathedral, that familiar autocrat, James VI, would gladly share a bottle of wine with George Heriot the goldsmith. Up on the Pentland Hills, that so quietly look down on the Castle with the city lying in waves around it, those mad and dismal fanatics, the Sweet Singers, haggard from long exposure on the moors, sat day and night with 'tearful psalms' to see Edinburgh consumed with fire from heaven, like another Sodom or Gomorrah. There, in the Grass-Market, stiff-necked, covenanting heroes offered up the often unnecessary, but not less honourable, sacrifice of their lives, and bade eloquent farewell to sun, moon, and stars, and earthly friendships, or died silent to the roll of drums. Down by yon outlet rode Grahame of Claverhouse and his thirty dragoons, with the town beating to arms behind their horses' tails—a sorry handful thus riding for their lives, but with a man at the head who was to return in a different temper, make a dash that staggered Scotland to the heart, and die happily in the thick of fight. There Aikenhead was hanged for a piece of boyish incredulity; there, a few years afterwards, David Hume ruined Philosophy and Faith, an undisturbed and well-reputed citizen; and thither, in yet a few years more, Burns came from the plough-tail to an academy of gilt unbelief and artificial letters.

R. L. STEVENSON, *Edinburgh* (Chatto and Windus).

*116. HYDER ALI'S ATROCITIES

Then ensued a scene of woe, the like[1] of which no eye had seen, no heart conceived, and which no tongue can adequately tell. All the horrors of war before known or heard of were mercy to[2] that new havoc. A storm of universal fire blasted every field, consumed every house, destroyed every temple. The miserable inhabitants, flying from their flaming villages, in part were slaughtered; others, without regard to sex, to age, to the respect of rank, or sacredness of function, fathers torn from children, husbands from wives, enveloped in a whirlwind of cavalry, and amidst the goading spears of drivers, and the trampling of pursuing horses, were swept into[3] captivity, in an unknown and hostile land. Those who were able to evade[4] this tempest, fled to the walled cities. But escaping from fire, sword, and exile, they fell into the jaws of famine.

For eighteen months, without intermission, this destruction raged from the gates of Madras to the gates of Tanjore; and so completely did[5] these masters in their art, Hyder Ali and his more ferocious son, absolve themselves of their impious vow, that when the British armies traversed,[6] as they did, the Carnatic for hundreds of miles in all directions, through the whole line of their march they did not see one man, not one woman, not one child, not one four-footed beast of any description whatever.[7] One dead, uniform silence reigned over[8] the whole region.

EDMUND BURKE, *Speech on the Nabob of Arcot's Debts.*

1 Turn as if: 'such as has been seen by no eye, conceived by no heart'. 2 to = compared with = *au prix de.*   3 *étaient balayés vers.*   4 *se soustraire à cette tourmente.*   5 The more normal French order is: *ces maîtres...s'acquittèrent si complètement de,* etc.   6 *parcoururent.*   7 *de quelque espèce que ce fût.*   8 *régnait dans.*

*117. PREMATURE REJOICINGS

In the city of Oxford there stands, in an open space not far from Magdalen Bridge, a stone bearing an inscription. The inscription tells of the great peace made in 1814, which was welcomed by all the nations of the world as the end of more than twenty years' continuous war. Well might the people of Oxford rejoice that peace had come at last, for it seemed as if peace were for ever banished from the earth. Children had been born in the midst of war time, they had grown to manhood, had married, and their children had in turn been born into a world in which the sound of the cannon...still drowned the voice of peace....But what is the date upon this stone? It is 1814....After all the rejoicings of Oxford and of the entire kingdom, it turned out that peace was not to return for yet another year, and that the man who so long had plunged Europe into war was once more and for the last time, to draw the sword and set the world aflame.... In the month of March, 1815, news reached the capitals of Europe that Buonaparte had succeeded in escaping from Elba and had landed at Cannes, in the South of France.

H. O. ARNOLD-FORSTER, *A History of England* (Cassell).

**118. THE ROAD TO BRUSSELS

By a stroke of fortune for the conservative cause the allied sovereigns and ministers were still gathered[1] in Vienna when it was learnt (7 March 1815) that Napoleon was once more on the soil of France. To wind up the work[2] of the Congress, to proclaim Napoleon suspect and outlaw, and to frame terms of military alliance against him was the work[3] of a fortnight. Before a blow had been struck every diplomatic card had been taken from Napoleon's hands. Had the issue on the field of Waterloo gone otherwise, he would still have succumbed to the united strength of Europe.

Yet of all modes of conducting his desperate adventure a campaign aimed at Brussels[4] offered the fairest chance of rallying the support of France. For centuries, seeing that it brought with it the great estuary of the Rhine, Belgium had possessed a symbolic, almost mysterious, value in the eyes of the French people. Over and over again the soil of this little country had been watered with French blood, nor had the ambition to acquire it ever failed to haunt the imagination of French statesmen. As the conquest of Belgium had been the first and principal glory of the young French Republic and its loss the most damaging commentary on the Empire, so its recovery now would be a prize than which none would be more welcome to the heart of France. Napoleon, then, was right to strike for Brussels, and Wellington, taking station on the field of Waterloo, was right to deny the road.

H. A. L. FISHER, *History of Europe*, III, p. 869
(Eyre and Spottiswoode).

1 *assemblés.*   2 *Terminer les travaux.*   3 *l'affaire.*   4 *ayant Bruxelles pour but.*

*119. THE BATTLE OF NAVARINO

The advance of the Allied Squadron into the bay on the 20th was majestic but ominous. They approached in perfect order and in perfect silence, Codrington anchoring the *Asia* opposite the Turkish and Egyptian flagships. In a few moments a dispute between boats' crews brought on a general action. For a time the fighting was very fierce. At one period Codrington, though the tallest man on his own quarter-deck, was the only one unwounded. The mizzen-mast fell and missed him by a hair's-breadth. Four bullets pierced his hat or his clothing, and a fifth smashed his watch. His own gunners of the *Asia* made the Egyptian flagship a wreck in ten minutes; and in three-quarters of an hour they sent the Turkish flagship drifting mastless out of the battle with five-sixths of the crew disabled! Many Turkish ships were soon dismasted or shattered, and, as night fell, the sound and sight of '37 beautiful explosions' showed the Turks themselves were destroying such ships as had escaped Codrington. His general order ran the next day, 'of the Turkish Fleet there remain only one frigate and fifteen smaller vessels in a state ever again to be put to sea'. Even Nelson could not have desired a more complete victory for his old captain.

H. TEMPERLEY, *The Foreign Policy of Canning* (Bell).

*120. AN EARLY VISIT

The dawn came through the trees at Kensington, and the little green before the palace slept on beneath its elms. The sun rose higher,[1] and the clock in its preposterous clock-tower above the gate[2] was pointing to five,[3] when a sound of wheels broke[4] the cool silence of the morning. A dusty carriage rumbled up and halted at the gate; two anxious gentlemen alighted;[5] but the sleeping palace was profoundly unaware of their arrival. They knocked, they pulled the bell,[6] they thumped until[7] a sleepy porter admitted[8] them to the little courtyard, where their progress was arrested once again. For the front door[9] was tightly shut; and when finally it opened, the visitors were turned adrift[10] into an empty room on the ground floor and left to their own devices. The minutes passed: and as their presence seemed to have been quite forgotten in a sleeping household, they rang the bell. When it was answered,[11] they desired explicitly that the attendant of the Princess Victoria might inform Her Royal Highness that the Archbishop of Canterbury and the Lord Chamberlain requested[12] an audience[13] on important business.[14]

PHILIP GUEDALLA, *The Hundred Years*
(Hodder and Stoughton).

1 Is this *se lever* or *s'élever*? See p. 8, § 11, DAYLIGHT.   2 What sort of 'gate'? See p. 5, § 6, FIELDS.   3 *marquait cinq heures.*   4 Is *interrompit* enough? See p. 16, § 18, To BREAK.   5 Supply 'from it'. See p. 42, § 35.   6 *le cordon de la cloche.*   7 Is *jusqu'à ce que* essential here? See p. 67, § 59, TILL.   8 Use *faire entrer.*   9 *la grande porte d'entrée.*   10 Use *lâcher.*   11 *Quand on vint à leur appel.*   12 *sollicitaient.*   13 See p. 15, § 18, AUDIENCE.   14 *pour affaire d'importance.*

*121. THE RETREAT FROM CABUL

The retreat began sadly. It was winter, and amidst those lofty mountains snow and ice lay thickly on the path. Akbar Khan did what he could to protect the retreating soldiers, but he could not do much. Crowds of fierce Afghans were posted on the rocks and on the steep sides of the hills through which the army had to struggle, shooting down the fugitives as they passed. Amongst the soldiers were English ladies, some with children to care for. When they reached the end of a narrow pass through which they had to go, scarcely a thousand men were left out of four thousand who had started from Cabul. To save the women and children they were delivered up to Akbar Khan, who promised to treat them kindly. He kept his word, and no harm happened to them. The men had to march on to death. They reached another narrow pass. The cruel Afghans were already on the rocks on either side, and shot them down without mercy. Very few lived to reach the other end. Those few pushed on, hoping to reach Jellalabad, where there was a British garrison. When they were still sixteen miles from Jellalabad, only six were alive. The pony on which one of these, Dr Brydon, rode was so worn out, and he himself was so utterly fatigued, that he lagged behind. The other five pushed on and were slain by the Afghans. Believing that the last Englishman had been killed, these Afghans went off to tell the tale. Weary and unnoticed, Dr Brydon came on slowly. At last he reached Jellalabad. He was the one man who arrived to tell the tale of the great disaster.

    S. R. GARDINER, *Outline of English History* (Longmans).

**122. AUGUST, 1914

It is perhaps a weakness[1] of British Cabinets that they shrink from facing distant and hypothetical questions. What Great Britain would do in the event of a violation of Belgian neutrality, or a German attack on Morocco, or a general war arising out of[2] the Serbian question, was at no time closely examined or narrowly defined in Downing Street. The theory was that the ultimate decision would lie[3] with Parliament, and that Parliament would act according to its understanding of the moral issues,[4] when the occasion arose. The Germans were, however, warned by Haldane in Berlin that a violation of Belgian neutrality would be gravely viewed in England, and Metternich, the capable German

Ambassador in London, was given[5] to understand by the same statesman that British public opinion would not permit[6] the destruction of France. It has sometimes been contended that bolder and more emphatic[7] declarations from the British Cabinet would have averted war. There can be no certainty on such a point. From 1912 onwards the real power in Berlin had not rested[8] with the Emperor alone, but in an increasing measure with the General Staff. These able soldiers rated the possible war effort[9] of England on the continent very low. That the English would be troublesome at sea was conceded. But Berlin was of opinion that, were war to break out, the campaign on the western front would be decided in a very few weeks. The presence of a British Expeditionary Force on the soil of France, though it would increase[10] the casualty list, would hardly affect[11] the time-table.

H. A. L. FISHER, A History of Europe, III
(Eyre and Spottiswoode).

1 *un défaut...d'hésiter à envisager les problèmes.* 2 *résultant de.* 3 Work in: *décider en dernier ressort.* 4 Say, *e.g., des questions morales que la situation soulèverait.* 5 Turn by the active: 'the same statesman gave Metternich to understand'. 6 Use *tolérer.* 7 See p. 19, § 18, EMPHATIC. 8 *n'appartenait pas.* 9 *l'effort militaire que l'Angleterre pourrait fournir en Europe.* 10 *tout en augmentant.* 11 *ne modifierait guère l'horaire prévu.*

****123. THE LIFE OF A TREATY

Nations should be willing to abide by two rules. They should abstain from imposing conditions which, on any just and reasonable view of human affairs, cannot be expected to be kept. And they should conclude their treaties as commercial treaties are usually concluded, only for a term of years.

If these principles are sound, it remains to be considered how they are to be applied to past treaties, which, though containing stipulations which, to be legitimate, must be temporary, have been concluded without such limitation, and are afterwards violated, or, as by Russia at present, repudiated, on the assumption of a right superior to the faith of engagements.

It is the misfortune of such stipulations, even if as temporary arrangements they might have been justifiable, that if concluded for permanency they are seldom to be got rid of without some lawless act on the part of the nation bound by them. If a lawless act, then, has been committed in the present instance, it does not entitle those who imposed the conditions to consider the lawlessness only, and to dismiss the more important consideration, whether, even if it was wrong to throw off the obligation, it would not be still more wrong to persist in enforcing it. If, though not fit to be perpetual, it has been imposed in perpetuity, the question when it becomes right to throw it off is but a question of time. No time having been fixed, Russia fixed her own time, and naturally chose the most convenient. She had no reason to believe that the release she sought would be voluntarily granted on any conditions which she would accept; and she chose an opportunity which, if not seized, might have been long before it occurred again, when the other contracting parties were in a more than usually disadvantageous position for going to war.   JOHN STUART MILL (1870).

V. CHARACTERS

**124. LOUIS XI

Brave enough for every useful and political purpose,[1] Louis XI had not a[2] spark of that romantic valour, or of the pride generally associated with it, which fought on[3] for the point of honour, when the point of utility had long been gained. Calm, crafty, and profoundly attentive to his own interest, he made every sacrifice,[4] both of pride[5] and passion,[5] which could interfere with it. He was careful in disguising his real sentiments and purposes from[6] all who approached him, and frequently used the expressions that 'the king knew not how to reign who[7] knew not how to dissemble; and that, for himself, if he thought his very cap knew[8] his secrets, he would throw it into the fire'. No man of his own[9] or of any other time better understood[10] how to avail himself[11] of the frailties of others, and when to avoid giving any advantage[12] by the untimely indulgence of his own.[13] He was by nature vindictive and cruel, even to the extent of finding pleasure in the frequent executions which he commanded. But, as no touch of mercy[14] ever induced[15] him to spare, when he could with safety condemn, so no sentiment of vengeance ever stimulated[15] him to violence.

SIR WALTER SCOTT, *Quentin Durward.*

1 *tout ce qui servait ses desseins.* 2 Use *la moindre.* See p. 32, § 19 (*b*). 3 Expand, *e.g.,* to *qui voulait qu'on continuât à se battre.* 4 Turn by a verb, *e.g., il lui sacrifiait tout ce qui pouvait le contrecarrer.* 5 Is the article required? See p. 34, § 21 (*b*). 6 Construction after *cacher?* See p. 64, § 57, FROM. 7 The order of words should be changed so that *qui* comes next its antecedent noun: *un roi qui ne savait pas dissimuler,* etc. 8 Use *pénétrer.* 9 *de son époque.* 10 Past Historic. See p. 47, § 44. 11 *exploiter.* 12 *éviter d'offrir la moindre prise sur lui.* 13 Say, for greater clearness: 'his own weaknesses'. 14 *aucun grain de pitié.* 15 Use *pousser.* Tense?

**125. VILLON QUITS THE CAPITAL

Villon was probably not followed out of Paris, like Antoine Fradin, the popular preacher, another exile of a few years later, by weeping multitudes; but I dare say one or two rogues of his acquaintance would keep him company for a mile or so on the south road, and drink a bottle with him before they turned. For banished people, in those days, seem to have set out on their own responsibility, in their own guard, and at their own expense. It was no joke to make one's way from Paris to Roussillon alone and penniless in the fifteenth century. Villon says he left a rag of his tails on every bush. Indeed, he must have had many a weary tramp, many a slender meal, and many a to-do with blustering captains of the Ordonnance. But with one of his light fingers, we may fancy that he took as good as he gave; for every rag of his tail, he would manage to indemnify himself upon the population in the shape of food, or wine, or ringing money; and his route would be traceable across France and Burgundy by housewives and inn-keepers lamenting over petty thefts, like the track of a single human locust.

A strange figure he must have cut in the eyes of the good country people: this ragged, blackguard city poet, with a smack of the Paris student, and a smack of the Paris street arab, posting along the highways, in rain or sun, among the green fields and vineyards. For himself, he had no taste for rural loveliness; green fields and vineyards would be mighty indifferent to Master Francis; but he would often have his tongue in his cheek at the simplicity of rustic dupes, and often, at city gates, he might stop to contemplate the gibbet with its swinging bodies, and hug himself on his escape.

R. L. STEVENSON, Men and Books (Chatto and Windus).

***126. Queen Elizabeth[1]

On the whole, she was English. On the whole, though she was infinitely subtle, she was not cruel; she was almost humane for her times; and her occasional bursts[2] of savagery were the results of fear or temper. In spite of superficial resemblances, she was the very opposite of her most dangerous enemy—the weaving spider of the Escurial. Both were masters[3] of dissimulation and lovers of delay; but the leaden foot of Philip was the symptom of a dying organism, while Elizabeth[1] temporised for the contrary reason—because vitality can afford[4] to wait. The fierce old hen sat still, brooding over the English nation, whose pullulating energies[5] were coming swiftly to ripeness and unity under her wings. She sat still; but every feather bristled; she was tremendously alive. While the Spanish ambassador declared that ten thousand devils possessed her, the ordinary Englishman saw in King Hal's full-blooded[6] daughter a Queen after his own heart. She swore; she spat; she struck with her fist when she was angry; she roared with laughter when she was amused.[7] And she was often amused. A radiant atmosphere of humour coloured[8] and softened the harsh lines of her destiny, and buoyed her up[9] along the zigzags of her dreadful path. Her response[10] to every stimulus was immediate and rich: to the folly of the moment, to the clash and horror of great events, her soul leapt out with a vivacity, an abandonment, a complete awareness[11] of the situation, which made her, which makes her still, a fascinating spectacle. She could play with life as with an equal,[12] wrestling with it, making fun of it, admiring it, watching its drama, intimately relishing the strangeness of circumstance, the sudden freaks of fortune, the perpetual unexpectedness of things. 'Per molto variare la natura è bella' was one of her favourite aphorisms.

LYTTON STRACHEY, *Elizabeth and Essex*
(Chatto and Windus).

1 Spelling? See p. 85, § 25 (a). 2 Simplify, *e.g.*, *si parfois elle se montrait tout d'un coup féroce, c'était l'effet de....* 3 *passés maîtres en.* 4 Use: *se permettre de.* 5 *l'énergie en plein germe.* 6 *au sang généreux.* 7 *gaie.* 8 *rehaussait.* 9 *la soutenait d'allégresse.* 10 *La promptitude de ses réactions.* 11 *conscience* (f.). 12 *d'égale à égale.*

****127. QUEEN ELIZABETH (*continued*)

The variations in her own behaviour were hardly less frequent than nature's. The rough hectoring dame with her practical jokes, her out-of-door manners, her passion for hunting, would suddenly become a stern-faced woman of business, closeted for long hours with secretaries, reading and dictating despatches, and examining with sharp exactitude the minutiae of accounts. Then as suddenly, the cultivated lady of the Renaissance would shine forth. For Elizabeth's accomplishments were many and dazzling. She was mistress of six languages besides her own, a student of Greek, a superb calligraphist, an excellent musician. She was a connoisseur of painting and poetry. She danced, after the Florentine style, with a high magnificence that astonished beholders. Her conversation, full, not only of humour, but of elegance and wit, revealed an unerring social sense, a

charming delicacy of personal perception. It was this
spiritual versatility which made her one of the supreme
diplomatists of history. Her protean mind, projecting itself
with extreme rapidity into every sinuous shape conceivable,
perplexed the most clear-sighted of her antagonists and
deluded the most wary. But her crowning virtuosity was
her command over the resources of words. When she wished,
she could drive in her meaning up to the hilt with hammer
blows of speech, and no one ever surpassed her in the
elaborate confection of studied ambiguities. Her letters she
composed in a regal mode of her own, full of apophthegm
and insinuation. In private talk she could win a heart by
some quick felicitous *brusquerie*; but her greatest moments
came when, in public audience, she made known her wishes,
her opinions, and her meditations to the world. Then the
splendid sentences, following one another in a steady
volubility, proclaimed the curious workings of her intellect
with enthralling force; while the woman's inward passion
vibrated magically through the loud high uncompromising
utterance and the perfect rhythms of her speech.

LYTTON STRACHEY, *Elizabeth and Essex*
(Chatto and Windus).

***128. CROMWELL

Your Cromwell, what good could it do him[1] to be 'noticed'
by noisy crowds of people?[2] God his Maker already noticed
him. He, Cromwell, was already there;[3] no notice would
make *him* other than he already was. Till his hair was grown
gray, and Life from the downhill slope[4] was all seen to be
limited, not infinite but finite, and all a measurable matter
how it went,—he had been content[5] to plow the ground, and
read his Bible. He in his old days could not support it any
longer, without selling himself to Falsehood, that he might[6]
ride in gilt carriages to Whitehall, and have clerks with
bundles of papers haunting him, 'Decide[7] this, decide that',
which in utmost sorrow of heart no man can perfectly
decide! What could gilt carriages do for this man? From of

old, was there not in his life a weight of meaning, a terror, and a splendour as of Heaven itself? His existence there[8] as man set him beyond the need of gilding Death, Judgment and Eternity; these already lay as the background[9] of whatsoever he thought or did. All his life lay begirt as in a sea of nameless Thoughts, which no speech of a mortal could name. God's Word, as the Puritan prophets of that time had read it; this was great,[10] and all else was little to him. To call such a man 'ambitious',[11] to figure him as the prurient windbag[12] described above, seems to me the poorest solecism.[13] Such a man will say: 'Keep your gilt carriages and huzzaing mob; keep your red-tape clerks, your influentialities, your important businesses. Leave me alone,[14] leave me alone; there is too much of life in me already!'   THOMAS CARLYLE.

1 *quel bien cela pouvait-il lui faire d'être*, etc.   2 Omit.   3 *Lui...Il était déjà Cromwell.*   4 Say, e.g., *en redescendant la pente des années.*   5 Rather *avait vécu content* à than *avait été content* de.   6 *à seule fin de pouvoir aller à Whitehall en carrosse doré.*   7 *trancher* seems the best word; *trancher ce point-ci, ce point-là, points que nul homme*, etc.   8 = in this world = *ici-bas.*   9 *au fond de.*   10 *voilà qui était grand.*   11 *Traiter d'ambitieux un tel homme.*   12 Use, e.g., *une nullité bouffie d'ambition.*   13 *contre-sens* (m.).   14 See p. 70, § 60.

****129. MILTON

Milton was, like Dante, a statesman and a lover; and, like Dante, he had been unfortunate in ambition and in love. He had survived his health and his sight, the comforts of his home, and the prosperity of his party. Of the great men by whom he had been distinguished at his entrance into life, some had been taken away from the evil to come; some had carried into foreign climates their unconquerable hatred of oppression; some were pining in dungeons; and some had poured forth their blood on scaffolds. Venal and licentious scribblers, with just sufficient talent to clothe the thoughts of a pandar in the style of a bellman, were now the favourite writers of the Sovereign and of the public. It was a loathsome herd, which could be compared to nothing so fitly as to the rabble of Comus, grotesque monsters, half bestial, half human, dropping with wine, bloated with gluttony, and reeling in obscene dances. Amidst these that fair Muse was placed, like the chaste lady of the Masque, lofty, spotless, and serene, to be chattered at, and pointed at, and grinned at, by the whole rout of Satyrs and Goblins.

If ever despondency and asperity could be excused in any man, they might have been excused in Milton. But the strength of his mind overcame every calamity. Neither blindness, nor gout, nor age, nor penury, nor domestic afflictions, nor political disappointments, nor abuse, nor neglect, had power to disturb his sedate and majestic patience. His spirits do not seem to have been high, but they were singularly equable. His temper was serious, perhaps stern; but it was a temper which no sufferings could render sullen or fretful. Such as it was when, on the eve of great events, he returned from his travels, in the prime of health and manly beauty, loaded with literary distinctions, and glowing with patriotic hopes, such it continued to be when, after having experienced every calamity which is incident to our nature, old, poor, sightless, and disgraced, he retired to his hovel to die.

LORD MACAULAY, *Essay on Milton.*

**130. HOSPITALITY

As we lived near the road, we often had the traveller or stranger visit[1] us; our cousins, too, even to the fortieth remove, all remembered their affinity...and came very frequently. Some of them did us no great honour by these claims[2] of kindred, as we had the blind, the maimed and the halt among the number. But my wife always desired that, as they were the same *flesh and blood*, they should sit[3] with us at the same table. So that if we had not very rich, we generally had very happy friends about us; for this remark will hold good[4] through life, that the poorer[5] the guest the better pleased[6] he ever[7] is with being treated; and as some men gaze with admiration at the colours of a tulip or the wing of a butterfly, so I was[8] by nature an admirer of happy human faces. However, when any one of our relations was found to be a person of bad character,[9] a troublesome guest, or one[10] we desired to get rid of, upon his leaving my house I ever took care to lend him a riding-coat or a pair of boots[11] or sometimes a horse of small value, and I always had the satisfaction of finding[12] he never came back to return them. By this[13] the house was cleared of such as we did not like, but never[14] was the family of Wakefield[15] known to turn[16] the traveller or the poor dependent from its door.

OLIVER GOLDSMITH, *The Vicar of Wakefield*.

1 *la visite de voyageurs et d'étrangers.*   2 Transpose: *e.g.,* En *revendiquant ces liens de parenté, certains ne nous,* etc.   3 See p. 55, § 51, SIT.   4 *se vérifie dans toutes les circonstances de la vie.*   5 Order of words? See p. 33, § 20 (*b*).   6 *satisfait.*   7 Omit.   8 *moi, je suis* comes more naturally in French.   9 *de mauvaise réputation,* not *'mauvais caractère'* = ill-tempered.   10 *quelqu'un.*   11 Is this *bottes* = riding-boots? Or *souliers* = ordinary boots?   12 Use *constater.*   13 Use *ainsi.*   14 *jamais on ne put dire.*   15 Not "*la famille Wakefield*"; it is a place-name here.   16 Use *fermer la porte à.*

*131. GIBBON AT HIS HOME

As my stay at Buriton was always voluntary, I was received and dismissed with smiles; but the comforts of m y retirement did not depend on the ordinary pleasures of the country. My father could never inspire me with his love and knowledge of farming. I never handled a gun, I seldom mounted a horse, and my philosophic walks were soon terminated by a shady bench, where I was long detained by the sedentary amusement of reading or meditation. At home I occupied a pleasant and spacious apartment; the library on the same floor was soon considered as my particular domain, and I might say with truth that I was never less alone than when by myself. My sole complaint, which I piously suppressed, arose from the kind restraint imposed on the freedom of my time. By the habit of early rising I always secured a sacred portion of the day, and many scattered moments were stolen and employed by my studious industry. But the family hours of breakfast, of dinner, of tea, and of supper were regular and long.

EDWARD GIBBON, *Memoirs.*

**132. SCOTT'S 'FAITHLESSNESS'[1]

Thus, the most startling fault of the age being its faithlessness, it is necessary[2] that its greatest man should be faithless. Nothing is more notable or sorrowful in Scott's mind[3] than its incapacity of steady belief in anything. He cannot even resolve hardily to believe in a ghost, or a water-spirit; always explains them away in an apologetic manner, not believing, all the while, even in his own explanation. He never can clearly ascertain whether there is anything behind the arras but rats;[4] never draws sword, and thrusts at it[5] for life or death; but goes on looking at it timidly, and saying, 'It must be the wind'. He is educated[6] a Presbyterian, and remains one, because it is the most sensible thing he can do if he is to live in Edinburgh; but he thinks Romanism more picturesque, and profaneness[7] more gentlemanly; does not see that anything affects human life[8] but love, courage, and destiny; which are, indeed, not matters of faith at all, but of sight.[9] Any gods but those are very misty in outline to him; and when the love is laid ghastly in poor Charlotte's coffin; and[10] the courage is no more of use,—the pen having fallen from between the fingers; and destiny is sealing the scroll,—the God-light is dim[11] in the tears that fall on it.

He is in all this the epitome of his epoch.

JOHN RUSKIN, *Modern Painters.*

1 *l'incrédulité.* 2 Is this *il faut que*? Or *il faut bien que*? 3 Transpose: '*chez Scott que l'impuissance de son esprit à croire fermement à*', etc. 4 *autre chose que des rats.* 5 *lui pousse une botte.* 6 Use *par éducation.* 7 *la libre pensée.* 8 *à ses yeux rien ne touche la vie*, etc. 9 *des questions d'optique.* 10 Supply *que.* See p. 66, § 58. 11 *bien pâle est l'éclat de la lumière divine dans*, etc.

***133. Byron's Last Journey

It would be idle to pretend that Byron set out upon his last journey with any very spirited enthusiasm, either for the cause which he was embracing or for the particular functions which he would be called upon to fulfil. Nor would it be honest to portray as some reckless Elizabethan, intent upon the gain and glory of a new endurance, the irresolute and dyspeptic little man who, on that July evening, limped gloomily up the gangway of the *Hercules*. For when it had come to packing up, and destroying old letters, and explaining to Barry what was to be done with the books, and totting up the accounts, and sending the horses down to the harbour, and finding everything at the Casa Saluzzo hourly more disintegrated and uncomfortable, he began, definitely and indignantly, to curse the whole undertaking. It was always like that: people never left one alone; there he was, good-natured and kindly, and they came along and took advantage of him, and extracted promises, and imposed upon him generally. Once again he had been caught in a chain of circumstances: there had been his first visit to Greece, and *Childe Harold*, and *The Corsair*, and that silly passage about the 'hereditary bondsmen'; and there had been Hobhouse (damn Hobhouse!), and that egregious ass Trelawny. And as a result here was he, who had never done any harm to anyone, sitting alone in the Casa Saluzzo, with his household gods once again dismantled around him, and his bulldog growling now and then at the distant voice of Trelawny thundering orders to the servants.

HAROLD NICOLSON, *Byron: The Last Journey* (Constable).

***134. Mrs Touchett

Mrs Touchett was certainly a person of many oddities,[1] of which[2] her behaviour on returning to her husband's house after many months was a noticeable specimen.[2] She had her own way of doing all that she did, and that is the simplest description of a character which, although by no means without liberal motions,[3] rarely succeeded in giving an impression of suavity. Mrs Touchett might[4] do a great deal of good, but she never pleased. This way of her own, of which she was so fond, was not intrinsically offensive[5]—it was just unmistakably distinguished from the way of others. The edges of her conduct were so very clear-cut[6] that for susceptible persons it sometimes had a knife-like effect.

That hard fineness came out in her deportment during the first hours of her return from America, under circumstances in which it might have seemed[7] that her first act[8] would have been to exchange greetings[9] with her husband and son. Mrs Touchett, for reasons which she deemed excellent, always retired on such occasions into impenetrable seclusion, postponing the more sentimental ceremony until she had repaired the disorder of dress[10] with a completeness which had the less reason[11] to be of high importance as neither beauty nor vanity were concerned in it. She was a plain-faced old woman, without graces and without any great elegance, but with an extreme respect for her own motives. She was usually prepared to explain these—when[12] the explanation was asked as a favour; and in such a case they proved totally different from those that had been attributed to her.

HENRY JAMES, *The Portrait of a Lady* (Macmillan).

1 *singularités.*   2 *dont...fournit un remarquable exemple.*   3 *aucune-ment incapable d'élans généreux.*   4 Use, *e.g., avoir beau.*   5 *n'avait en soi rien de blessant.*   6 Say, *e.g., Ses actions avaient en quelque sorte des arêtes si tranchantes.*   7 *où l'on aurait pu penser.*   8 *occupation.*   9 *échanger des marques d'affection.*   10 *sa toilette.*   11 *dont la haute importance se justifiait d'autant moins que.*   12 Say, *e.g., pour peu qu'on le lui demandât.*

**135. MISS STILES

Miss Stiles, who came in, was not handsome. She was large and fat, with a round red face like a sun, and she wore colours too bright for her size. She had a slow soft voice like the melancholy moo of a cow. She was not a bad woman, but, temperamentally, was made unhappy by the success or good fortune of others. Were you in distress, she would love you, cherish you, never abandon you. She would share her last penny with you, run to the end of the world for you, defend you before the whole of humanity. Were you, however, in robust health, she would hint to every one of a possible cancer; were you popular, it would worry her terribly and she would discover a thousand faults in your character; were you successful in your work, she would pray for your approaching failure lest you should become arrogant. She gossiped without cessation, and always, as it were, to restore the proper balance of the world, to pull down the mighty from their high places, to lift the humble only that they in their turn might be pulled down. She played fluently and execrably on the piano. She spent her day in running from house to house.

HUGH WALPOLE, *The Cathedral* (Macmillan).

*136. CHILDHOOD MEMORIES

I learned to speak from my family and chiefly from my mother. None of us spoke well; our common idioms were poor and bad; we mispronounced many words, and long words we avoided as something dangerous and pretentious. I had very few toys: a tin railway-engine I remember, some metal soldiers, and an insufficient supply of wooden building bricks.[1] There was no special place for me to play, and if I laid out[2] my toys on the living-room table, a meal was sure to descend and sweep them away. I remember a great longing to play with the things in the shop, and especially with the bundles of firewood[3]..., but my father discouraged such ambitions. He did not like to have[4] me about the shop until I was[5] old enough to help, and the indoor part of most of my days was spent in the room above it or in the underground room below it.

After the shop was closed[6] it became a very cold, cavernous, dark place to a little boy's imagination[7]; there were dreadful shadows in which terrible things might lurk,[8] and even holding fast[9] to my mother's hand on my way to bed, I was filled with fear to traverse it. It had always a faint, unpleasant smell, a smell of decaying vegetation varying with the particular fruit or vegetable that was most affected,[10] and a constant element of paraffin. But on Sundays when it[11] was closed all day, the shop was different, no longer darkly threatening but very very still.

H. G. WELLS, *The Dream* (Cape).

1 *pièces de jeux de construction.*   2 *si je disposais.*   3 *fagotins.*
4 *me voir au magasin.*   5 Translate: 'so long as I was not'.   6 *Après la fermeture le magasin devenait....*   7 Transpose: 'of the little boy that I was': use *que*; see p. 44, § 89.   8 Transpose: 'lurked perhaps'.   9 Use *serrer fort.*   10 *atteint.*   11 *le magasin.*

**137. OUR ELDERS

These elders, our betters by a trick of chance, commanded no respect, but only a certain blend of envy—of their good luck—and pity—for their inability to make use of it. Indeed, it was one of the most hopeless features in their character (when we troubled ourselves to waste a thought on them, which wasn't often) that, having absolute license to indulge in the pleasures of life, they could get no good of it. They might dabble in the pond all day, hunt the chickens, climb trees in the most uncompromising Sunday clothes; they were free to issue forth and buy gunpowder in the full eye of the sun—free to fire cannons and explode mines on the lawn: yet they never did any one of these things. No irresistible Energy haled them to church o' Sundays; yet they went there regularly of their own accord, though they betrayed no greater delight in the experience than ourselves.

On the whole, the existence of these Olympians seemed to be entirely void of interests, even as their movements were confined and slow, and their habits stereotyped and senseless. To anything but appearances they were blind. For them the orchard (a place elf-haunted, wonderful!) simply produced so many apples and cherries: or it didn't—when the failures of Nature were not infrequently ascribed to us. They

never set foot within fir-wood or hazel-copse, nor dreamt of
the marvels hid therein. The mysterious sources, sources as
of old Nile, that fed the duck-pond had no magic for them.

KENNETH GRAHAME, *The Golden Age*
(John Lane, The Bodley Head).

***138. A MAN OF ENERGY

He left home at sixteen (this was about 1833) spurred on by
the sympathy[1] of a strong-minded mother. I have still in
the attic of his old house, the little hair-covered trunk[2]
which he took with him, and which contained all his
worldly possessions.

From that time on, until his old age, he never came home[3]
except to rest in the occasional, very brief intervals of
incessant and almost appalling activity, both intellectual
and physical. With only a little help from his family he
earned his way through college, and then put himself
through[4] a Theological Seminary in record time.

With him, as with other manifestants of the mid-century
explosion of energy in America, it was as if[5] the long generations of vegetating country-dwellers had, like other vegetating[6] matter of bygone ages, turned to rich veins of highly
combustible material,[7] which this descendant of theirs
mined out, at top speed, and cast by great shovelfuls into the
furnace of his personality. He seems always to have been
incandescent,[8] the whole six-feet-three of him, with motive-
power which he could not, try as he might,[9] use up fast
enough to cool off. All his life he burned hot with a vitality
at which[10] an ever-widening circle of other human beings,
rich and poor, young and old, learned and ignorant, warmed
their hands[11] and their hearts.

D. CANFIELD, *Raw Material* (Cape).

1 *l'approbation.*   2 *malle couverte en tissu de crin.*   3 Is this *revenait?*
Or *revint?* See p. 47, § 44.   4 *passa par.*   5 *on eût dit que.*   6 Use
végétatif.   7 *d'une matière extrêmement inflammable.*   8 *en état per-
pétuel d'incandescence.*   9 *quoi qu'il fît.*   10 *à la flamme de laquelle.*
11 *venaient se réchauffer les mains,* etc.

**139. ACTIVITY

The gales that winter appeared to be never ending. Without cease the wind roared and bellowed and blustered: but in weather when, unless business called them, other people stayed at home, Joanna chose to go out, to walk, enjoying with her large young frame the physical impact of the wind, the battling against it and throwing herself upon it, or being blown along as though Mercury's wings were fastened to her feet. Almost alone of things in Newborough, this afforded her a sense of life, made her forget her worries, the possible developments of the future, in the struggle of the present. Her skin felt cool and fresh as an apple, and every muscle strengthened, when the fingers of the wind had played up and down them....But these hours were inevitably followed by a stronger and more melancholy reaction.

The sea, too, fascinated and drew her down to it. The buttressed, battlemented terrace of the Winter Gardens showed through its apertures no prying heads at this season of the year, no drone of pseudo-military bands drifted down to be muffled by the waves, and the long wide expanse of sand, those placid golden lawns, freshly mown, trimmed daily by the tides, lay empty. Only on the nearer, sickle-curved stretch, between the Hotel Superbe and the broken Norman castle on the hill—those two landmarks, both equally, it seemed, the relics of a forgotten age—some little show of activity manifested itself.

OSBERT SITWELL, *Those were the Days* (Macmillan).

****140. ACTIVITY (*continued*)

In one place, for example, a hockey-ground had been drawn out,[1] and violent combat raged between two teams of fat-calfed, short-skirted, flustered and dishevelled girls from the local schools for Young Ladies. The special aim of these establishments—as opposed to that of the 'finishing-off' schools,[2] which, after the continental fashion, placed a premium on culture—was the more native one of training the pupils interned therein up to the point where 'they could hold their own with men':[3] In pursuit of this romantic yet useful ideal—in defiance, equally, of the fact that men and women were not made in the same mould[4] and that, most emphatically, the same muscles do not need exercising in them—the mistresses organised these matches. The players, their faces striped and blotched with red patches[5] (a tribute to 'the healthy school diet which prevails'), and now rendered still more purple by the system of semi-strangulation to which the tight elastic bands running under their chins, placed there in order to keep their floppy caps on, subjected them, rushed frantically—and in accordance,[6] no doubt, with the guidance of some esoteric code—from point to point, hitting out with their clubs;[7] the weapons, seemingly, of some barbarian and autochthonous tribe. A few teachers, their severe, rather[8] masculine faces painted and tattooed by the cold to resemble African fetish masks, their bones rattling[9] in the wind, watched them, guarded them, while, from time to time, their blue, thin lips shaped the strangest and most epicene[10] cries: 'Go it, Stumpy!' 'Worry her, Carrots!' 'Bravo, Goggles, old gal!'...But no one seemed to be surprised: it was a daily sight, at the same time a way of forgetting and a preparation for the lives that were to follow.   OSBERT SITWELL, *Those were the Days* (Macmillan).

1 *on avait tracé un terrain de hockey.*   2 *Écoles de perfectionnement.*
3 *lutter de pair avec les hommes dans n'importe quel jeu.*   4 *n'ont pas été coulés dans le même moule.*   5 *dont les visages, zébrés...s'empourpraient pour l'instant davantage.*   6 *et, semblait-il, selon les règles d'un code ésotérique.*   7 *distribuant de grands coups de crosses.*   8 Is this *assez?* Or *plutôt?* See p. 61, § 54, RATHER.   9 *et dont les os s'entrechoquaient sous la violence du vent.*   10 *les moins féminins.*

***141. AN EIGHTEENTH-CENTURY ATMOSPHERE

Besides a millionaire's fortune in money, he came into possession of all the Hertford-Wallace treasures in Paris. To remember all those treasures now, as I remember them, is to look back into another age,—an age when culture and elegance seemed permanent, privileged, and secure; an age

when a taste in fine books, furniture, and pictures formed
part of a gentleman's equipment, as much as a taste in good
food and noble wines. It scarcely seems to belong to this
uneasy century at all. The connoisseurship and splendid
living which descended as the mantle of Elijah on the
shoulders of John Murray Scott surrounded not only him
but also his friends with an atmosphere of the eighteenth
rather than the twentieth century.

It was not so much in his London house as in Paris that
one could savour this atmosphere to the full. In Paris he
seemed to expand, as though the full flower of his jovial
benevolence opened under the influence of its own con-
genial incarnation of benign hospitality, desirous only that
everyone should be happy as his guest, dispensing, in his
lavish way, all the store of courtesy, intellect and fine fare
at his disposal. For he was a great giver, and he had much
to give. His vast apartment on the first floor, turning the
corner of the Boulevard des Italiens and the rue Lafitte, with
twenty windows opening on either street (not so very far
from the hotel where my grandfather had originally made
Pepita's acquaintance), was in itself a treasure-house which
brought visitors from every part of Europe. I shall never
forget the enchantment of that house. From the moment
one had pulled the string and the big door had swung open,
admitting one to the interior courtyard where grooms in
wooden clogs seemed perpetually to be washing carriages,
the whole house belonged to him, though he reserved only
the first floor for himself and a number of odd and secret
little apartments tucked away on various floors and in
various corners. Thus in one corner, quite separate, were the
rooms for the linen, under the charge of the *lingère*, such
linen as I have never seen since, stacks and stacks of it, with
lavender bags between each layer, and blue and pink
ribbons tying it up; sheets as fine as a cambric handkerchief,
towels you could almost have threaded through a ring. The
lingère used to sit there all day darning and ironing, with a
canary singing in a cage at an open window.

V. SACKVILLE WEST, *Pepita* (Hogarth Press).

**142. GASTON

I must not let that name go by without a word for the best[1] of all good fellows now gone down into the dust. We shall never again see Gaston in his forest costume—he was Gaston with all the world, in[2] affection, not in[2] disrespect— nor hear him wake the echoes of Fontainebleau with the woodland horn. Never again shall his kind smile put peace[3] among all races of artistic men, and make the Englishman at home in France. Never more shall the sheep, who were not more innocent at heart[4] than he, sit all unconsciously[5] for his industrious pencil. He died too early,[6] at the very moment when he was beginning to put forth fresh sprouts,[7] and blossom[8] into something worthy of himself; and yet none who knew him will think he lived in vain. I never knew[9] a man so little, for whom yet I had so much affection; and I find it a good test of others, how much they had learned to understand[10] and value him. His was indeed a good influence in life while he was[11] still among us; he had a fresh laugh, it did you good to see him; and however sad he may have been at heart,[4] he always bore a bold and cheerful countenance,[12] and took fortune's worst as it were the showers of spring.

R. L. STEVENSON, *An Inland Voyage* (Chatto and Windus).

1 *sans dire un mot du meilleur*, etc.   2 in = out of = *par*.   3 Use *faire régner la paix*.   4 *au fond*.   5 *sans le savoir*.   6 See p. 58, § 53. 7 *donner de nouvelles pousses*.   8 *parvenait à un épanouissement*. 9 Simplify by transposing: 'I never felt (*éprouver*) so much affection for a man I knew so little.'   10 Simplify by adding *voir*, e.g., *voir jusqu'à quel point ils étaient parvenus à le comprendre*.   11 Is this *aussi longtemps qu'il était des nôtres*? Or *fut*? See p. 47, § 44.   12 *il faisait toujours fière et joyeuse mine*.

**143. FRENCH AND ENGLISH CHARACTER

The Frenchman's habitation, like himself, is open, cheerful, bustling and noisy. All is clatter and chatter. He is talkative and good-humoured with his servants, sociable with his neighbours, and complaisant with all the world. He lives in part of a great hotel, with wide portal, paved court, a spacious staircase, and a family on every floor. The Englishman, on the contrary, ensconces himself in a snug brick mansion, which he has all to himself; locks the front door; puts broken bottles along his walls, and spring-guns and man-traps in his gardens; exults in his quiet and privacy, shrouds himself with trees and window-curtains. Yet whoever gains admittance is apt to find a warm heart and a warm fireside within.

The French excel in wit, the English in humour; the French have gayer fancy, the English richer imagination. The vivacity of the French is apt to sparkle up and be frothy; the gravity of the English to settle down and grow muddy. When the two characters can be fixed in a medium, the French kept from effervescence and the English from stagnation, both will be found excellent.

WASHINGTON IRVING, *Wolfert's Roost* (adapted).

***144. FRENCH INDEPENDENCE

At last I saw a nice old man and his wife looking at me with some interest, so I gave them good day and pulled up alongside.[1] I began with a remark[2] upon their dog, which had somewhat the look of a pointer; thence I slid into a compliment on Madame's flowers, and thence into a word in praise[3] of their way of life.

If you ventured[4] on such an experiment in England you would get a slap in the face at once. The life would be shown[5] to be a vile one, not without a side-shot[6] at your better fortune. Now, what I like so much in France is the clear unflinching recognition[7] by everybody of his own luck. They all know on what side their bread is buttered, and take a pleasure in showing it to others, which is surely the better part of religion.[8] And they scorn to make a poor mouth over their poverty, which I take to be the better part of manliness. I have heard a woman, in quite a better position at home, with a good bit of money in hand,[9] refer to her own child with a horrid whine as 'a poor man's child'. I would not say such a thing to the Duke of Westminster. And the French are full of[10] this spirit of independence. Perhaps it is the result of republican institutions, as they call them. Much more likely it is because there are so few people really poor,[11] that the whiners are not enough to keep each other in countenance.[12]

R. L. STEVENSON, *An Inland Voyage* (Chatto and Windus).

1 *j'accostai*; the speaker was in a canoe.   2 *J'entrai en matière avec une remarque.*   3 *quelques mots flatteurs sur.*   4 *Si vous tentiez.*   5 *On vous dépeindrait....*   6 *non sans décocher de biais quelque allusion à.*   7 Turn by: *cette manière nette et résolue dont chacun*, etc.   8 *l'essentiel de la religion.*   9 *et avec pas mal d'argent de côté.*   10 *imbus de.*   11 *si peu de vrais pauvres.*   12 *pour s'enhardir.* Should *mutuellement* be added? See p. 45, § 41.

****145. ENGLISH AND FRENCH IN THE MIDDLE EAST

The Englishmen in the Middle East divided into two classes. Class one, subtle and insinuating, caught the characteristics of the people about him, their speech, their conventions of thought, almost their manner. He directed men secretly, guiding them as he would. In such frictionless habit of influence his own nature lay hid, unnoticed.

Class two, the John Bull of the books, became the more rampantly English the longer he was away from England. He invented an Old Country for himself, a home of all remembered virtues, so splendid in the distance that, on return, he often found reality a sad falling off and withdrew his muddle-headed self into fractious advocacy of the good old times. Abroad, through his armoured certainty, he was a rounded sample of our traits. He showed the complete Englishman. There was friction in his track, and his direction was less smooth than that of the intellectual type: yet his stout example cut wider swathe.

Both sorts took the same direction in example, one vociferously, the other by implication. Each assumed the Englishman a chosen being, inimitable, and the copying him blasphemous or impertinent. In this conceit they urged on people the next best thing. God had not given it them to be

English; a duty remained to be good of their type. Consequently we admired native custom; studied the language; wrote books about its architecture, folklore, and dying industries. Then one day, we woke up to find this chthonic spirit turned political, and shook our heads with sorrow over its ungrateful nationalism—truly the fine flower of our innocent efforts.

The French, though they started with a similar doctrine of the Frenchman as the perfection of mankind (dogma amongst them, not secret instinct), went on, contrarily, to encourage their subjects to imitate them; since, even if they could never attain the true level, yet their virtue would be greater as they approached it. We looked upon imitation as a parody; they as a compliment.

T. E. LAWRENCE, *The Seven Pillars of Wisdom* (Cape).

VI. CONVERSATIONAL

*146. A SECRET CONVERSATION

Soon after sunrise in the morning[1] Nell stole out from the tent, and rambling into[2] some fields at a short distance, plucked a few wild roses and such humble flowers, purposing to make them into[3] little nosegays and offer them to the ladies in the carriages when the company arrived.[4] Her thoughts were not idle[5] while she was thus employed; when she returned[4] and was seated beside the old man in one corner of the tent, tying her flowers together, while the two men lay dozing in another corner, she plucked him by the sleeve, and slightly glancing towards them, said in a low voice:

'Grandfather, don't look at those I talk of, and don't seem as if I spoke of anything but what I am about.[6] What was that you told me before we left the old house? That if they knew what we were going to do, they would say you were mad, and part us?'

The old man turned to her with an aspect[7] of wild terror, but she checked him by a look, and bidding him hold some flowers while she tied them up, and so bringing her lips closer to his ear,[8] said:

'I know that was what you told me.... Grandfather, these men suspect that[9] we have secretly left our friends, and mean to carry us before some gentleman[10] and have us taken care of[11] and sent back.'

CHARLES DICKENS, *Old Curiosity Shop.*

1 To avoid absurdity, begin by *Le lendemain matin.* 2 *et allant à l'aventure entra.* 3 = 'make with them' = *en faire.* 4 It will lighten the French sentence if a noun is substituted for the verb; e.g., *quand, après son retour, assise,* etc. 5 *Son esprit ne chômait point.* 6 *ce à quoi je m'occupe.* 7 *une expression.* 8 Avoid too concrete expressions: see p. 71, § 60. 9 = *nous soupçonnent d'avoir.* 10 = 'a magistrate'; say, e.g., '*chez Monsieur le Juge*' (child's language). 11 *pour qu'on s'occupe de nous.*

*147. TOM AND MAGGIE

Tom had not heard anything from home for some weeks—a fact which did not distress him, for his father and mother were not apt to manifest their affection in unnecessary letters—when, to his great surprise, on the morning of a dark cold day near the end of November, he was told, soon after entering the study at nine o'clock, that his sister was in the drawing-room. It was Mrs Stelling who had come into the study to tell him, and she left him to enter the drawing-room alone. Maggie...was tall now, almost as tall as Tom, though she was only thirteen; and she really looked older than he did at that moment. She had thrown off her bonnet, her heavy braids were pushed back from her forehead, as if it would not bear that extra load, and her young face had a strangely worn look as her eyes turned anxiously towards the door. When Tom entered she did not speak, but only went up to him, put her arms round his neck, and kissed him earnestly....'Why, how is it you're come so early this cold morning, Maggie?...How is it you're not at school? The holidays have not begun yet?'— 'Father wanted me at home', said Maggie, with a slight trembling of the lip. 'I came home three or four days ago.'

GEORGE ELIOT, *The Mill on the Floss.*

*148. DEBTS

'No, dear father!'[1] Maggie burst out entreatingly;[2] 'it's a very long while since all that: you've been ill a great many weeks—more than two months—everything is changed.'

Mr Tulliver looked at them all three alternately with a startled gaze: the idea that much had happened of which he knew nothing[3] had often transiently[4] arrested him before,[5] but it came upon him now with entire novelty.

'Yes, father', said Tom, in answer to the[6] gaze. 'You needn't trouble your mind about business[7] until you are quite well. Everything is settled about that for the present —about the mill and the land and the debts....'

'Don't you take on too much about it, sir', said Luke. 'You'd have paid everybody if you could....'

Good Luke felt, after the manner of contented, hard-working men whose lives have been spent in servitude, that sense of natural fitness in rank[8] which made[9] his master's downfall a tragedy to him. He was urged,[10] in his slow way, to say something that would express[11] his share in the family sorrow, and these words...were the most ready to his tongue. They were just the words to lay the most painful hold on his master's bewildered mind.

GEORGE ELIOT, *The Mill on the Floss.*

1 *père chéri.*   2 *d'un ton suppliant.*   3 It is simpler to use *ignorer*; see p. 60, § 54, NOT.   4 *un instant.*   5 *déjà.*   6 *ce.*   7 *vous tracasser au sujet des affaires.*   8 *avait...ce sentiment naturel de la hiérarchie.* 9 Construction? see p. 53, § 51, To MAKE.   10 *Il eut à cœur de dire, lentement suivant sa manière.*   11 Subjunctive: *qui exprimât.*

**149. THE HISTORICAL BLOOD-STAIN

Suddenly Mrs Otis caught sight of a dull red stain on the floor just by the fireplace and, quite unconscious of what it really signified, said to Mrs Umney, 'I am afraid something has been spilt there'.

'Yes, madam', replied the old housekeeper in a low voice, 'blood has been spilt on that spot.'

'How horrid', cried Mrs Otis; 'I don't at all care for blood-stains in a sitting-room. It must be removed at once.' The old woman smiled, and answered in the same low, mysterious voice, 'It is the blood of Lady Eleanore de Canterville, who was murdered on that very spot by her own husband, Sir Simon de Canterville, in 1575. Sir Simon survived her nine years, and disappeared suddenly under very mysterious circumstances. His body has never been discovered, but his guilty spirit still haunts the Chase. The blood-stain has been much admired by tourists and others, and cannot be removed.'

'That is all nonsense', cried Washington Otis; 'Pinkerton's Champion Stain Remover and Paragon Detergent will clean it up in no time', and before the terrified housekeeper could interfere he had fallen upon his knees, and was rapidly scouring the floor with a small stick of what looked like a black cosmetic. In a few moments no trace of the blood-stain could be seen.

'I knew Pinkerton would do it', he exclaimed triumphantly, as he looked round at his admiring family; but no sooner had he said these words than a terrible flash of lightning lit up the sombre room, a fearful peal of thunder made them all start to their feet, and Mrs Umney fainted.

'What a monstrous climate!' said the American Minister calmly, as he lit a long cheroot. 'I guess the old country is so overpopulated that they have not enough decent weather for everybody. I have always been of opinion that emigration is the only thing for England.'

'My dear Hiram,' cried Mrs Otis, 'what can we do with a woman who faints?'

'Charge it to her like breakages,' answered the Minister; 'she won't faint after that'; and in a few moments Mrs Umney certainly came to.

OSCAR WILDE, *The Canterville Ghost*
(Collins and Mr Vyvyan Holland).

*150. EXPLOSIVE CLOCKS

'Explosive clocks',[1] said Herr Winckelkopf, 'are not very good things for foreign exportation,[2] as, even if they succeed in passing the Custom House, the train service is so irregular, that they usually go off before they have reached their proper destination. If, however, you want one[3] for home use,[4] I can supply you with an excellent article, and guarantee that you will be satisfied with the result. May I ask for whom it is intended?[5] If it is for[5] the police, or for anyone connected with Scotland Yard, I am afraid I cannot do anything for you. The English detectives are really our best friends, and I have always found[6] that by relying on[7] their stupidity, we can do exactly what we like.[8] I could not spare one of them.'

'I assure you', said Lord Arthur, 'that it has nothing to do with the police at all. In fact, the clock is intended for the Dean of Chichester.'

'Dear me! I had no idea that you felt so strongly about religion, Lord Arthur. Few young men do[9] nowadays.'

'I am afraid you overrate me, Herr Winckelkopf', said Lord Arthur, blushing. 'The fact is, I really know nothing about theology.'

'It is a purely private matter then?'

'Purely private.'

OSCAR WILDE, *Lord Arthur Savile's Crime*
(Collins and Mr Vyvyan Holland).

1 *Les pendules explosives.* 2 *de très bons articles d'exportation.*
3 Supply *en.* 4 *la consommation intérieure.* 5 Use *(destiné) à.*
6 *constaté.* 7 *en nous en remettant à.* 8 *ce qui nous plaît.* 9 *sont dans ce cas.*

*151. EXPLOSIVE CLOCKS (*continued*)

Herr Winckelkopf shrugged his shoulders, and left the room, returning in a few minutes with a round cake of dynamite about the size of a penny, and a pretty little French clock, surmounted by an ormolu figure of Liberty trampling on the hydra of Despotism.

Lord Arthur's face brightened up when he saw it. 'That is just what I want,' he cried, 'and now tell me how it goes off.'

'Ah! there is my secret', answered Herr Winckelkopf, contemplating his invention with a justifiable look of pride; 'let me know when you wish it to explode, and I will set the machine to the moment.'

'Well, to-day is Tuesday, and if you could send it off at once—'

'That is impossible; I have a great deal of important work on hand for some friends of mine in Moscow. Still, I might send it off to-morrow.'

'Oh, it will be quite time enough!' said Lord Arthur politely, 'if it is delivered to-morrow night or Thursday morning. For the moment of the explosion, say Friday at noon exactly. The Dean is always at home at that hour.'

'Friday, at noon', repeated Herr Winckelkopf, and he made a note to that effect in a large ledger that was lying on a bureau near the fireplace.

OSCAR WILDE, Lord Arthur Savile's Crime
(Collins and Mr Vyvyan Holland).

**152. THE PHILOSOPHER AT THE POLICE BARRACKS

'I want to give myself up',[1] said the Philosopher.

The policeman looked at him:

'A man as old as you are', said he, 'oughtn't to be a fool.[2] Go home now, I advise you, and don't say a word to anyone whether you did it[3] or not. Tell me this now,[4] was it found out, or are you only making a clean breast of it?'

'Sure I must give myself up', said the Philosopher.

'If you must, you must, and that's an end of it. Wipe your feet on the rail[5] there and come in—I'll take your deposition.'

'I have no deposition for you,' said the Philosopher, 'for I didn't do a thing at all.'

The policeman stared at him again.

'If that's so', said he, 'you needn't come in at all, and

you needn't have awakened me out of my sleep either.
Maybe, tho',⁶ you are the man that fought the badger⁷ on
the Naas Road—Eh?'

'I am not,' replied the Philosopher: 'but I was arrested
for killing my brother and his wife, although I never touched
them.'

'Is that who you are?'⁸ said the policeman; and then,
briskly, 'You're as welcome as the cuckoo, you are so.
Come in and make yourself comfortable till⁹ the men
awaken, and they are the lads that'll be¹⁰ glad to see you.'

            JAMES STEPHENS, *The Crock of Gold* (Macmillan).

1 *me constituer prisonnier.*   2 *faire l'imbécile.*   8 Use *faire le coup =*
'do the deed (trick', etc.).   4 *Dites-moi un peu.*   5 *le décrottoir.*
6 *Peut-être, après tout, est-ce vous l'homme.*   7 *le colporteur.*   8 *C'est ça
que vous êtes?*   9 *en attendant que.*   10 *vous parlez si ces gars-là seront.*

*153. A LONG WAIT

Meantime the three children were on the platform at
Sethley Bridge, on the Midland main line, two miles from
home. They waited one hour. A train came—he was not
there. Down the line the red and green lights shone. It was
very dark and very cold.

'Ask him if the London train's come', said Paul to Annie,
when they saw a man in a tip cap.

'I'm not', said Annie. 'You be quiet—he might send us
off.'

But Paul was dying for the man to know they were
expecting someone by the London train: it sounded so
grand. Yet he was much too much scared of broaching any
man, let alone one in a peaked cap, to dare to ask. The three
children could scarcely go into the waiting-room for fear of
being sent away, and for fear something should happen
whilst they were off the platform. Still they waited in the
dark and cold.

'It's an hour an' a half late', said Arthur pathetically.

'Well,' said Annie, 'it's Christmas Eve.'

They all grew silent. He wasn't coming. They looked
down the darkness of the railway. There was London! It

seemed the uttermost of distance. They thought anything might happen if one came from London. They were all too troubled to talk. Cold, and unhappy, and silent, they huddled together on the platform.

At last, after more than two hours, they saw the lights of an engine peering round, away down the darkness. A porter ran out. The children drew back with beating hearts. A great train bound for Manchester drew up. Two doors opened, and from one of them, William. They flew to him. He handed parcels to them cheerily, and immediately began to explain that this great train had stopped for *his* sake at such a small station as Sethley Bridge: it was not booked to stop.   D. H. LAWRENCE, *Sons and Lovers* (Heinemann and Mrs Frieda Lawrence).

**154. UNDESIRABLE BOARDERS

'I've given these Boutwoods notice',[1] said Sarah Gailey suddenly, the tray in her hands ready to lift.

'Not really?'

'They were shockingly late[2] for breakfast again this morning, both of them. And Mr Boutwood had the face to ask for another[3] egg. Hettie came and told me, so I went in myself. I told him[4] breakfast was served in my house at nine o'clock, and there was a notice to that effect in the bedrooms, not to mention the dining-room. And as good a breakfast as they'd get in any of their hotels, I lay![5] If the eggs are cold at ten o'clock and after, that's not my fault. They're both of them perfectly healthy, and yet they're bone-idle. They never want to go to bed and they never want to get up. It isn't as if they went to theatres and got home late and so on. I could make excuses for that[6]—now and then. No! It's just idleness and carelessness. And if you saw their bedroom! Oh, my! A nice example to servants![7] Well, he was very insulting—most insulting.[8] He said he paid me to give him not what I wanted, but what *he* wanted! He said if I went into a shop, and they began to tell me what I ought to want and when[9] I ought to want it,

I should be annoyed. I said I didn't need anyone to tell me that, I said! And my house wasn't a shop. He said it was a shop, and if it wasn't, it ought to be! Can you imagine it?'[10]   ARNOLD BENNETT, *Hilda Lessways* (Methuen).

1 *J'ai donné congé à.*   2 *horriblement en retard.*   3 Meaning of 'another'? See p. 14, § 18.   4 To avoid ambiguity: *Je lui ai dit, à ce Monsieur.*   5 *je parie!*   6 *je passerais bien là-dessus.*   7 *Quel exemple pour les domestiques!*   8 *grossier, ce qui s'appelle grossier.*   9 *à quel moment.*   10 *A-t-on jamais vu?*

*155. TALKING TO A NATIVE

When the mosque, long and domeless, gleamed at the turn of the road, she exclaimed, 'Oh, yes—that's where I got to—that's where I've been.'

'Been there when?' asked her son.

'Between the acts.'

'But, mother, you can't do that sort of thing.'

'Can't mother?' she replied.

'No, really not in this country. It's not done. There's the danger of snakes for one thing. They are apt to lie out in the evening.'

'Ah yes, so the young man there said.'

'This sounds very romantic', said Miss Quested, who was exceedingly fond of Mrs Moore, and was glad she should have had this little escapade. 'You meet a young man in a mosque, and then never let me know!'

'I was going to tell you, Adela, but something changed the conversation and I forgot. My memory grows deplorable."

'Was he nice?'

She paused, then said emphatically: 'Very nice.'

'Who was he?' Ronny enquired.

'A doctor. I don't know his name.'

'A doctor? I know of no young doctor in Chandrapore. How odd! What was he like?'

'Rather small, with a little moustache and quick eyes. He called out to me when I was in the dark part of the mosque—about my shoes. That was how we began talking.

He was afraid I had them on, but I remembered luckily. He told me about his children, and then we walked back to the club. He knows you well.'

'I wish you had pointed him out to me. I can't make out who he is."

'He didn't come into the club. He said he wasn't allowed to.'

Thereupon the truth struck him, and he cried 'Oh, good gracious! Not a Mohammedan? Why ever didn't you tell me you'd been talking to a native? I was going all wrong.'

'A Mohammedan! How perfectly magnificent!' exclaimed Miss Quested. 'Ronny, isn't that like your mother? While we talk about seeing the real India, she goes and sees it, and then forgets she's seen it.'

E. M. FORSTER, *A Passage to India* (Arnold).

*156. VERE

Vere had been a thorn in her mother's side....She ought to have been born[1] a boy....She looked like a jolly boy, being blessed with[2] a disarming grin and most powerful muscles. With the gloves (she subscribed to buy[3] a set) Vere could hold her own[4] with a brother a year older than herself. She climbed trees and robbed nests; she played cricket when she got the chance and loathed the piano. She mimicked dear Mrs Pogany to her face.[5] Rose adored her.

It was Vere who shouted with laughter when Mrs Easter was reading aloud *The Pillars of the House* to Rose and the other children.

'It's such fun',[6] she replied, when Mrs Easter paused to inquire the reason of this mistimed hilarity.

'Fun?'

'Rather—isn't it, Rose?'

'Yes', said Rose now giggling convulsively.

'I can enjoy a joke[7] as well as anybody,' remarked her mother, 'but Miss Yonge is not trying to be funny, I can assure you.'

'That's it,' spluttered Vere, 'she's funny without knowing it—isn't she, Rose?'

'Yes', said Rose.

'If you would kindly explain to[8] my limited intelligence what you both mean, I should be obliged.'

Vere considered this soberly, understudying her father.

'One can't explain jokes to people who don't see them.'

HORACE A. VACHELL, *Blinds Down* (Smith, Elder and Co.).

1 Omit.   2 *dotée de.*   8 *pour s'en payer une paire.*   4 *était de force à tenir en respect.*   5 *en sa présence même.*   6 *C'est si drôle.*   7 *Je sais apprécier les plaisanteries.*   8 *à l'usage de.*

157. 'ARE YE STEPPING WEST?'

'Are ye stepping west, Hermiston?' said she, giving him his territorial name after the fashion of the country-side.

'I was,' said he, a little hoarsely, 'but I think I will be about the end of my stroll now. Are you like me, Miss Christina? The house would not hold me. I came here seeking air.'

He took his seat at the other end of the tombstone and studied her, wondering what was she. There was infinite import in the question alike for her and him.

'Ay', said she. 'I couldna bear the roof either. It's a habit of mine to come up here about the gloaming when it's quaiet and caller.'

'It was a habit of my mother's also', he said gravely. The recollection half startled him as he expressed it. He looked around. 'I have scarce been here since. It's peaceful', he said, with a long breath.

'It's no' like Glasgow', she replied. 'A weary place, yon Glasgow! But what a day have I had for my hame-coming, and what a bonny evening!'

'Indeed, it was a wonderful day', said Archie. 'I think I will remember it years and years until I come to die. On days like this—I do not know if you feel as I do—but everything appears so brief, and fragile, and exquisite, that I am afraid to touch life. We are here for so short a time;

and all the old people before us—Rutherfords of Hermiston, Elliotts of the Cauldstaⁿeslap—that were here but a while since riding about and keeping up a great noise in this quiet corner—making love too, and marrying—why, where are they now? It's deadly commonplace, but, after all, the commonplaces are the great poetic truths.'

R. L. STEVENSON, *Weir of Hermiston* (Chatto and Windus).

**158. 'ARE YE STEPPING WEST?' (*continued*)

He was sounding her, semi-consciously, to see if she could understand him; to learn if she were only an animal the colour of flowers,[1] or had a soul in her to keep her sweet.[2] She, on her part, her means well in hand, watched, woman-like, for any opportunity to shine, to abound in his humour, whatever that might be. The dramatic artist, that lies dormant or only half awake in[3] most human beings, had in her sprung to his feet[4] in a divine fury, and chance had served her well. She looked upon him with a subdued twilight[5] look that became the hour of the day and the train of thought; earnestness shone through her[6] like stars in the purple west; and from the great but controlled upheaval of her whole nature there passed into her voice, and rang in her lightest words, a thrill of emotion.

'Have you mind of Dand's song?' she answered. 'I think he'll have been trying to say[7] what you have been thinking.'

'No, I never heard it', he said. 'Repeat it to me, can you?'

'It's nothing wanting the tune', said Kirstie.

'Then sing it me', said he.

'On the Lord's Day? That would never do, Mr Weir!'

'I am afraid I am not so strict a keeper[8] of the Sabbath, and there is no one in this place to hear us, unless the poor old ancient under the stone.'

'No' that I'm thinking that really', she said. 'By my way of thinking, it's just as serious as a psalm. Will I sooth[9] it to ye, then?'

'If you please', said he, and, drawing near to her on the tombstone, prepared[10] to listen.

R. L. STEVENSON, *Weir of Hermiston* (Chatto and Windus).

1 *une créature animale, brillante comme une fleur.*   2 *qui lui conservât son parfum.*   3 *chez.*   4 *s'était d'un bond dressé en elle.*   5 Transpose: *qui convenait aux pensées de cette heure crépusculaire.*   6 *transparaissait en elle.*   7 Say *y exprimer.*   8 *observateur.*   9 *chanter...* *tout doucement.*   10 *se disposa à.*

159. A FAIRY-TALE?

That evening when Michael's prayers were concluded and he was lying very still in his bed, he waited for his mother's tale.

'Once upon a time', she began, 'there was a very large and enormous forest—' 'No, don't tell about a forest', Michael interrupted. 'Tell about that man in the picture.'

Mrs Fane was staring out of the window, and after a moment's hesitation she turned round.

'Because there *are* fairy-tales without a prince', said Michael apologetically.

'Well, once upon a time', said his mother, 'there lived in an old old country house three sisters whose mother had died when they were quite small.'

'Why did she die?'—'She was ill.'

Michael sighed sympathetically.

'These three sisters', his mother went on, 'lived with their father, an old clergyman.'—'Was he kind to them?'—'According to his own ideas he was very kind. But the youngest sister always wanted to have her own way and one day when she was feeling very cross because her father had told her she was to go and stay with an aunt, who should come riding along a lane but—' 'That man', interrupted Michael, greatly excited.

'A rider on horseback. And he said good morning, and she said good morning, though she had no business to.'—'Why hadn't she?'—'Because it isn't right for girls to speak to riders on horseback without being introduced. But the

rider was very handsome and brave and after that they met very often, and then one day he said, 'Won't you ride away with me?' and she rode away with him and never saw her father or her sisters or the old house any more.'
Mrs Fane had turned her face to the sunset again.
'Is that all?' Michael asked.—'That's all.'—'Was they happy ever afterwards?' 'Very happy—too happy.'—'Are they happy now?'—'Very happy—too happy.' 'Did they live in a castle?'—'Sometimes, and sometimes they lived in a beautiful ship and went sailing away to the most beautiful cities in the world.'—'Can't Michael go with you?' he asked. 'Darling boy, it's a fairy-tale.'—'Is it?' he said doubtfully.
COMPTON MACKENZIE, *Sinister Street* (Compton Mackenzie).

VII. LANGUAGE AND LITERATURE

***160. WHY GREAT LITERATURE IS IMMORTAL

Let us consider, too, how differently young and old are affected by the words[1] of some classic author, such as Homer or Horace. Passages, which to a boy[2] are but rhetorical common-places, neither better nor worse than a hundred others which any clever writer might supply,[3] which he gets by heart and thinks very fine, and imitates, as he thinks, successfully, in his own flowing versification, at length come home to him, when long years have passed, and he has had experience of life,[4] and pierce him, as if he had never before known them, with their sad earnestness and vivid exactness.

Then[5] he comes to understand how it is that lines, the birth[6] of some chance morning or evening at an Ionian festival, or among the Sabine hills, have lasted generation after generation, for thousands of years, with[7] a power over the mind, and a charm, which the current literature of his own day, with[8] all its obvious advantages, is utterly unable to rival. Perhaps this is the reason of the mediaeval opinion about Virgil,[9] as if a prophet or magician; his single words and phrases, his pathetic half-lines, giving utterance,[10] as the voice of Nature herself, to that pain and weariness, yet hope of better things, which is the experience of her children in every time.   J. H. NEWMAN, *The Grammar of Assent.*

1 *à la lecture.*   2 *aux yeux d'un collégien.*   3 *offrir.* Remember that in a relative clause (see p. 49, § 50) Inversion is permissible and sometimes desirable.   4 *a acquis l'expérience de la vie.*   5 *Alors?* Or *C'est alors que?*   6 *nés comme par hasard un matin.*   7 *exerçant.*   8 *malgré.*   9 *l'opinion que le moyen âge se faisait de Virgile.*   10 *qui expriment...* *cette peine.*

**161. THE JARGON

The Church would have Latin spoken by everybody except the working folk, Abélard replied; for the Church wishes the world to remain in ignorance, reserving learning to itself, as its exclusive possession; a mistaken view, for in spite of the Church the jargon, as the ecclesiastics are apt to call it, has become the language of music, and poetry and music and the arts, I have often thought, are as powerful as dialectics. We have therefore art and reason on our side; and the Church will not prevail against us in the end, though the end be far distant. But why, then, asked Héloïse, do you not lecture in French? I should be understood, he answered, only by a handful, for the French spoken in one district is not exactly the same as in another; the language is in the process of formation, and Latin will dominate the lecture-room for many a year to come. But the language of the future is the French language; even the ecclesiastics are obliged to speak it when they call assemblies to urge the people to enlist in Raymond's army, and the welcome given to Pope Urban was really given to the French language. I will never speak of the jargon again, but always of the French language, Héloïse said, half to herself, half to Abélard.

GEORGE MOORE, *Héloïse and Abélard* (Heinemann).

***162. The Poetry of Villon

It is in death that Villon finds his truest inspiration; in the
swift and sorrowful change that overtakes beauty; in the
strange revolution by which great fortunes and renowns are
diminished[1] to a handful of churchyard dust; and in the
utter passing away[2] of what was once lovable and mighty.
It is[3] in this that the mixed texture of his thought enables
him to reach such poignant and terrible effects, and to
enhance[4] pity with ridicule, like a man cutting capers to[5] a
funeral march. It is[6] in this, also, that he rises out of himself into the higher spheres of art. So, in the ballade by
which he is best known,[7] he rings the changes on names that
once stood for[8] beautiful and queenly women, and are now
no more than letters[9] and a legend.[9] 'Where are the snows of
yester year?' runs[10] the burden.... Alas, and with so pitiful
an experience of life, Villon can offer us nothing but terror[9]
and lamentation[9] about death! No one has ever more
skilfully[11] communicated his own disenchantment; no one
ever blown a more ear-piercing[12] note of sadness. This un-
repentant thief can attain neither to Christian confidence,
nor to the spirit of[13] the bright saying, that[14] whom the gods
love die early.[15] It is a poor heart, and a poorer age, that
cannot accept the conditions of life with some heroic
readiness.[16]

R. L. STEVENSON, *Men and Books* (Chatto and Windus).

1 Turn by the active: *qui réduit.* 2 *la disparition.* 3 For clarity:
C'est lorsqu'il chante la mort que, etc. 4 *rehausser...par.* 5 *à
la musique de.* 6 *C'est alors, aussi, qu'il s'élève au-dessus de lui-même
et pénètre dans.* 7 *à laquelle il doit surtout sa renommée.* 8 *désignaient.*
9 Omit the article; see p. 34, § 22 (a). 10 *dit.* 11 *avec plus d'art.*
12 Use simply *perçant.* 13 'of' can, as often, be rendered here by *que*+
verb, *e.g., aux sentiments que produit cette parole,* etc. 14 Omit *que* and
put a colon. See p. 77, § 68. 15 *les hommes aimés des dieux.* 16 *em-
pressement.*

**163. THE GLORY OF THE POET

Shakespeare wrote at a time when solitary great men were gathering to themselves the fire that had once flowed hither and thither among all men, when individualism in work and thought and emotion was breaking up the old rhythms of life, when the common people, no longer uplifted by the myths of Christianity and of still older faiths, were sinking into the earth.

The people of Stratford-on-Avon have remembered little about him, and invented no legend to his glory. They have remembered a drinking-bout of his, and invented some bad verses for him, and that is about all. Had he been some hard-drinking, hard-living, hard-riding, loud-blaspheming Squire, they would have enlarged his fame by a legend of his dealings with the devil; but in his day the glory of a Poet, like that of all other imaginative powers, had ceased, or almost ceased outside a narrow class. The poor Gaelic rhymer leaves a nobler memory among his neighbours, who will talk of Angels standing like flames about his death-bed, and of voices speaking out of bramble-bushes that he may have the wisdom of the world. The Puritanism that drove the theatres into Surrey was but part of an inexplicable movement that was trampling out the minds of all but some few thousands born to cultivated ease.

W. B. YEATS, *Ideas of Good and Evil* (Macmillan).

**164. THE ART OF RACINE

Virgil's poetry is intended to be read, Racine's to be declaimed; and it is only in the theatre that one can experience to the full the potency of his art. In a sense we can know him in[1] our library, just as we can hear the music of Mozart with silent eyes.[2] But, when the strings begin, when the whole volume of that divine harmony engulfs us,[3] how differently then we understand and feel! And so, at the theatre, before one of those high tragedies, whose interpretation has taxed to the utmost[4] ten generations of the

greatest actresses of France, we realise, with the shock[5] of
a new emotion, what we had but half-felt before. To hear
the words of Phèdre spoken by the mouth of Bernhardt,[6] to
watch, in the culminating horror[7] of crime and of remorse,
of jealousy, of rage, of desire, and of despair, all the dark
forces of destiny crowd down upon[8] that great spirit, when
the heavens and the earth reject her, and Hell opens, and
the terrific urn of Minos thunders and crashes to the
ground—that indeed is to come close to immortality, to
plunge shuddering through infinite abysses, and to look, if
only for a moment, upon eternal light.

LYTTON STRACHEY, *Books and Characters*
(Chatto and Windus).

1 *sans quitter.*   2 *par le muet truchement des yeux.*   3 *quand cette
divine harmonie nous baigne de toutes ses ondes.*   4 *a mis à dure épreuve.*
5 *nous concevons, sous le choc.*   6 *prononcées par la bouche de Sarah Bernhardt.*   7 *dans l'horreur croissante.*   8 *s'abattre en foule sur.*

**165. ANDROMACHE

One while he appeared much concerned about Andromache;
and a little while after as much for Hermione; and was
extremely puzzled to think what would become of Pyrrhus.
When Sir Roger saw Andromache's obstinate refusal to her
lover's importunities, he whispered me in the ear that he was
sure she would never have him; to which he added with a
more than ordinary vehemence, 'You cannot imagine, sir,
what it is to have to do with a widow.' Upon Pyrrhus his
threatening afterwards to leave her, the knight shook his
head, and muttered to himself, 'Ay, do if you can'. This
part dwelt so much upon my friend's imagination, that at
the close of the third act, as I was thinking of something else
he whispered in my ear, 'These widows, sir, are the most
perverse creatures in the world. But pray (says he), you that
are a critic, is this play according to your dramatic rules, as
you call them? Should your people in tragedy always talk
to be understood? Why, there is not a single sentence in this
play that I do not know the meaning of.'[8] . . . Upon Hermione's

going off with a menace to Pyrrhus, the audience gave a loud clap; to which Sir Roger added, 'On my word, a notable young baggage!'   JOSEPH ADDISON, *Spectator*.

***166. THE THIRST FOR NEWS

There is no humour[1] in my countrymen which I am[2] more inclined to wonder at than their general thirst after news.[3] There are about half a dozen ingenious men, who live very plentifully upon this curiosity of their fellow-subjects. They all of them receive the same advices from abroad, and very often in the same words; but their way of cooking[4] it is so different, that there is no citizen, who has an eye to[5] the public good, that can leave the coffee-house with peace of mind before he has given every one of them a reading. These several dishes of news are so very agreeable to the palate of my countrymen, that they are not only pleased with them when they are served up hot, but when they are again set cold[6] before them, by those penetrating politicians, who oblige the public with their reflections and observations upon every piece of intelligence[7] that is sent us from abroad. The text is given us by one set of writers, and the comment by another.

But notwithstanding[8] we have the same tale told us in so many different papers, and if occasion requires[9] in so many articles of the same paper; notwithstanding[8] a scarcity of foreign posts, we hear the same story repeated, by different advices from Paris, Brussels, The Hague, and from every great town in Europe; notwithstanding the multitude of annotations, explanations, reflections, and various readings[10] which it passes through, our time lies heavy on our hands till the arrival of a fresh mail: we long to receive further particulars, to hear what will be the next step, or what will be the consequences of that which has been already taken. A westerly[11] wind keeps the whole town in suspense and puts a stop to conversation.

JOSEPH ADDISON, *Spectator* 452 (8 August 1712).

1 *trait* (m.) *de caractère.*   2 Mood?   3 *la soif des nouvelles qu'ils ont tous.*   4 *accommoder.*   5 *pas un citoyen soucieux de,* etc.   6 *quand ils leur sont représentés froids.*   7 *chaque nouvelle.*   8 Use *avoir beau.*   9 *au besoin.*   10 *variantes.*   11 See p. 8, § 1, NORTH.

***167. The Literary Life

I believe, if anyone, early in his life, should contemplate the dangerous fate of authors, he would scarce be of their number on any consideration. The life of a Wit is a warfare upon earth; and the present spirit of the learned world is such, that to attempt to serve it (any way) one must have the constancy of a martyr, and a resolution to suffer for its sake. I could wish people would believe what I am pretty certain they will not, that I have been much less concerned about Fame than I durst declare till this occasion, when methinks I should find more credit than I could heretofore; since my writings have had their fate already, and it is too late to think of prepossessing the reader in their favour.... I confess it was want of consideration that made me an author; I writ because it amused me; I corrected because it was as pleasant to me to correct as to write; and I published because I was told I might please such as it was a credit to please. To what degree I have done this, I am really ignorant: I had too much fondness for my productions to judge of them at first, and too much judgment to be pleased with them at last. But I have reason to think they can have no reputation which will continue long, or which deserves to do so: for they have always fallen short not only of what I read of others, but even of my own Idea of Poetry.

ALEXANDER POPE, *Preface* to *Poetical Works.*

**168. Voltaire

To[1] men of letters who could by no possibility[2] be his rivals, Voltaire was, if they behaved well to him, not merely just. not merely courteous, but often a hearty friend and a munificent benefactor. But to[1] every writer who rose[3] to a celebrity approaching his own, he became either a disguised

15-2

or an avowed enemy. He slily depreciated Montesquieu and Buffon. He publicly, and with violent outrage, made war on Rousseau. Nor had he the art of hiding his feelings under the semblance[5] of good humour or of contempt. With all his great talents, and all his long experience of the world, he had no more self-command than a petted child or a hysterical woman. Whenever he was mortified,[6] he exhausted the whole rhetoric of anger and sorrow to express his mortification.[7] His torrents of bitter words, his stamping and cursing, his grimaces and his tears of rage, were a rich feast[8] to those abject natures, whose delight[9] is in the agonies[10] of powerful spirits and in the abasement of immortal names. These creatures had now found out a way of galling him to the very quick. In one walk,[11] at least, it had been admitted by envy itself[12] that he was without a living competitor....At length, a rival was announced.

LORD MACAULAY, *Essay on Frederick the Great.*

1 *Pour.*   2 *ne pouvaient en aucune façon.*   3 *atteignait.*   4 Repeat *ennemi.*   5 *les dehors.*   6 *blessé dans son amour-propre.*   7 *son dépit.*   8 *spectacle* (m.).   9 *qui trouvent leur plaisir dans.*   10 Not *agonie* (see p. 14, § 18); use, *e.g., souffrances.*   11 *Dans un genre.*   12 Turn by active form: *les envieux eux-mêmes avaient reconnu.*

***169. A TREND TOWARDS THE ROMANTIC

Alas! to us, who know not La Dumesnil, to us whose *Mérope* is nothing more than a little sediment of print, the precious stone of our forefathers has turned out to be a simple piece of paste. Its glittering was the outcome of no inward fire, but of a certain adroitness in the manufacture; to use our modern phraseology, Voltaire was able to make up for his lack of genius by a thorough knowledge of 'technique', and a great deal of 'go'.

And to such titles of praise let us not dispute his right. His vivacity, indeed, actually went so far as to make him something of an innovator. He introduced new and imposing spectacular effects; he ventured to write tragedies in which no persons of royal blood made their appearance; he was so bold as to rhyme 'père' with 'terre'. The wild diversity of his incidents shows a trend towards the romantic, which, doubtless, under happier influences, would have led him much further along the primrose path which ended in the bonfire of 1830.

But it was his misfortune to be for ever clogged by a tradition of decorous restraint; so that the effect of his plays is as anomalous as would be—let us say—that of a shilling shocker written by Miss Yonge. His heroines go mad in epigrams, while his villains commit murder in inversions. Amid the hurly-burly of artificiality, it was all his cleverness could do to keep its head to the wind; and he was only able to remain afloat at all by throwing overboard his humour. The Classical tradition has to answer for many sins; perhaps its most infamous achievement was that it prevented Molière from being a great tragedian. But there can be no doubt that its most astonishing one was to have taken—if only for some scattered moments—the sense of the ridiculous from Voltaire.

LYTTON STRACHEY, *Books and Characters*
(Chatto and Windus).

**170. WALPOLE'S CHARM

What then is the charm, the irresistible charm, of Walpole's writings? It consists, we think, in the art of amusing without exciting[1].... He had a strange ingenuity[2] peculiarly his own, an ingenuity which appeared in all that he did, in his building,[3] in his gardening, in his upholstery,[4] in the matter and in the manner of his writings. The Odd was his peculiar domain. In his villa, every apartment is a museum; every piece of furniture is a curiosity; there is something strange in the form of the shovel; there is a long story belonging to the bell-rope. We wander among a profusion of rarities, of trifling intrinsic value,[5] but so quaint in fashion, or connected with such remarkable names and events, that they may well detain[6] our attention for a moment. A moment is enough. Some new relic, some new unique,[7] some new carved work, some new enamel, is forthcoming in an instant. One cabinet of trinkets is no sooner closed than[8] another is opened. It is the same with Walpole's writings. It is not in their utility, it is not in their beauty, that their attraction lies. They are to the works of great historians and poets, what[9] Strawberry Hill is to the Museum of Sir Hans Sloane or to the Gallery of Florence.

LORD MACAULAY, *Essay on Horace Walpole*.

1 *sans passionner.*   2 Beware of homonyms; see p. 22, § 18, INGENUITY.
3 *dans sa façon de construire.*   4 *de se meubler.*   5 *d'une valeur in-trinsèque insignifiante.*   6 *méritent de retenir.*   7 *une nouvelle pièce unique.*   8 *se ferme à peine que.*   9 *ce que*; see p. 44, § 38.

***171. MME DU DEFFAND'S *SALON*

Besides the diplomats, nearly every foreign traveller of distinction found his way to the renowned salon; Englishmen were particularly frequent visitors; and among the familiar figures of whom we catch more than one glimpse in the letters to Walpole are Burke, Fox, and Gibbon. Sometimes influential parents in England obtained leave for their young sons to be admitted into the centre of Parisian refinement. The English cub, fresh from Eton, was introduced by his tutor into the red and yellow drawing-room, where the great circle of a dozen or more elderly important persons, glittering in jewels and orders, pompous in powder and rouge, ranged in rigid order round the fireplace, followed with the precision of a perfect orchestra the leading word or smile or nod of an ancient Sibyl, who seemed to survey the company with her eyes shut, from a vast chair by the wall. It is easy to imagine the scene, in all its terrifying politeness. Madame du Deffand could not tolerate young people; she declared that she did not know what to say to them; and they, no doubt, were in precisely the same difficulty. To an English youth, unfamiliar with the language and shy as only English youths can be, a conversation with that redoubtable old lady must have been a grim ordeal indeed. One can almost hear the stumbling, pointless observations, almost see the imploring looks cast, from among the infinitely attentive company, towards the tutor, and the pink ears growing still more pink.

LYTTON STRACHEY, *Books and Characters*
(Chatto and Windus).

⌐*172. GIBBON'S STYLE

Gibbon's style is detestable, but his style is not the worst thing about him. His history has proved an effectual bar[1] to all real familiarity with the temper and habits of imperial Rome. Few persons read the original authorities, even those which are classical; and certainly no distinct knowledge[2] of the actual state of the empire can be obtained from Gibbon's rhetorical sketches. He takes notice of nothing but what may produce an effect; he skips on from eminence to eminence, without ever taking you through the valleys[3] between: in fact, his work is little else but a disguised collection of all the splendid anecdotes which he could find in any book concerning any persons or nations from the Antonines to the capture of Constantinople. When I read a chapter in Gibbon, I seem[4] to be looking through a luminous haze or fog: figures come and go, I know not how or why, all larger than life,[5] or distorted or discoloured; nothing is real, vivid, true.

S. T. COLERIDGE, *Table Talk* (15 August 1833).

1 *s'est révélée comme un obstacle*, etc.   2 Say *on ne peut tirer une connaissance précise.*   3 *sans jamais vous faire traverser les vallées*, etc.
4 *j'ai l'impression de*, etc.   5 Use *plus grand que nature.*

**173. THE FRENCH AT THE THEATRE

I have been frequently puzzled with this exception to the butterfly, airy, thoughtless, fluttering character of the French—on which we compliment ourselves—and never more so than the first night I went to the theatre. The order, the attention, the decorum were such as would shame any

London audience. The attention was more like that of a learned society to a lecture on some scientific subject than of a promiscuous crowd collected together merely for amusement, and to pass away an idle hour.

There was a professional air, an unvarying gravity in the looks and demeanour of the whole assembled multitude, as if everyone had an immediate interest in the character of the national poetry, in the purity of the French accent, in the propriety of the declamation, in the conceptions of the actor, and the development of the story, instead of its presenting a mob of idle boys and girls, of ignorant gaping citizens, or supercilious box-lobby loungers, affecting a contempt for the performance, and for everyone around them. The least noise or irregularity called forth the most instant and lively disapprobation....Not only was the strictest silence observed, as soon as the curtain drew up, but no one moved or attempted to move. The spell thrown over the customary or supposed restlessness and volatility of the French was in this respect complete.

WILLIAM HAZLITT, *Notes of a Journey through France and Italy.*

**174. MY LITTLE LIBRARY

As often as I survey my bookshelves I am reminded of Lamb's 'ragged veterans'. Not that all my volumes came from the second-hand stall; many of them were neat enough[1] in new covers, some were even stately in fragrant bindings, when they passed into my hands. But so often have I[2] removed, so rough has been[2] the treatment of my little library at each change of place, and, to tell the truth, so little care have I given to[3] its well-being at normal times, (for in all practical matters I am idle and inept), that even the comeliest of my books show the results[4] of unfair usage. More than one has been foully injured by a great nail driven into a packing-case—this but the extreme instance of the wrongs they have undergone. Now that I have leisure and peace of mind, I find myself[5] growing more careful—an illustration of the great truth that virtue is made easy[6] by circumstance. But I confess that, so long as a volume hold together, I am not much troubled as to its outer appearance. I know men who say they had as lief read[7] any book in a library copy as in one[8] from their own shelf. To me that is unintelligible. For one thing, I know[9] every book of mine by[9] its *scent*, and I have but to put my nose between the pages to be reminded of all sorts of things. My Gibbon, for example, my well-bound eight-volume Milman edition, which I have read and read and read again for more than thirty years—never do I open it but the scent of the noble page restores to me[10] all the exultant happiness of that moment when I received it as a prize.

GEORGE GISSING, *The Private Papers of Henry Ryecroft*
(Constable).

1 *se présentaient assez proprement.*   2 No inversion.   8 *je me suis si peu préoccupé de.*   4 *portent les traces.*   5 *je me prends à.*   6 Translate as if 'it is easier to be virtuous when the circumstances lend themselves to it'.   7 *qui disent avoir autant de plaisir à lire.*   8 *que dans un exemplaire.*   9 *je reconnais...à.*   10 Use *ranimer en moi.*

*175. MODERN BIOGRAPHY

An irresistible impulse urges an increasing number of clever people to pounce upon the verdicts of history and turn them inside out. The vices of our typical saints are exposed, and the virtues of our accepted criminals are insisted upon. Clio is shown to have been invariably mistaken, and we are left we know not where, in a state of bewildered confusion. Tiberius was a good, kind nobleman, who organised pleasant Sunday-school treats in his palace at Capreæ. Judas Iscariot was a far-sighted financial genius, misunderstood by his Communist colleagues. If Henry VIII had a fault, it was a too-complacent indulgence towards his giddy wives, who for their part meant no harm. In the eyes of the biographical whitewasher nobody means any harm, except evil characters like Marcus Aurelius and Mrs Elizabeth Fry.

This tendency to accept the topsy-turvy position, in which the critic attracts attention by standing on his head, has invaded the admired seclusion of Haworth Parsonage. For seventy years, the three wonderful Brontë sisters have been seen radiant against the background of a deplorable brother, 'the dissolute and art-loving Branwell', as Sir Sidney Lee severely styles him. Suddenly, all that is changed, and we are called upon to believe that Branwell was not dissolute, and that he wrote his sisters' books. In fact, that he was the flower of the flock.

SIR EDMUND GOSSE, *Silhouettes* (Heinemann).

*176. DO YOU READ IN BED?

Hundreds of thousands,[1] possibly millions, of people every night[2] in England[2] read something in[3] bed.[2] They say nothing about it except 'I read for a little last night and then slept like a top', or 'I didn't feel like going to sleep last night, so I read for a bit', or 'I began reading so-and-so in bed last night, and I couldn't get to sleep until[4] I finished it'. Usually nothing at all is said;[5] if anything is said, it is very little. Yet what a large slice of each of our lives has gone[6] in this harmless occupation. We get our clothes off. We get our pyjamas[7] on. We wind our watches. We arrange the table and the light and get into bed. We pile up, or double up, the pillows. Then we settle down to it. Sometimes the book is so exciting[8] that all thought of sleep fades away, and we read on oblivious of everything except the unseen menace in that dark house, the boat gliding stealthily along that misty river, the Chinaman's eyes peering through that greenish-yellow[9] fog, or the sudden crack[10] of the revolver in that den of infamy. Sometimes we read for a while and then feel as though[11] we could go peacefully to sleep. We feel drunk and, dropping the book aside from lax hands,[12] just manage to get the light out before falling back into a dense and miry[13] slumber.

J. C. SQUIRE (SOLOMON EAGLE), *Essays at Large: Reading in Bed* (Heinemann).

1 *des centaines de mille.* N.B. *mille* = thousand never takes an *s*.   2 Distribute the adverbial phrases; see p. 78, § 69.   3 Preposition? See p. 64,

§ 57, IN.   4 Use *avant de.* See p. 67, § 59, TILL.   5 Use the active form. See p. 46, § 42 (*a*).   6 *quelle partie importante...a été consacrée à,* etc. 7 Singular. See p. 85, § 24.   8 *passionnant.*   9 See p. 10, § 13 (*c*). 10 *coup sec.*   11 Use *il nous semble que:* see p. 55, § 51, (IT) SEEMS. 12 *de nos mains sans forces.*   13 *trouble.*

***177. ON SPEAKING FRENCH

Wherever two Englishmen are speaking French to a Frenchman you may safely diagnose in the breast of one of the two humiliation, envy, ill-will, impotent rage, and a dull yearning for vengeance; and you can take it that the degree of these emotions is in exact ratio to the superiority of the other man's performance. In the breast of this other are contempt, malicious amusement, conceit, vanity, pity, and joy in ostentation; these, also, exactly commensurable with his advantage. Strange and sad that this should be so; but so it is. French brings out the worst in all of us—all, I mean, but the few, the lamentably far too few, who cannot aspire to stammer some colloquial phrases of it.

Even in Victorian days, when England was more than geographically, was psychologically an island, French made mischief among us, and was one of the Devil's favourite ways of setting brother against brother. But in those days the bitterness of the weaker brother was a little sweetened with disapproval of the stronger. To speak French fluently and idiomatically and with a good accent—or with an idiom and accent which to other rough islanders *seemed* good—was a rather suspect accomplishment, being somehow deemed incompatible with civic worth. Thus the weaker ones had not to drain the last lees of their shame, and the stronger could not wholly rejoice in their strength. But the old saving prejudice has now died out (greatly to the delight of the Devil), and there seems no chance that it will be revived.

MAX BEERBOHM, *And Even Now* (Heinemann).

***178. To Conquer or to Die

There were many good talkers on the ship; and I believe that good talking[1] of a certain sort is a common accomplishment among working men.... They could all tell a story with effect. I am sometimes tempted to think that the less literary class show always better[2] in narration; they have so much[3] more patience with detail, are so much less hurried to reach the points, and preserve so much juster a proportion among the facts. At the same time[4] their talk is dry; they pursue a topic ploddingly,[5] have not an agile fancy, do not throw sudden lights from unexpected quarters, and when the talk is over they often[6] leave the matter where it was. They mark time instead of marching. They think only to argue,[7] not to reach new conclusions, and use their reason[8] rather as a weapon of offence than as a tool for self-improvement. Hence the talk of some of the cleverest was unprofitable in result, because there was no give and take;[9] they would grant you as little as possible for premise,[10] and begin to dispute under an oath[11] to conquer or to die.[12]

R. L. STEVENSON, *The Amateur Emigrant*
(Chatto and Windus).

1 *l'art de bien parler, dans un certain genre, est assez répandu.*   2 *se montrent toujours à leur avantage.*   3 *tellement.*   4 *Cependant.*   5 *lourdement.*   6 Is *souvent* quite enough here? see p. 60, § 54, OFTEN.   7 *pour discuter.*   8 *leur raison leur est plutôt une arme offensive.*   9 *il ne comportait point d'échange.*   10 Use *concéder...dans les prémisses.*   11 *en se jurant de vaincre.*   12 *ou de mourir?* Or *ou mourir?* See p. 62, § 56.

VIII. PHILOSOPHICAL AND REFLECTIVE

**179. Meditation among the Tombs

I know that entertainments of this nature are apt to raise dark and dismal thoughts in timorous minds and gloomy imaginations; but for my own part, though I am always serious, I do not know what it is to be melancholy; and can therefore take a view of nature in her deep and solemn scenes, with the same pleasure as in her most gay and delightful ones. By these means I can improve myself with those objects which others consider with terror.

When I look upon the tombs of the great, every emotion of envy dies in me; when I read the epitaphs of the beautiful, every inordinate desire goes out; when I meet with the grief of parents upon a tombstone, my heart melts with compassion; when I see the tomb of the parents themselves, I consider the vanity of grieving for those whom we must quickly follow; when I see kings lying by those who deposed them, when I consider rival wits placed side by side, or the holy men that divided the world with their contests and disputes, I reflect with sorrow and astonishment on the little competitions, factions, and debates of mankind. When I read the several dates of the tombs, of some that died yesterday, and some six hundred years ago, I consider that great day when we shall all of us be contemporaries, and make our appearance together.

JOSEPH ADDISON, *Spectator.*

***180. THE SEARCH AFTER TRUTH

But the comparative study of the beliefs and institutions of mankind is fitted to be much more than a means of satisfying an enlightened curiosity and of furnishing materials for the researches of the learned. Well handled,[1] it may become a powerful instrument to expedite progress if it lays bare certain weak spots in the foundations on which modern society is built—if it shows that much[2] which we are wont to regard as solid[3] rests on the sands of superstition rather than on the rock of nature. It is indeed a melancholy and in some respects thankless task to strike at[4] the foundations of beliefs in which, as in a strong tower, the hopes and aspirations of humanity through long ages have sought a refuge from the storm and stress of life.[5] Yet sooner or later it is inevitable that the battery of the comparative method should breach these venerable walls, mantled over with the mosses and ivy and wild flowers of a thousand tender and sacred associations....[6]

The task of building up[7] into fairer and more enduring forms the old structures so rudely shattered is reserved for other hands, perhaps for other and happier ages. We cannot foresee, we can hardly even guess, the new forms into which thought and society will run in the future. Yet this uncertainty ought not to induce[8] us, from any consideration of expediency or regard for antiquity, to spare the ancient moulds, however beautiful, when those are proved to be worn out. Whatever comes of it, wherever it leads us, we must follow truth alone. It is our only guiding star.

SIR JAMES G. FRAZER, *The Golden Bough* (Macmillan).

1 *En des mains habiles.*   2 *beaucoup de choses.*   3 *solidement établies.*
4 *saper.*   5 Simplify, *e.g., loin des orages de la vie.*   6 *souvenirs.*
7 Say, *e.g., Rebâtir en donnant des formes...aux...est une tâche réservée à,* etc.   8 *nous amener, au nom de quelque opportunisme...à.*

*181. THE WALLS OF BALCLUTHA

I have seen the walls of Balclutha, but they were desolate. The fire had resounded in the halls: and the voice of the people is heard no more. The stream of Clutha was removed from its place, by the fall of the walls. The thistle shook, there, its lonely head: the moss whistled to the wind. The fox looked out from the windows, the rank grass of the wall waved round its head. Desolate is the dwelling of Moina, silence is in the house of her fathers. Raise the song of mourning, O bards! over the land of strangers. They have but fallen before us: for, one day, we must fall. Why dost thou build the hall, son of the winged days? Thou lookest from thy towers to-day; yet a few years, and the blast of the desert comes; it howls in thy empty court, and whistles round thy half-worn shield. And let the blast of thy desert come! we shall be renowned in our day! The mark of my arm shall be in battle; my name in the song of bards. Raise the song; let joy be heard in my hall!

JAMES MACPHERSON, *Ossian: Carthon.*

***182. HALF A DOZEN GRASSHOPPERS

I have often been astonished, considering[1] that we are divided from you but by a slender dyke of about twenty-four miles, and that the mutual intercourse between the two countries has lately been very great,[2] to find how little you seem to know of us. I suspect that this is owing[3] to your forming a judgment of this nation from[4] certain publications which do very erroneously, if they do at all,[5] represent the opinions and dispositions generally prevalent in England. The vanity, restlessness, petulance,[6] and spirit of intrigue[7] of several petty cabals, who attempt to hide their total want of consequence in[8] bustle and noise makes you imagine that our contemptuous neglect of their abilities is a general mark of acquiescence in their opinions. No such thing, I assure you. Because[9] half-a-dozen grasshoppers under a fern make the field ring with their importunate chink, whilst thousands of great cattle,[10] reposed beneath the shadow[11] of the British oak, chew the cud and are silent, pray do not imagine that those who make the noise are the only inhabitants of the field; that, of course,[12] they are many in number; or that, after all, they are other than the little shrivelled, meagre, hopping, though loud and troublesome[13] insects[14] of the hour.

EDMUND BURKE, *Reflections on the Revolution in France.*

1 Transpose to: 'Considering that we...great, I have often', etc.   2 *les relations mutuelles entre nos deux pays se sont récemment beaucoup développées.*   3 *Cela tient, je crois, à ce que,* etc.   4 *d'après.*   5 *représentent d'une façon fausse, si tant est qu'elles les représentent.*   6 For 'petulance', here = *l'esprit chagrin,* see p. 25, § 18.   7 *le caractère intrigant.*   8 *à force d'agitation,* etc.   9 Here, rather *De ce que* than *Parce que.*   10 *des milliers de têtes de gros bétail.* See p. 5, § 6, FLOCKS.   11 *se reposant à l'ombre.*   12 *par suite.*   13 *pour bruyants...qu'ils soient.*   14 *insectes* (m.) *éphémères.*

*183. THE DRUIDS' STONE

The temples of the mighty and skilful Roman have crumbled to dust in its neighbourhood; the churches of the Arian Goth, his successor in power, have sunk beneath the earth, and are not to be found; and the mosques of the Moor, the conqueror of the Goth, where and what are they? Upon the rock, masses of hoary and vanishing ruin. Not so the Druids' stone. There it stands on the hill of winds, as strong and as freshly new as the day, perhaps thirty centuries back, when it was first raised, by means which are a mystery. Earthquakes have heaved it, but its copestone has not fallen; rain-floods have deluged it, but failed to sweep it from its station; the burning sun has flashed upon it, but neither split nor crumbled it; and Time, stern old Time, has rubbed it with his iron tooth, and with what effect let those who view it declare. He who wishes to study the literature, the learning, and the history of the ancient Celt, may glean from that blank stone the whole known amount.

GEORGE BORROW, *The Bible in Spain.*

***184. ADORATION

It is to far happier, far higher, exaltation that we owe those fair fronts[1] of variegated mosaic, charged with wild fancies and dark hosts of imagery,[2] thicker and quainter than ever filled the depth[3] of midsummer dream; those vaulted gates, trellised with close leaves;[4] those window labyrinths of twisted tracery and starry light; those misty masses of multitudinous pinnacle and diademed tower;[5] the only witnesses, perhaps, that remain to us of the faith and fear of nations. All else for which the builders[6] sacrificed has passed away—all their living interests, and aims, and achievements. We know not for what they laboured, and we see no evidence[7] of their reward. Victory, wealth, authority, happiness—all have departed, though bought by many a bitter sacrifice. But of them and their life and their toil upon the earth, one reward, one evidence,[8] is left to us in[9] those grey heaps of deep-wrought stone. They have taken with them to the grave their powers, their honours, and their errors; but they have left us their adoration.

JOHN RUSKIN, *The Seven Lamps of Architecture.*

1 *ces beaux frontons.*   2 *d'une sombre foule d'images.*   3 *que celles qui ont jamais peuplé les profondeurs.*   4 *feuillages serrés.*   5 *tours portant diadème.*   6 *bâtisseurs.*   7 *preuve certaine.*   8 *un seul monument.* 9 *sous la forme de.*

**185. LOOKING AT THE SKY

If, in our moments of utter idleness and insipidity, we turn to the sky as a last resource, which of its phenomena do we speak of? One says, it has been wet; and another, it has been windy; and another, it has been warm. Who, among the whole chattering crowd, can tell me of the forms and the precipices of the chain of tall white mountains that girded the horizon at noon yesterday? Who saw the narrow sun-beam that came out of the south, and smote upon their summits until they melted and mouldered away in a dust of blue rain? Who saw the dance of the dead clouds when the sunlight left them last night and the west wind blew them before it like withered leaves? All has passed, un-regretted as unseen; or if the apathy be ever shaken off, even for an instant, it is only by what is gross, or what is extraordinary; and yet it is not in the broad and fierce manifestations of the elemental energies, nor in the clash of the hail, nor the drift of the whirlwind, that the highest characters of the sublime are developed. God is not in the earthquake, nor in the fire, but in the still small voice.

JOHN RUSKIN, *Modern Painters.*

**186. GRASS

It seems to me not to have been without a peculiar signi-ficance, that our Lord, when about to work the miracle[1] which, of all that he showed, appears to have been felt by the multitude as[2] the most impressive—the miracle of the loaves—commanded the people to sit down by companies 'upon the green grass'. He was about to[3] feed them with the principal produce of earth and the sea, the simplest representations[4] of the food of mankind. He gave them the *seed* of the herb; He bade them sit down upon the herb itself, which was as great a gift, in its fitness[5] for their joy and rest, as its perfect fruit,[6] for their sustenance; thus, in this single order and act, when rightly understood,[7] indicating for evermore how the Creator had entrusted the comfort,[8] consolation,[8] and sustenance of man, to the simplest and most despised of all the leafy families[9] of the earth.

And well does it fulfil its mission. Consider what we owe merely to the meadow grass, to the covering[10] of the dark ground by that glorious enamel, by the companies of those soft, and countless, and peaceful spears. The fields! Follow but forth for a little time the thoughts of all that we ought to recognize in those words. All spring and summer[11] is in them,—the walks by silent, scented paths,—the rests in noonday heat,—the joy of herds and flocks,[12]—the power of all shepherd life and meditation,—the life of sunlight upon the world, falling in emerald streaks, and falling in soft blue shadows, where else it would have struck upon the dark mould, or scorching dust,—pastures beside[13] the pacing brooks,—soft banks and knolls of lowly hills,—thymy slopes of down overlooked by the blue line of lifted sea.[14]

JOHN RUSKIN, *Modern Painters.*

1 *au moment d'accomplir le miracle.* 2 *comme étant.* 3 *allait.* 4 *spécimens.* 5 *dans son adaptation à.* 6 Supply 'was'=*l'était.* 7 *à les bien entendre.* 8 Both 'comfort' and 'consolation' are included in French *consolation.* 9 *espèces feuillues.* 10 *au revêtement...par.* 11 Say 'and all summer'. 12 *des troupeaux de gros et menu bétail.* 13 *bordant.* 14 *de la mer soulevée sur un fond de ciel.*

****187. TRUTH

The cruellest lies are often told in silence. A man may have sat in a room for hours and not opened his teeth, and yet come out of that room a disloyal friend or a vile calumniator. And how many loves have perished because, from pride, or spite, or diffidence, or that unmanly shame which withholds a man from daring to betray emotion, a lover, at the critical point of the relation, has but hung his head and held his tongue? And, again, a lie may be told by a truth, or a truth conveyed through a lie. Truth to facts is not always truth to sentiment; and part of the truth, as often happens in answer to a question, may be the foulest calumny. A fact may be an exception; but the feeling is the law, and it is that which you must neither garble nor belie. The whole tenor of a conversation is a part of the meaning of each separate statement; the beginning and the end define and travesty the intermediate conversation. You never speak to God; you address a fellow-man, full of his own tempers; and to tell truth, rightly understood, is not to state the true facts, but to convey a true impression; truth in spirit, not truth to letter, is the true veracity. To reconcile averted friends a Jesuitical discretion is often needful, not so much to gain a kind hearing as to communicate sober truth. Women have an ill name in this connection; yet they live in as true relations; the lie of a good woman is the true index of her heart.

R. L. STEVENSON, *Virginibus Puerisque* (Chatto and Windus).

***188. CHANGED TIMES

Changed times, indeed, when we must sit[1] all night, beside the fire, with folded hands; and a changed world for most of us, when we find we can pass the hours without discontent, and be happy thinking.[2] We are in such haste to be doing, to be writing, to make our voice audible a moment in the derisive silence of eternity, that we forget that one thing, of which these are but the parts[3]—namely, to live. We fall in love, we drink hard, we run to and fro upon the earth like frightened sheep. And now you are to ask yourself if, when all is done, you would not have been better to sit by the fire at home and be happy thinking.[4] To sit still and contemplate, to be pleased by the great deeds of men without envy, to be everything and everywhere in sympathy, and yet content to remain where and what you are—is not this to know both wisdom and virtue, and to dwell with happiness? After all, it is not they who carry flags, but they who look upon it from a private chamber,[5] who have the fun of the procession.

R. L. STEVENSON, *Virginibus Puerisque* (Chatto and Windus).

1 *rester.* 2 *trouver notre joie à penser.* 3 *dont tout cela n'est qu'une partie.* 4 *prendre plaisir à méditer.* 5 *de chez eux.*

*189. THE POWER OF MONEY

You tell me that money cannot buy the things most precious. Your commonplace proves that you have never known the lack of it. When I think of all the sorrow and the barrenness that has been wrought in my life by want of a few more pounds per annum than I was able to earn, I stand aghast at money's significance. What kindly joys have I lost, those simple forms of happiness to which every heart has claim, because of poverty! Meetings with those I loved made impossible year after year; sadness, misunderstanding, nay, cruel alienation, arising from inability to do the things I wished, and which I might have done had a little money helped me; endless instances of homely pleasure and content-ment curtailed or forbidden by narrow means. I have lost friends merely through the constraints of my position; friends I might have made have remained strangers to me; solitude of the bitter kind, the solitude which is enforced at times when mind or heart longs for companionship, often cursed my life solely because I was poor. I think it would scarce be an exaggeration to say that there is no moral good which had not to be paid for in coin of the realm.

GEORGE GISSING, *The Private Papers of Henry Ryecroft*
(Constable).

**190. OUR VILLAGE

Of all situations for[1] a constant residence, that which appears to me most delightful is a little village far in the country; a small neighbourhood,[2] not[3] of fine mansions finely peopled,[2] but of cottages and cottage-like houses, 'messuages and tenements',[4] as a friend of mine called such ignoble and nondescript dwellings, with inhabitants whose faces are[5] as familiar to us as the flowers in our garden; a little world of our own, close-packed[6] and insulated like ants in an ant-hill, or bees in a hive, or sheep in a fold, or nuns in a convent, or sailors in a ship; where we know[5] every one, are known[5] to every one, interested in every one, and authorized to hope that every one feels an interest in us. How pleasant it is to learn to know and to love the people about us, with all their peculiarities, just as we learn to know and to love the nooks and turns of the shady lanes and sunny commons that we pass every day.

MISS MITFORD, Our Village.

1 possibles pour.   2 Translate according to the sense, e.g., avec un modeste voisinage...aux nobles habitants.   3 What form of the negative is required? See p. 60, § 54, NOT.   4 'locations et logements'.   5 Rather the Conditional than the Present tense, since it is all a supposition.   6 où nous serions lassés.

*191. WHAT YOU SHOULD SEE IN LONDON

I hope the two ladies from the country who have been writing to the newspapers to know what sights they ought to see in London during their Easter holiday will have a nice time. I hope they will enjoy the Tube and have fine weather for the Monument..., and see the dungeons at the Tower and the seats of the mighty at Westminster, and return home with a harvest of joyful memories. But I can promise them that there is one sight they will not see. They will not see me. Their idea of a holiday is London. My idea of a holiday is forgetting there is such a place as London.

Not that I dislike London. I should like to see it. I have long promised myself that I would see it. Some day, I have said, I will surely have a look at the place. It is a shame, I have said, to have lived in it so long and never to have seen it. I suppose I am not much worse than other Londoners. Do you, sir, who have been taking the morning bus from Balham for heaven knows how many years—do you, when you are walking down Fleet Street, stand still with a shock of delight as the dome of St Paul's and its cross of gold burst on your astonished sight?...Did you ever see London as those two ladies from the country will see it this Easter as they pass breathlessly from wonder to wonder? Of course not. You need a holiday in London as I do. You need to set out with young Tom (aged ten) on a voyage of discovery and see all the sights of this astonishing city as though you had come to it from a far country.

A. G. GARDINER, *On Taking a Holiday. Windfalls* (Dent).

192. LOSING ONE'S TRAIN

The clocks up at the villa[1] must have been[2] all wrong, or else my watch did not go with them,[3] or else I had not looked often enough at it while rambling about the town on my way to the station. Certain it is that when I got there, at the gallop of my cab-horse, the express was gone. There is something hatefully inexorable about expresses: it is useless to run after them, even in Italy. The next train took an hour and a quarter instead of forty minutes to cover[4] the nineteen miles between Pistoia and Florence. Moreover, that next train was not till eight in the evening, and it was now half-past five.

I felt all it was proper to feel on the occasion, and said, if anything, rather more. Missing a train is a terrible business, even if[5] you miss nothing else in consequence; and the inner disarray, the blow and wrench[6] to thoughts and feelings, is most often far worse than any mere upsetting of arrangements. A chasm suddenly gapes between present and future, and the river of life flows backwards,[7] if but for a second. It is most fit and natural to lose one's temper; but the throwing out of so much moral ballast[8] does not help one to overtake that train. I mention this, lest I should pass for heartless; and now proceed to say that, after a few minutes given to wrath and lamentation, I called the cab back and went in search of a certain very ancient church, containing[9] a very ancient pulpit, which I had never succeeded in seeing before.

VERNON LEE, *Hortus Vitae: Losing One's Train* (John Lane, The Bodley Head).

1 *Là-haut, à la villa, les pendules...?* Or *Les pendules là-haut à la villa?* Which seems the better order? 2 When put into the Present tense, this

is 'must be' = *doivent être*. The past tense corresponding to *doivent* is therefore = 'must have been'.   3 Give the sense.   4 *parcourir*.   5 *quand
même*. For tense, see p. 67, § 59, IF.   6 *le coup porté, la violence
faite aux sentiments*, etc.   7 *remonte vers sa source*.   8 *tant de lest
ainsi lâché par l'esprit*.   9 *possédant*.

***193. WATER MUSIC

The house in which I live is haunted by the noise of dripping
water. Always, day and night, summer and winter, something is dripping somewhere. For many months an unquiet
cistern kept up within its iron bosom a long, hollow-toned
soliloquy. Now it is mute; but a new and more formidable
drip has come into existence. From the very summit of the
house a little spout—the overflow, no doubt, of some unknown receptacle under the roof—lets fall a succession of
drops that is almost a continuous stream. Down it falls,
this all but stream, a sheer forty or fifty feet on to the
stones of the basement steps, thence to dribble ignominiously
away into some appointed drain. The cataracts blow their
trumpets from the steep; but my lesser waterfalls play a
subtler, I had almost said a more 'modern' music. Lying
awake at nights, I listened with a mixture of pleasure and
irritation to its curious cadences.

The musical range of a dripping tap is about half an
octave. But within the bounds of this major fourth, drops
can play the most surprising and varied melodies. You will
hear them climbing laboriously up small degrees of sound,
only to descend at a single leap to the bottom. More often
they wander unaccountably about in varying intervals,
familiar or disconcertingly odd. And with the varying pitch
the time also varies, but within narrower limits. For the
laws of hydrostatics, or whatever other science claims
authority over drops, do not allow the dribblings much
licence either to pause or to quicken the pace of their falling.
It is an odd sort of music. One listens to it as one lies in bed,
slipping gradually into sleep, with a curious, uneasy
emotion.

ALDOUS HUXLEY, *On the Margin* (Chatto and Windus).

***194. An Empty House

So with the house empty and the doors locked and the mattresses rolled round,[1] those stray airs, advance guards of great armies, blustered in,[2] brushed bare boards, nibbled and fanned, met nothing in bedroom or drawing-room that wholly resisted[3] them but only hangings that flapped, wood that creaked, the bare legs of tables, saucepans and china already furred, tarnished, cracked. What people had shed and left[4]—a pair of shoes, a shooting cap, some faded skirts and coats in wardrobes—those alone kept the human shape and in the emptiness indicated how once they were filled and animated;[5] how once hands were busy with hooks and buttons; how once the looking-glass had held[6] a face; had held[6] a world hollowed out in which a figure turned, a hand flashed, the door opened, in came children rushing[7] and tumbling; and went out again. Now, day after day, light turned, like a flower reflected in water, its clear image[8] on the wall opposite. Only the shadows of the trees, flourishing in the wind, made obeisance on the wall, and for a moment darkened the pool in which light reflected itself; or birds, flying, made a soft spot flutter[8] slowly across the bedroom floor.

VIRGINIA WOOLF, *To the Lighthouse* (Hogarth Press).

1 Simply *roulés.*   2 *faisaient bruyamment irruption.*   3 Mood? See p. 47, § 44.   4 *Les vêtements dont on s'était défait...étaient seuls à conserver,* etc.   5 *que les vies naguère s'y étaient moulées.*   6 *encadré.* 7 *c'était* (see p. 55, § 51, THERE ARE) *une ruée, une bousculade d'enfants.* 8 *promenait sa claire image sur.*

**195. The English Aristocracy

The English aristocracy remained a race of country gentlemen. They never became mere loungers or triflers, kicking their heels about a Court and amusing themselves with tedious gallantries and intrigues. They threw themselves into country life and government, and they were happiest away from London. The great swarms of guests that settled on such country seats as Holkham were like gay and bois-

terous schoolboys compared with the French nobles who
had forgotten how to live in the country and were tired of
living at Versailles. If anything could exceed Grey's
reluctance to leave his great house in Northumberland for
the excitements of Parliament, it was Fox's reluctance to
leave his little house in Surrey. The taste for country
pleasures and for country sports was never lost, and its
persistence explains the physical vitality of the aristocracy.
This was a social fact of great importance, for it is health
after all that wins half the battles of classes. No quantity
of Burgundy and Port could kill off a race that was continually restoring its health by life in the open air; it did not
matter that Squire Western generally spent the night under
the table if he generally spent the day in the saddle. This
inheritance of an open-air life is probably the reason that
in England, in contrast to France and Italy, good looks are
more often to be found in the aristocracy than in other
classes of society.

J. L. HAMMOND and BARBARA HAMMOND, *The Village
Labourer* 1760–1832 (Longmans).

***196. DEFINITION OF A GENTLEMAN

It is almost a definition of a gentleman[1] to say he is one who
never inflicts pain. This description is both refined and, as
far as it goes,[2] accurate. He is mainly occupied in merely
removing the obstacles which hinder the free and unem-
barrassed action of those about him; and he concurs with
their movements rather than takes[3] the initiative himself....
The true gentleman carefully avoids whatever may cause a
jar or a jolt in the minds of those with whom he is cast;[4]...
his great concern being to make every one at their ease and
at home.[5] He has his eyes on all his company; he is tender
towards[6] the bashful, gentle towards the distant, and merci-
ful towards the absurd; he can recollect to whom he is
speaking; he guards against unseasonable allusions, or
topics which may irritate;[7] he is seldom prominent[8] in
conversation, and never wearisome. He makes light of

favours while he does them, and seems to be receiving when he is conferring. He never speaks of himself except when compelled, never defends himself by a mere retort, he has no ears for slander[9] or gossip, is scrupulous in imputing motives to those who interfere with him,[10] and interprets everything for the best.   J. H. NEWMAN, *The Idea of a University.*

1 Say, *e.g., C'est presque définir le* (see p. 82, § 19 (*b*)) *gentleman que de dire.* 2 *dans ses limites.*   3 *plutôt qu'il ne prend.*   4 *ceux avec lesquels il se trouve.*   5 *de mettre tout le monde en confiance et à l'aise.*   6 *il fait preuve de délicatesse envers.*   7 *qui risquent de froisser.*   8 Use *se mettre en avant.*   9 *il ne prête point l'oreille aux médisances.*   10 *ceux qui le gênent.*

*197. FRANCE

When wayfaring in France as a tourist the towers of a château seen among the woods from the roadside, or a prefecture standing in its park in a country town, or the modest home of a rural priest beneath the shadow of a church, had always filled me with wondering desire to know what manner of people dwelt within those walls; so having read and imagined much about the lives they led, it would not have been surprising if some disillusion had followed my first entry into this novel society. Nothing of the sort occurred, and the memory of my opening journey as a resident in France is a series of pleasing pictures. . . .

Even now, when I know the French provinces as few foreigners can know them, the familiar scenes of daily life which meet the casual view give me pleasurable sensations as keen as when I was a passing stranger. A bishop blessing little children in the aisles of his cathedral, a group of white-coifed peasant women in a market-place, or a red-legged regiment swinging through a village to the strains of a bugle-march, has now for me not merely the sentimental or picturesque interest of former days. I know, indeed, that the lives of many of these people are neither ideal nor idyllic, but I recognize now in these provincials, with all their failings, the true force of France, which keeps her in

the front rank of nations, in spite of the follies, govern-
mental and otherwise, committed in her beautiful capital.

J. E. C. BODLEY, *France.*

**198. To Die Young

One inevitable result of war is the death of many young
men who might well[1] have expected to live longer.[2] Since[3]
to attain a rational attitude of mind towards death[4] is the
chief problem of human life, we may well consider the case
of the young soldier who became acquainted with[5] the
problem earlier in life than is usual. Although we all know
that we are seated at play[6] with an opponent who is certain
to checkmate in something less than three score and ten
moves, the end seems so remote to most lads of eighteen that
they don't really believe in it. Yet earthly life is a losing
game which is to be played out with what propriety we can
manage, and which should be lost without rancour. Soldiers
learn to live and die in that fashion. It is virtuous[7] and not
vicious to be indifferent to death, provided that you are as
indifferent to your own as to your neighbour's. Religious
faith is rarely so strong as to support a man against[8]
selfish mourning when death takes his friends; but military
honour, when it teaches him to go to his own death with a
smile, helps him to a little virtue. To die young is by no
means an unmitigated misfortune; to die gaily in the
unselfish pursuit of what you believe to be a righteous cause
is an enviable and not a premature end.

CHARLES EDMONDS, *A Subaltern's War* (Peter Davies).

1 Omit.   2 *davantage.*   3 Transpose to: 'Since the chief problem...
is to attain'.   4 *parvenir devant la mort à une attitude,* etc.   5 *qui fut
mis aux prises avec.*   6 *nous sommes assis à la table de jeu en face d'un,* etc.
7 *C'est montrer de la vertu, et non un défaut, que d'être indifférent devant la
mort.*   8 Say, *e.g., pour empêcher un homme de tomber dans.*

*199. Lasting Peace

Victor and vanquished alike have bravely played their parts.
We are above the meanness of jeering over our triumph.
They need feel no humiliation in their defeat, and therefore,

when the wounds which have been made are healed over, when the scars which have been left begin to fade, then let us see to it as Englishmen worthy of the name that we do nothing to recall the regretted animosities of the past. We must show our readiness to welcome our new fellow-subjects to all the privileges of a greater and a freer Empire than the world has ever known. We must give to them equality in all things with ourselves, and we must ask of them something in return. It is with them now that the future lies. We hold out our hand to them; we ask them to take it, and to take it without any *arrière pensée*, but frankly and in the spirit in which it is offered. Let us try whether out of these two great and kindred races we cannot make a fusion—a nation stronger in its unity than either of its parts would be alone. That is the future of South Africa to which all patriots must aspire, and which is within the bounds of a reasonable aspiration.

JOSEPH CHAMBERLAIN, *Speech at Durban*, 27 Dec. 1902.

***200. THE SHAPE OF THINGS TO COME

'And whatever's this I can see in yours, Nannie? My lands![1] I believe it's a wedding cake!'

'It's no such thing', said Nannie primly. 'It's a nice big new work-basket, that's what it is. Just the thing I need, with[2] the amount of stockings they all manage to wear out down here.'

'Well, well, we'll see', said Mrs Adie darkly. 'Wedding cake or work-basket, what will be will be, and one thing leads to[3] another.'

There she goes again,[4] thought Mrs Miniver with an inward chuckle. Rhythm and alliteration: the phrase-makers always get the last word. She herself was sitting in a big wicker armchair at one side of the range. She had drawn back a little because of the heat, and from where she sat, half in shadow, the scene looked strangely theatrical. Mrs Adie, with a flush on her high cheek-bones and her usually neat[5] hair a little dishevelled, was reaching forward to fish out Judy's 'fortune';[6] and, opposite, the six fire-lit faces were awaiting, with varying degrees of credulity, her next pronouncement. It didn't much matter, after all, thought Mrs Miniver, whether the fortunes came true, or whether anybody believed in them; what mattered was that here at least was one small roomful[7] of warmth and happiness, shut in by frail window-panes from a freezing, harsh, and inexplicable world. All one could do was to be thankful for moments like these. During the next 12 months, perhaps, the remaining odds and ends of their civilization would have been tipped into the melting-pot; and not even Mrs Adie—.

But she became aware that her own fortune had just been told out of the seventh bowl and that she had not heard a word of it.

'Thank you so much, Mrs Adie', she said with a smile, taking the cold, queer-shaped[8] lump of metal on to her palm. So far as she could remember, it was almost exactly the same shape as the one she had had last year. So that was all right; for herself, she could think of nothing better.[9]

'Mrs Miniver', *The Times*, 2nd January 1939
(Chatto and Windus and Miss Jan Struther).

1 Vulgarly, *Mes aïeux!*   2 *étant donné.*   3 *entraîne.*   4 *La voilà qui continue.*   5 *bien peignés.*   6 '*la bonne aventure*'.   7 *toute une petite pièce heureuse et bien au chaud.*   8 *de forme bizarre.*   9 *ne pouvait rien rêver de mieux.*

MODEL TRANSLATIONS BY PRO-
FESSORS IN FRENCH AND OTHER
UNIVERSITIES

G. BONNARD, Professor in the University of Lausanne.
   THOMAS HARDY, *Far from the Madding Crowd*: 'Heaven opened then...',
   p. 256.
   VIRGINIA WOOLF, *The Waves*: 'The sun had not yet risen...', p. 258.

C. CESTRE, Professor in the University of Paris.
   NATHANIEL HAWTHORNE, *The Birthmark*: 'The next day Aylmer...',
   p. 260.
   EDWIN ARLINGTON ROBINSON, *The Man against the Sky*: 'Between
   me and the sunset...', p. 262.

J. DOUADY, Inspecteur-Général, Paris.
   DICKENS, *Nicholas Nickleby*: 'Nicholas was prepared...', p. 264.

A. J. FARMER, Professor in the University of Bordeaux.
   JAMES THOMSON, *The Castle of Indolence*: 'In lowly dale...', p. 266.
   H. G. WELLS, *Tono-Bungay*: 'Head and centre of our system...', p. 270.

R. LAS VERGNAS, Professor in the University of Lille.
   CHARLES KINGSLEY, *Yeast*: 'He tried to think, but the river...',
   p. 272.
   OSBERT SITWELL, *The Man Who Lost Himself*: 'The smell of paint
   fought...', p. 274.

PIERRE LEGOUIS, Professor in the University of Lyons.
   MILTON, *The Reason of Church Government*: 'How happy were it...',
   p. 276.
   BROWNING, *Fra Lippo Lippi*: 'I am poor brother Lippo...', p. 280.

F. C. ROE, Professor in the University of Aberdeen.
   Mrs GASKELL, *Cranford*: 'In a few minutes tea was brought...', p. 284.
   GEORGE ELIOT, *The Mill on the Floss*: 'Why, what a nice little lady...',
   p. 284.

W. THOMAS, sometime Professor in the University of Lyons.
   RUSKIN, *Modern Painters*: 'The pine rises in serene resistance...',
   p. 286.
   R. L. STEVENSON, *Edinburgh*: 'Into no other city...', p. 288.

Heaven opened then, indeed. The flash was almost too novel for its inexpressibly dangerous nature to be at once realized, and they could only comprehend the magnificence of its beauty. It sprang from east, west, north, south. It was a perfect dance of death. The forms of skeletons appeared in the air, shaped with blue fire for bones—dancing, leaping, striding, racing around, and mingling altogether in unparalleled confusion. With these were intertwined undulating snakes of green. Behind these was a broad mass of lesser light. Simultaneously came from every part of the tumbling sky what may be called a shout; since, though no shout ever came near it, it was more of the nature of a shout than of anything else earthly. In the meantime one of the grisly forms had alighted upon the point of Gabriel's rod, to run invisibly down it, down the chain, and into the earth. Gabriel was almost blinded, and he could feel Bathsheba's warm arm tremble in his hand—a sensation novel and thrilling enough; but love, life, everything human, seemed small and trifling in such close juxtaposition with an infuriated universe.

Oak had hardly time to gather up these impressions into a thought, and to see how strangely the red feather of her hat shone in this light, when the tall tree on the hill before mentioned seemed on fire to a white heat, and a new one among those terrible voices mingled with the last crash of those preceding. It was a stupefying blast, harsh and pitiless, and it fell upon their ears in a dead, flat blow, without that reverberation which lends the tones of a drum to more distant thunder. By the lustre reflected from every part of the earth and from the wide domical scoop above it, he saw that the tree was sliced down the whole length of its tall, straight stem, a huge riband of bark being apparently flung off. The other portion remained erect, and revealed the bared surface as a strip of white down the front. The lightning had struck the tree. A sulphurous smell filled the air; then all was silent, and black as a cave in Hinnom.

THOMAS HARDY, *Far from the Madding Crowd*
(Macmillan and the Trustees of the Hardy estate).

Le ciel se déchira. L'éclair était presque trop surprenant pour qu'on en comprît aussitôt le caractère infiniment redoutable. Ils ne purent en saisir que la majestueuse beauté. Il bondit à la fois de l'est et de l'ouest, du sud et du nord. Ce fut une vraie danse de la mort. Des sortes de squelettes apparurent dans les airs, des flammes bleues figurant leurs os. Tout autour du ciel ces formes dansaient, bondissaient, semblaient ouvrir d'immenses enjambées et lutter à la course; elles se mêlèrent enfin en une confusion sans exemple. D'ondoyants serpents de feu vert s'enlaçaient à elles. Au delà s'étendait une énorme lueur. En même temps, de tous les côtés du ciel bouleversé vint à eux comme un aboi formidable; jamais aucun aboi n'en approcha, mais cela tenait plus de l'aboi que d'aucun autre bruit terrestre. Cependant un de ces fantômes horribles s'était posé sur la pointe de la tringle de Gabriel, la descendait invisible, suivait la chaîne et s'enfonçait dans la terre. Gabriel fut presque aveuglé; il pouvait sentir trembler dans sa main le bras chaud de Bethsabée—sensation nouvelle et enivrante certes—mais l'amour, la vie, toutes les choses humaines lui paraissaient insignifiantes en présence de cet univers en furie.

A peine Oak avait-il eu le temps de rassembler en une pensée ces impressions, de voir de quel étrange éclat la plume rouge du chapeau de Bethsabée brillait dans cette lumière, que le grand arbre au haut de la colline dont j'ai déjà parlé, parut prendre feu, puis devenir incandescent; une encore de ces voix terribles se mêla au dernier fracas de celles qui l'avaient précédée. Ce fut comme une explosion étourdissante, brutale et cruelle, qui s'abattit sur eux comme un coup de massue, sans ces échos qui prêtent au tonnerre éloigné les roulements du tambour. A la clarté que réfléchissaient et le pays tout entier et le dôme immense qui se creusait au-dessus, il vit l'arbre déchiré sur toute la hauteur de son fût élancé; un énorme ruban d'écorce en avait été violemment arraché. L'arbre restait debout et montrait sa chair mise à nu comme une bande blanche du haut en bas du tronc. La foudre avait frappé l'arbre. Une odeur de soufre remplit l'air. Puis tout fut silencieux, et noir comme une caverne des Enfers. G. BONNARD.

The sun had not yet risen. The sea was indistinguishable from the sky, except that the sea was slightly creased as if a cloth had wrinkles in it. Gradually as the sky whitened a dark line lay on the horizon dividing the sea from the sky and the grey cloth became barred with thick strokes moving, one after another, beneath the surface, following each other, pursuing each other, perpetually.

As they neared the shore each bar rose, heaped itself, broke and swept a thin veil of white water across the sand. The wave paused, and then drew out again, sighing like a sleeper whose breath comes and goes unconsciously. Gradually the dark bar on the horizon became clear as if the sediment in an old wine-bottle had sunk and left the glass green. Behind it, too, the sky cleared as if the white sediment there had sunk, or as if the arm of a woman couched beneath the horizon had raised a lamp and flat bars of white, green and yellow spread across the sky like the blades of a fan. Then she raised her lamp higher and the air seemed to become fibrous and to tear away from the green surface flickering and flaming in red and yellow fibres like the smoky fire that roars from a bonfire. Gradually the fibres of the burning bonfire were fused into one haze, one incandescence which lifted the weight of the woollen grey sky on top of it and turned it to a million atoms of soft blue. The surface of the sea slowly became transparent and lay rippling and sparkling until the dark stripes were almost rubbed out. Slowly the arm that held the lamp raised it higher and higher until a broad flame became visible; an arc of fire burnt on the rim of the horizon, and all round it the sea blazed gold.

The light struck upon the trees in the garden, making one leaf transparent and then another. One bird chirped high up; there was a pause; another chirped lower down. The

Le soleil ne s'était pas encore levé. On ne distinguait pas la mer du ciel, sauf que la mer était légèrement ridée, comme quand une nappe fait des plis. Peu à peu, à mesure que le ciel blanchissait, une ligne sombre s'épaissit à l'horizon, séparant la mer du ciel, et la nappe grise se raya de lourdes barres qui s'avançaient sous sa surface, l'une après l'autre, et qui se succédaient, et qui se poursuivaient, indéfiniment.

En s'approchant du rivage, chaque vague se soulevait, se ramassait sur elle-même, puis déferlait et balayait le sable d'un léger voile d'eau blanche. La vague s'arrêtait, puis se retirait en soupirant comme un dormeur dont la respiration va et vient sans qu'il en ait conscience. Peu à peu la barre sombre à l'horizon s'éclaircit, comme quand dans une vieille bouteille de vin la lie se dépose, rendant au verre sa transparence verte. Derrière elle, le ciel aussi s'éclaircissait comme si là-bas une cendre blanche s'était déposée à son tour, ou comme si une femme couchée au-dessous de l'horizon levait une lampe à bout de bras ; et, tout au travers du ciel, de larges raies blanches, vertes et jaunes s'étendirent comme les branches d'un éventail. Elle leva plus haut sa lampe. L'air parut alors se cristalliser en mille petites flammes vacillantes ; on eût dit qu'il se détachait brusque-ment du fond vert du ciel, sous la forme de filaments jaunes et rouges comme les flammes mêlées de fumée qui s'élèvent en grondant d'un feu. Peu à peu les flammèches du feu qui flambait se fondirent en une seule et même vapeur lumineuse, en une seule et même incandescence qui souleva au-dessus d'elle la pesanteur du ciel laineux et gris qu'elle transforma en des millions d'atomes d'un bleu tendre. La surface de la mer lentement devint transparente. Elle se couvrit de mille rides étincelantes au point que les barres sombres en furent presque effacées. Lentement le bras qui tenait la lampe l'éleva plus haut, plus haut encore jusqu'à ce qu'une grande flamme devînt visible ; un arc de feu brûla au bord de l'horizon, et tout autour la mer s'embrasa d'une coulée d'or.

La lumière vint frapper les arbres du jardin, rendant transparente une feuille, puis une autre. Un oiseau, un seul, gazouilla, haut perché ; il y eut un silence ; un autre

sun sharpened the walls of the house, and rested like the tip of a fan upon a white blind and made a blue finger-print of shadow under the leaf by the bedroom window. The blind stirred slightly, but all within was dim and unsubstantial. The birds sang their blank melody outside.

VIRGINIA WOOLF, *The Waves* (Hogarth Press).

The next day Aylmer apprised his wife of a plan that he had formed whereby he might have opportunity for the intense thought and constant watchfulness which the proposed operation would require; while Georgiana, likewise, would enjoy the perfect repose essential to its success. They were to seclude themselves in the extensive apartments occupied by Aylmer as a laboratory, and where, during his toilsome youth, he had made discoveries in the elemental powers of Nature that had roused the admiration of all the learned societies in Europe. Seated calmly in this laboratory, the pale philosopher had investigated the secrets of the highest cloud region and of the profoundest mines; he had satisfied himself of the causes that kindled and kept alive the fires of the volcano; and had explained the mystery of fountains, and how it is that they gush forth, some so bright and pure, and others with such rich medicinal virtues, from the dark bosom of the earth. Here, too, at an earlier period, he had studied the wonders of the human frame, and attempted to fathom the very process by which Nature assimilates all her precious influences from earth and air, and from the spiritual world, to create and foster man, her masterpiece. The latter pursuit, however, Aylmer had long laid aside in unwilling recognition of the truth—against which all seekers sooner or later stumble—that our great creative Mother, while she amuses us with apparently working in the broadest sunshine, is yet severely careful to keep her own secrets, and, in spite of her pretended openness, shows us nothing but results. She permits us, indeed, to mar, but seldom to mend, and, like a jealous patentee, on no account to make. Now,

gazouilla à son tour, plus bas. Le soleil éclaira les murs de
la maison et vint se poser comme l'extrémité d'un éventail
sur un rideau blanc, faisant, au-dessous de la feuille près de
la fenêtre, une ombre bleue semblable à l'empreinte d'un
doigt. Le rideau bougea légèrement, mais à l'intérieur tout
était obscur et comme irréel. Dehors les oiseaux s'étaient mis
à pépier étourdiment. G. BONNARD.

Le lendemain, Aylmer fit part à sa femme d'un plan qu'il
avait formé, devant lui permettre le travail de pensée
intense et la surveillance constante qu'exigerait l'opération
projetée, tandis que Georgiana, aussi bien, jouirait du repos
parfait essentiel au succès. Ils se retireraient dans le grand
appartement occupé par Aylmer comme laboratoire, et où,
pendant sa jeunesse laborieuse, il avait fait des découvertes
dans l'ordre des forces élémentaires de la nature, qui avaient
suscité l'admiration de toutes les sociétés savantes d'Europe.
Installé dans le calme de ce laboratoire, le pâle philosophe
avait étudié les secrets des régions les plus élevées des
nuages et les plus profondes des mines; il s'était assuré des
causes qui enflamment et maintiennent allumés les volcans;
il avait expliqué le mystère des sources, et comment il se fait
qu'elles jaillissent, les unes claires et pures, les autres
chargées de riches vertus médicinales, des entrailles obscures
de la terre. Là aussi, à une époque plus ancienne, il s'était
penché sur les merveilles de l'organisme humain, et avait
essayé de sonder le processus même par lequel la Nature
emprunte toutes ses précieuses influences à la terre, à l'air
et au monde spirituel, pour créer et maintenir l'Homme,
son chef-d'œuvre. Ces dernières recherches, cependant,
Aylmer les avait laissées de côté depuis longtemps, obligé
malgré lui de reconnaître cette vérité, où achoppent tôt ou
tard tous les investigateurs, que notre grande Mère créatrice,
laquelle nous amuse en semblant œuvrer à la claire lumière
du plein jour, toutefois prend minutieusement soin de garder
son secret, et, en dépit d'une prétendue franchise, ne nous
livre que les résultats. Elle nous permet, il est vrai, de
gâter, mais rarement de réparer, et, comme le possesseur

however, Aylmer resumed these half-forgotten investigations; not, of course, with such hopes or wishes as first
suggested them; but because they involved much physiological truth and lay in the path of his proposed scheme for
the treatment of Georgiana.

As he led her over the threshold of the laboratory,
Georgiana was cold and tremulous. Aylmer looked cheer-
fully into her face, with intent to reassure her, but was so
startled with the intense glow of the birthmark upon the
whiteness of her cheek that he could not restrain a strong
convulsive shudder. His wife fainted.

NATHANIEL HAWTHORNE, *Mosses from an Old Manse:*
The Birthmark.

Between me and the sunset, like a dome
Against the glory of a world on fire,
Now burned a sudden hill,
Bleak, round, and high, by flame-light height made higher,
With nothing on it for the flame to kill
Save one who moved and was alone up there
To loom before the chaos and the glare
As if he were the last god going home
Unto his last desire.

.   .   .   .

Again, he may have gone down easily,
By comfortable altitudes, and found,
As always, underneath him solid ground
Whereon to be sufficient and to stand
Possessed already of the promised land,
Far stretched and fair to see:
A good sight, verily,
And one to make the eyes of her who bore him
Shine glad with hidden tears.
Why question of his ease of who before him,
In one place or another where they left
Their names as far behind them as their bones,
And yet by dint of slaughter, toil and theft,
And shrewdly sharpened stones,

jaloux d'un brevet, en aucune façon de créer. Voici, cependant, qu'Aylmer reprenait ces investigations à demi
oubliées; non pas, bien sûr, avec les espérances ou les désirs
qu'elles avaient suggérés au début; mais parce qu'elles
impliquaient de grandes vérités physiologiques et ouvraient
la voie au plan formé par lui de traiter Georgiana.

Au moment où il lui fit franchir le seuil du laboratoire,
Georgiana, toute tremblante, sentit son sang se glacer.
Aylmer dirigea vers elle un regard joyeux, dans l'intention de
la rassurer, mais il fut si bouleversé de l'éclat intense de la
marque sur la pâleur de sa joue qu'il ne put réprimer un
violent frisson convulsif. Sa femme s'évanouit.   c. CESTRE.

Entre le couchant et moi, comme un dôme
Contre la gloire d'un univers en feu,
Lors flamba une soudaine éminence,
Désolée, arrondie, haute, rendue plus haute par l'immensité
    embrasée,
N'ayant rien sur son flanc que la flamme pût dévorer,
Qu'un homme qui avançait et était là seul,
Dressé devant le chaos et le rougeoiement,
Comme s'il était le dernier dieu faisant route
    Vers son dernier désir.

.   .   .   .

Il se peut qu'il descende sans peine,
Par des altitudes aisées, et trouve,
Comme toujours, sous ses pas le sol ferme
Et s'y tienne debout satisfait,
Déjà maître de la terre promise,
Immense et belle à voir:
Beau spectacle, en vérité,
A faire briller les yeux de celle qui l'a enfanté
De l'éclat joyeux de larmes secrètes.
Pourquoi troubler sa quiétude en évoquant
Ceux qui l'ont précédé, là ou ailleurs, laissant
Leur nom aussi loin derrière eux que leurs os,
Taillant par le labeur, la rapine et le meurtre,
Et à l'aide de pierres astucieusement aiguisées,

Carved hard the way for his ascendency
Through deserts of lost years?
Why trouble him now who sees and hears
No more than what his innocence requires,
And therefore to no other height aspires
Than one at which he neither quails nor tires?
He may do more by seeing what he sees
Than others eager for iniquities;
He may, by seeing all things for the best,
Incite futurity to do the rest.
EDWIN ARLINGTON ROBINSON, *The Man against the Sky*
(Collected Poems, Macmillan, New York).

Nicholas was prepared for something odd, but not for
something quite so odd as the sight he encountered. At the
upper end of the room were a couple of boys, one of them
very tall and the other very short, both dressed as sailors—
or at least as theatrical sailors, with belts, buckles, pigtails,
and pistols complete—fighting what is called in play-bills a
terrific combat with two of those short broadswords with
basket hilts which are commonly used at our minor theatres.
The short boy had gained a great advantage over the tall
boy, who was reduced to mortal strait, and both were
overlooked by a large heavy man, perched against the
corner of a table, who emphatically adjured them to strike
a little more fire out of the swords, and they couldn't fail to
bring the house down on the very first night.

The two combatarts went to work afresh, and chopped
away until the swords emitted a shower of sparks....

The engagement commenced with about two hundred chops
administered by the short sailor and the tall sailor alternately, without producing any particular result until the
short sailor was chopped down on one knee, but this was
nothing to him, for he worked himself about on the one
knee with the assistance of his left hand, and fought most

Le rude chemin qui mène à la souveraineté
A travers des déserts d'années perdues?
Pourquoi l'importuner, lui qui ne voit et n'entend
Que ce que demande sa simplicité
Et n'aspire à d'autres cimes
Que celles dont la vue ne l'émeut, ni ne le lasse?
Ne se peut-il, qu'en voyant ce qu'il voit,
Il accomplisse plus que d'autres, acharnés à sonder l'iniquité?
Ne se peut-il qu'en voyant toutes choses pour le mieux,
Il incite l'avenir à faire le reste?   C. CESTRE.

Nicolas s'attendait à quelque chose de bizarre, mais moins bizarre assurément que le spectacle qui s'offrit à lui. A l'autre extrémité de la salle étaient deux jeunes gens, l'un très grand, l'autre très petit, tous deux en costumes de marins, ou plus exactement de marins de théâtre, avec tout leur attirail, ceinturon, boucles, queue postiche, pistolets. Ils se livraient ce qu'on appelle sur les affiches un combat à mort, armés de ces sabres d'abordage avec garde en coquille dont on se sert habituellement sur les petites scènes. Le plus petit avait pris nettement l'avantage sur le plus grand qui en était réduit à la dernière extrémité. Ils travaillaient tous deux sous la surveillance d'un gros homme de haute taille, perché sur un coin de table, qui les conjurait avec énergie de faire jaillir de leurs sabres un peu plus d'étincelles, et alors ils ne pourraient manquer de faire crouler la salle sous les applaudissements dès la première représentation.

Les deux combattants se remirent à l'œuvre de nouveau, et ferraillèrent à tout rompre, au point qu'une pluie d'étincelles jaillissait de leurs sabres....

L'engagement commença par environ deux cents coups de sabre administrés alternativement par le petit matelot et par le grand, sans résultat apparent, jusqu'au moment où le petit matelot reçut un coup qui le força à mettre un genou en terre, mais peu lui importait car il pivotait sur son unique genou avec l'aide de sa main gauche, se battant comme un lion jusqu'au moment où le grand

desperately until the tall sailor chopped his sword out of his grasp. Now the inference was, that the short sailor, reduced to this extremity, would give in at once and cry quarter, but instead of that he all of a sudden drew a large pistol from his belt and presented it at the face of the tall sailor, who was so overcome at this (not expecting it) that he let the short sailor pick up his sword and begin again. Then the chopping recommenced, and a variety of fancy chops were administered on both sides, such as chops dealt with the left hand and under the leg and over the right shoulder and over the left; and when the short sailor made a vigorous cut at the tall sailor's legs, which would have shaved them clean off if it had taken effect, the tall sailor jumped over the short sailor's sword, wherefore to balance the matter and make it all fair, the tall sailor administered the same cut and the short sailor jumped over *his* sword. After this there was a good deal of dodging about and hitching up of the inexpressibles in the absence of braces, and then the short sailor (who was the moral character evidently, for he always had the best of it) made a violent demonstration and closed with the tall sailor, who, after a few unavailing struggles, went down and expired in great torture as the short sailor put his foot upon his breast and bored a hole in him through and through.   CHARLES DICKENS, *Nicholas Nickleby.*

In lowly dale, fast by a river's side,
With woody hill o'er hill encompassed round,
A most enchanting wizard did abide,
Than whom a fiend more fell is nowhere found.
It was, I ween, a lovely spot of ground;
And there a season atween June and May,
Half prankt with spring, with summer half imbrowned,
A listless climate made, where, sooth to say,
No living wight could work, ne carèd e'en for play.

matelot lui fit sauter le sabre des mains. On se serait
attendu à ce que le petit matelot, réduit à cette extrémité,
se fût rendu à l'instant et eût demandé quartier; mais
au lieu de cela il tira soudain de son ceinturon un grand
pistolet qu'il braqua au visage du grand matelot, lequel, ne
s'y attendant pas, en fut tellement saisi qu'il laissa le petit
matelot ramasser son sabre et reprendre le combat. Alors
on se remit à ferrailler en administrant de part et d'autre une
série de coups de fantaisie, tels que coups de la main gauche,
coups par-dessous la jambe, par-dessus l'épaule droite,
par-dessus la gauche; lorsque le petit matelot lança contre
les jambes du grand un vigoureux coup de taille qui les lui
aurait fauchées net s'il avait porté, le grand matelot sauta
par-dessus le sabre du petit; conséquemment, pour équilibrer
le combat et égaliser la partie, le grand matelot porta le
même coup au petit, qui sauta par-dessus le sabre de l'autre.
Il y eut ensuite parades sur parades, et amarrages des
pantalons qui tombaient faute de bretelles; finalement le
petit matelot, qui était évidemment le personnage vertueux,
car il avait toujours le dessus, fit une attaque désespérée, en
vint au corps à corps avec le grand qui, après s'être débattu
en vain, tomba et expira au milieu de cruelles tortures car le
petit matelot, lui mettant le pied sur la poitrine, le troua de
part en part.   J. DOUADY.

Dans une vallée profonde, tout près du bord d'une rivière,
Entourée de collines boisées s'étageant l'une sur l'autre,
Habitait un magicien aux sortilèges puissants:
Nulle part on ne trouve démon plus malfaisant.
C'était, je pense, un délicieux coin de terre: 5
Et là, une saison qui n'était ni juin ni mai,
A demi parée par le printemps, à demi bronzée par l'été,
Faisait régner un climat langoureux sous lequel, à dire vrai,
Aucun être ne pouvait travailler, ni n'avait même le goût de
    jouer.

Was nought around but images of rest:
Sleep-soothing groves, and quiet lawns between;
And flowery beds that slumbrous influence kest,
From poppies breathed; and beds of pleasant green,
Where never yet was creeping creature seen.
Meantime, unnumbered glittering streamlets played,
And hurlèd everywhere their waters sheen;
That, as they bickered through the sunny glade,
Though restless still themselves, a lulling murmur made.

Joined to the prattle of the purling rills
Were heard the lowing herds along the vale,
And flocks loud-bleating from the distant hills,
And vacant shepherds piping in the dale;
And now and then, sweet Philomel would wail,
Or stockdoves plain amid the forest deep,
That drowsy rustled to the sighing gale;
And still a coil the grasshopper did keep:
Yet all these sounds yblent inclinèd all to sleep.

Full in the passage of the vale, above,
A sable silent solemn forest stood,
Where nought but shadowy forms was seen to move,
As Idless fancied in her dreaming mood.
And up the hills, on either side, a wood
Of blackening pines, aye waving to and fro,
Sent forth a sleepy horror through the blood;
And where this valley winded out, below,
The murmuring main was heard, and scarcely heard, to
    flow.   JAMES THOMSON, *The Castle of Indolence.*

Rien alentour que des images de repos: 10
Des bosquets propices au sommeil, séparées par de paisibles
  pelouses,
Des parterres de fleurs où flottait un parfum assoupissant,
Exhalé par les pavots, et des tapis de riante verdure,
Où jamais on ne vit créature rampante.
Cependant, d'innombrables ruisselets jouaient, étincelants, 15
Précipitant de tous côtés leurs eaux brillantes
Qui, dans leur cours rapide le long des clairières ensoleillées,
Bien que sans cesse agitées, faisaient entendre un murmure
  berceur.

En même temps que le babil des ruisseaux clapotants,
On entendait le meuglement des troupeaux le long de la 20
  vallée,
Le bêlement sonore des moutons dans les collines lointaines,
Et la flûte des bergers insouciants dans le val.
De temps en temps montait le chant mélancolique et doux
  de Philomèle
Ou la plainte des tourterelles dans la forêt profonde,
Qui bruissait, endormie, au soupir du vent; 25
Et sans cesse le criquet menait son vacarme.
Cependant, tous ces bruits fondus invitaient tous les êtres
  au sommeil.

En plein travers de la vallée, en haut,
Se dressait une forêt noire, silencieuse, auguste,
Où l'on ne voyait passer que des ombres vagues, 30
Telles qu'en imagine l'Oisiveté dans ses rêveries.
Et plus haut sur les collines, de chaque côté, un bois
De pins sombres, qui ondulaient sans cesse,
Faisait passer dans le sang une crainte assoupie;
A l'endroit où la vallée sinueuse s'ouvrait, en bas, 35
On entendait—mais à peine perceptible—le murmure des
  flots de l'océan. A. J. FARMER.

22 *la flûte*: var. *le pipeau*. 33 Var. *l'ondulation incessante.*

Head and centre of our system was Lady Drew, her 'leddy-ship', shrivelled, garrulous, with a wonderful memory for genealogies, and very, very old; and beside her and nearly as old, Miss Somerville, her cousin and companion. These two old souls lived like dried-up kernels in the great shell of Bladesover House, the shell that had once been gaily full of fops, of fine ladies in powder and patches and courtly gentlemen with swords; and when there was no company they spent whole days in the corner parlour just over the housekeeper's room, between reading and slumber and caressing their two pet dogs. When I was a boy, I used always to think of these two poor old creatures as superior beings living, like God, somewhere through the ceiling. Occasionally they bumped about a bit and one even heard them overhead, which gave them a greater effect of reality without mitigating their vertical predominance. Sometimes, too, I saw them. Of course if I came upon them in the park or in the shrubbery (where I was a trespasser) I hid or fled in pious horror, but I was upon due occasion taken into the Presence by request. I remember her 'leddyship' then as a thing of black silks and a golden chain, a quavering in-junction to me to be a good boy, a very shrunken, loose-skinned face and neck, and a ropy hand that trembled a half-crown into mine. Miss Somerville hovered behind, a paler thing of broken lavender and white and black, with screwed-up, sandy-lashed eyes. Her hair was yellow and her colour bright, and when we sat in the housekeeper's room of a winter's night warming our toes and sipping elder-wine, her maid would tell us the simple secrets of that belated flush.　　　　H. G. WELLS, *Tono Bungay* (Collins).

La tête et le centre de notre système, c'était Lady Drew, 'milady', ratatinée, bavarde, avec une mémoire merveilleuse pour les généalogies, et très, très vieille; auprès d'elle, et presque aussi vieille, Miss Somerville, sa cousine et dame de compagnie. Ces deux vieux êtres habitaient, telles des 5 amandes desséchées, l'immense coque du château de Bladesover qu'emplissait jadis une brillante assemblée de petits-maîtres, de nobles dames avec leur poudre et leurs mouches, et de galants gentilshommes portant l'épée. Quand il n'y avait pas de visites, elles passaient des journées 10 entières au petit salon d'angle, juste au-dessus de la chambre de la femme de charge, à lire, à somnoler et à caresser les deux chiens favoris. Quand j'étais jeune et que je pensais à ces deux pauvres vieilles, c'était toujours comme à des êtres supérieurs vivant, ainsi que Dieu, quelque part au-15 delà du plafond. De temps en temps, elles faisaient quelque bruit en se remuant, et même on les entendait, ce qui leur donnait une apparence plus grande de réalité, sans diminuer en rien leur prédominance verticale. Quelquefois aussi je les voyais. Naturellement, si je tombais sur elles dans le 20 parc ou dans le bosquet (où j'étais en fraude), je me cachais ou m'enfuyais pieusement horrifié; mais j'étais, à l'occasion, dûment conduit en sa Présence, à sa requête. Et, dans ces moments, je me souviens de 'milady' comme d'une chose portant des soieries noires et une chaîne d'or, comme d'une 25 voix chevrotante qui m'enjoignait d'être un enfant sage, comme d'un visage et d'un cou à la peau flétrie et flasque, comme d'une main tremblante et noueuse qui insinuait dans la mienne une demi-couronne. Miss Somerville flottait derrière, falote, en lavande passée, en blanc et noir, avec des 30 yeux bridés aux cils roux. Elle avait les cheveux jaunes et la mine colorée, et quand, par une soirée d'hiver, nous étions assis dans la chambre de la femme de charge, réchauffant nos pieds et sirotant du vin de sureau, sa femme de chambre nous révélait les secrets élémentaires de cette rougeur 35 tardive.   A. J. FARMER.

5 *vieux êtres*: var. *vieilles créatures*.   12 *caresser*: var. *dorloter*.   13 Var. *Tout enfant, quand*, etc.   21 Var. (*où je n'avais par le droit d'être*). 30 *falote*: var. *effacée*.

He tried to think, but the river would not let him. It thundered and spouted out behind him from the hatches, and leapt madly past him, and caught his eyes in spite of him, and swept them away down its dancing waves, and then let them go again only to sweep them down again and again, till his brain felt a delicious dizziness from the everlasting rush and the everlasting roar.

And then below, how it spread, and writhed, and whirled into transparent fans, hissing and twining snakes, polished glass wreaths, huge crystal bells, which boiled up from the bottom, and dived again beneath long threads of creamy foam, and swung round posts and roots, and rushed blackening under dark weed-fringed boughs, and gnawed at the marly banks, and shook the ever restless bulrushes, till it was swept away and down over the white pebbles and olive weeds, in one broad rippling sheet of molten silver. towards the distant sea. Downwards it fleeted ever, and bore his thoughts floating on its oily stream; and the great trout, with their yellow sides and peacock backs, lounged among the eddies, and the silver grayling dimpled and wandered upon the shallows, and the May-flies flickered and rustled round him like water fairies, with their green gauzy wings; the coot clanked musically among the reeds; the frogs hummed their ceaseless vesper monotone; the king-fisher darted from his hole in the bank like a blue spark of electric light; the swallows' bills snapped as they twined and hawked above the pool; the swifts' wings whirred like musket-balls, as they rushed screaming past his head; and ever the river fleeted by, bearing his eyes away down the current, till its wild eddies began to glow with crimson beneath the setting sun.   CHARLES KINGSLEY, *Yeast.*

Il essaya de penser, mais le fleuve ne le lui permit pas. Sortant, par derrière lui, des vannes, il jaillissait dans un fracas de tonnerre, passait devant lui en bonds insensés, attirant malgré lui ses regards, les emportant d'un trait au fil de ses vagues dansantes, puis leur rendant de nouveau la liberté, mais seulement pour les emporter de nouveau tout là-bas, tant qu'à la fin son esprit éprouva un délicieux vertige en cet éternel élan et cet éternel grondement.

Et alors, tout en bas, comme ses éploiements, ses torsions, ses remous le transformaient en éventails transparents, en serpents sifflant et nouant leur étreinte, en volutes de verre poli, en géantes cloches de cristal, qui jaillissaient du fond en bouillonnant, plongeaient de nouveau sous de longs fils d'écume crémeuse, contournaient d'un bond poteaux et racines, se précipitaient, de plus en plus sombres, sous d'obscurs rameaux enchevêtrés d'herbes, rongeaient les berges marneuses, et agitaient les joncs à jamais frémissants, pour disparaître enfin, là-bas, d'un trait, par-dessus les cailloux blancs et les herbes vert-olive, en une vaste nappe ondoyante d'argent liquide, vers la mer lointaine. Vers l'aval il fuyait à tout jamais, entraînant ses pensées sur le flot de son cours moiré, et les belles truites aux flancs dorés et au dos ocellé flânaient dans les remous, et l'omble argenté passait en frétillant sur les bancs, et les demoiselles l'entouraient, telles des ondines, de leur voltigement et du bruissement de leurs vertes ailes de gaze; la foulque claquait en cadence dans les roseaux; les grenouilles fredonnaient sans trêve leurs vêpres monotones; le martin-pêcheur sortait comme une flèche de son trou sur la berge, tel une étincelle bleue de lumière électrique; les hirondelles happaient du bec, tout en décrivant leur vol plané au-dessus du 'dormant'; les ailes des martinets vibraient comme des balles de fusil, tandis qu'ils passaient au-dessus de sa tête en un vol rapide et criard; et à tout jamais fuyait le fleuve, entraînant ses regards là-bas au fil du courant, tant qu'à la fin le désordre de ses remous commença de s'empourprer sous les feux du couchant.   R. LAS VERGNAS.

The smell of paint fought against the country scents gently breathed out by every young leaf and crinkled blossom, and mingled with that of tar and petrol, for cars and taxicabs were purring softly over the watery black surface of the roads, shining and smooth as canals, through the amber and clouded heat of a hot London morning. Outside one square block of a house, a red and white awning was already being erected; large, rectangular vans drove up on their tiny wheels, and men hurried in and out—And Tristram thought of how, in the evening, the gondola-like cars would glide up to houses with a lacquered inevitability, and cascades and showers of golden light would splash and shiver down from the wide-open windows into the darkness—From them, too, would float the over-sympathetic hooting and sobbing of saxophones, as they gurgled and throbbed out those tunes which, in spite of their self-satisfied brazen rhythms and savage gorilla-like drummings that pretend to constitute an incitement to worship before Venus, have yet under them a good solid bottom of hell fire! For beneath every jazz rhythm was hidden the mournful whining of the Wesleyan Chapel, the austere howlings of the Pilgrim Fathers, as much as the comfortable self-righteousness of 'Hymns Ancient and Modern'—as dance music, it was, in fact, comparable to the daughter of a clergyman who earns renown by playing an unexpectedly daring part on the music-hall stage. Still, the traffic, even at this hour, would roar aloud above such melodious thumpings and moanings—At night its waves would arrange themselves into their wonted tiers, each one serving a different need or pleasure of the town—there would be the after-theatre wave, the later one of the pleasure-seekers returning home, both westward: and then the lorries, piled up with vegetables and provisions, would pound and lumber eastward.

OSBERT SITWELL, *The Man Who Lost Himself* (Duckworth).

L'odeur de la peinture contrariait les senteurs champêtres mollement exhalées par toutes ces jeunes feuilles et ces floraisons à peine écloses, et se mariait à celle du goudron et de l'essence, car les autos et les taxis parcouraient en un doux ronron la surface noire et miroitante de la chaussée, luisante et lisse comme un canal, dans l'ardeur ambrée et légèrement voilée d'une ardente matinée londonienne. Devant une maison dressée comme un bloc massif et carré, on était déjà en train de monter un tendelet blanc et rouge; de grands fourgons rectangulaires venaient de ranger, perchés sur leurs roues minuscules, et des hommes entraient et sortaient précipitamment. Et Tristram imaginait comment, dans la soirée, les autos viendraient aborder les maisons dans un glissement de gondoles avec une inéluctabilité lustrée, et les cascades et les averses de lumière d'or tomberaient en éclaboussures et en éclats de fenêtres ouvertes tout grand jusqu'au cœur de l'obscurité. D'elles aussi se déverseraient à flots le hululement et le sanglotement à l'excès fondants des saxophones, lançant le glouglou et les pulsations de ces airs qui, en dépit de leur rythme complaisamment effronté et de leur barbare tambourinage quasi-simiesque, lesquels prétendent constituer une invite au culte de Vénus, ont cependant sous eux un fond épars et solide de flammes infernales. Car, sous tous ces rythmes de jazz, se cachait le morne pleurnichement des chapelles wesleyennes, les sévères vociférations des 'Pères Pèlerins', tout autant que la piété commode et aisément satisfaite des 'Hymnes Anciens et Modernes'—en tant que musique de danse, c'était, en fait, comparable à la fille d'un pasteur qui acquiert un renom en jouant un rôle d'une audace inattendue sur une scène de music hall. Et pourtant la circulation, même à cette heure-là, dominerait de son bruyant tohu-bohu la mélodie de ces battements sourds et de ces gémissements. Dans la nuit, ses vagues viendraient se disposer en leurs alignements accoutumés, chacune desservant un besoin ou un plaisir différents de la ville—il y aurait la vague de la sortie des théâtres; celle, plus tardive, des coureurs d'amusements rentrant au logis; toutes deux vers l'ouest—et puis les gros camions, tout entassés de légumes et de provisions, se dirigeraient vers l'est, d'une allure poussive et empêtrée.   R. LAS VERGNAS.

How happy were it for this frail, and as it may be called
mortal life of man, since all earthly things which have the
name of good and convenient in our daily use, are withal so
cumbersome and full of trouble, if knowledge, yet which is
the best and lightsomest possession of the mind, were, as
the common saying is, no burden; and that what it wanted
of being a load to any part of the body, it did not with a
heavy advantage overlay upon the spirit! For not to speak
of that knowledge that rests in the contemplation of natural
causes and dimensions, which must needs be a lower wisdom,
as the object is low, certain it is, that he who hath obtained
in more than the scantiest measure to know anything
distinctly of God, and of his true worship, and what is
infallibly good and happy in the state of man's life, what in
itself evil and miserable, though vulgarly not so esteemed;
he that hath obtained to know this, the only high valuable
wisdom indeed, remembering also that God, even to a
strictness, requires the improvement of these his entrusted
gifts, cannot but sustain a sorer burden of mind, and more
pressing, than any supportable toil or weight which the
body can labour under, how and in what manner he shall
dispose and employ those sums of knowledge and illumination, which God hath sent him into this world to trade with.
And that which aggravates the burden more, is, that,
having received amongst his allotted parcels certain precious
truths, of such an orient lustre as no diamond can equal,
which nevertheless he has in charge to put off at any cheap
rate, yea, for nothing to them that will; the great merchants
of this world, fearing that this course would soon discover
and disgrace the false glitter of their deceitful wares, where-
with they abuse the people, like poor Indians with beads and
glasses, practise by all means how they may suppress the
vending of such rarities, and at such a cheapness as would
undo them, and turn their trash upon their hands. Therefore
by gratifying the corrupt desires of men in fleshly doctrines,
they stir them up to persecute with hatred and contempt all
those that seek to bear themselves uprightly in this their

Quel bonheur ce serait pour cette fragile, et, peut-on dire,
mortelle, vie humaine, attendu que toutes les choses
terrestres que nous appelons bonnes et commodes dans notre
usage quotidien sont néanmoins si encombrantes et si pleines
de tourment, quel bonheur ce serait si le savoir, qui est 5
encore la possession la meilleure et la moins pesante de
l'esprit, était, comme on le dit communément, le contraire
d'un fardeau, et qu'il ne compensât pas le poids qu'il n'impose à aucune partie du corps en accablant avec usure
l'âme ! Car, pour ne pas parler de ce savoir qui consiste dans 10
la contemplation des causes et des dimensions naturelles et
qui est nécessairement une sagesse inférieure puisque l'objet
en est bas, il est certain que celui qui a réussi dans une
mesure plus que très restreinte à connaître distinctement
quelque chose de Dieu, et de son vrai culte, et à reconnaître 15
ce qui est infailliblement bon et heureux dans la condition
humaine, ce qui est en soi mauvais et malheureux, quand
bien même le vulgaire en juge autrement; celui, dis-je, qui a
réussi à acquérir cette sagesse, la seule qui soit vraiment
d'un grand prix, s'il se rappelle aussi que Dieu exige, et 20
même avec rigueur, l'emploi profitable de ces dons qu'il nous
a confiés, ne peut éviter un fardeau spirituel plus pénible et
plus accablant qu'aucun faix de labeur supportable sous
lequel puisse peiner le corps, à savoir le choix de la manière
dont il devra disposer et user de ces valeurs de savoir et de 25
lumière avec lesquelles Dieu l'a envoyé commercer dans ce
monde. Et ce qui aggrave encore ce fardeau, c'est que, cet
homme ayant reçu parmi les lots qui lui sont attribués
certaines vérités précieuses, d'un lustre oriental tel que nul
diamant ne saurait les égaler, vérités dont il doit néanmoins 30
se défaire à n'importe quel prix, bien plus, pour rien, en
faveur de ceux qui en veulent; les grands négociants de ce
monde, craignant que cette pratique ne révélât et ne
discréditât bientôt le faux brillant de leurs marchandises
trompeuses, avec quoi ils abusent le peuple, comme on abuse 35
de pauvres Indiens avec des perles de verre, complotent par
tous les moyens d'empêcher la vente de telles raretés à un
prix si bas, concurrence qui les ruinerait et leur laisserait
leur pacotille sur les bras. Aussi, satisfaisant les désirs
corrompus des hommes avec des doctrines charnelles, les 40
excitent-ils à persécuter de leur haine et de leur mépris tous
ceux qui cherchent à se comporter droitement dans cette

spiritual factory: which they foreseeing, though they cannot but testify of truth, and the excellency of that heavenly traffic which they bring, against what opposition or danger soever, yet needs must it sit heavily upon their spirits, that being, in God's prime intention and their own, selected heralds of peace, and dispensers of treasure inestimable, without price, to them that have no peace, they find in the discharge of their commission, that they are made the greatest variance and offence, a very sword and fire both in house and city over the whole earth.

JOHN MILTON, *The Reason of Church Government urged against Prelaty*, Bk. ii.

This is the kind of text in which the translator must resist any temptation to amend his author's faults. Milton's periods should remain 'cumbersome', but not become more so in French. The reader may be given some guidance, but sparingly; otherwise any gain in ease or perspicuity entails loss in rhetoric and rhythm.

1 **cette fragile...vie, attendu que**: The English order of the adjectives has been kept, since the juxtaposition of *mortelle* and *puisque* would lead to ambiguity: the substitution for *puisque* of the heavier, more obtrusive *attendu que* is intended to show that the causal relation is not to one epithet, but to the whole of the main and hypothetical clauses.   5 **quel bonheur ce serait**: the repetition is useful not only for clarity but for euphony; the *si* = 'so' must be separated from the *si* = 'if'.   6 **la possession la meilleure**: *ce que l'esprit possède de meilleur* is more idiomatic and would be preferable but for its heaviness here.   **la moins pesante**: 'lightsomest', with its moral and physical meanings combined in a conceit, is difficult to render; "*la plus légère*" would sound like moral reproach.   7 **était... le contraire d'un fardeau**: "*n'était pas...un fardeau*" would mean the reverse of what Milton intends. He is about to propound a paradox. The impossibility in French of altering the place of the negative (except in philosophical jargon: *le non-moi, le non-être*) reduces a translator to makeshifts. **le contraire de**: var. *tout le contraire de*; (*tout*) *autre chose que*.   9 **avec usure**: cp. O.E.D., *s.v.* ADVANTAGE, sense 7.   10 **consiste dans**: cp. O.E.D., *s.v.* REST, *v.* sense 6c.   11 Var. *des causes naturelles et des dimensions spatiales*.   12 **inférieure**: it is to be hoped that the French reader will remember that *inférieur* is a comparative of *bas*.   13 **a réussi à**: cp. O.E.D., *s.v.* OBTAIN, sense 5c; *est parvenu à*.   15 **quelque chose**: var. (but heavier) *quoi que ce soit*.   **reconnaître**: required by the change of construction here.   18 **en juge**: In such cases as 'not so

factorerie spirituelle qui leur est propre; et comme ces justes prévoient cette hostilité, sans pouvoir s'abstenir de rendre témoignage à la vérité et à l'excellence de ces marchandises 45 célestes qu'ils apportent, en face de toute opposition et de tout danger que ce soit, cela doit pourtant peser lourdement sur leur cœur de s'apercevoir que, choisis comme messagers de paix dans l'intention première de Dieu et dans la leur et dispensateurs d'un trésor inestimable, sans prix, à ceux qui 50 ne possèdent pas la paix, ils deviennent, dans l'accomplissement de leur mission, la plus grande cause de discorde et de scandale, une véritable épée, un vrai brandon, dans la maison comme dans la cité sur toute la terre. P. LEGOUIS.

esteemed' French avoids the passive. 21 l'emploi profitable: cp. O.E.D., *s.v.* IMPROVEMENT, sense 1. The allusion is to the parable of the talents; as in Milton's own sonnet: 'And that one talent which is death to hide.' 23 faix: We take 'toil or weight' as together forming one idea, and rely on the literary and rhetorical force of *faix* and its reminiscences of La Fontaine's *Bûcheron*. 25 valeurs: cp. O.E.D., *s.v.* SUM, sense 1e. It seems stricter grammar to take 'with which' as going with 'hath sent' than as going with 'to trade'. 28 lots: cp. *des lots de marchandises*. 29 oriental: the noun *orient* is more familiar to French readers, but it has become restricted to pearls. 31 n'importe quel prix: we have to drop either 'any' or 'cheap'; var. *à bas prix*. 35 avec quoi: slightly archaic (and therefore not inappropriate here) for *avec lesquelles*. 36 perles de verre: it is convenient to take 'beads' and 'glasses' together: var. *colliers de verroterie* (more scornful—and more Miltonic). 38 concurrence: added, because otherwise the phrase might be construed as meaning the 'great merchants undo' themselves by selling too cheap. 39 pacotille: more appropriate than *camelote* as being older and continuing the metaphor, of Indian trade. satisfaisant: if 'gratify' means, as we think, 'indulge', this example is older than any in O.E.D., sense 5. We connect 'in fleshly doctrines' with 'gratifying'; cp. O.E.D., *s.v.* IN *prep.*, sense 13a. 42 cette factorerie: var. *ce comptoir*; both words were used in the Indian trade. 45 marchandises: cp. O.E.D., *s.v.* TRAFFIC, *sb.*, sense 4. 48 de s'apercevoir: the translation of 'find' must be put thus early in the sentence to avoid an unpleasant break in the rhythm; hence the similar change in the place of 'are made'—a Latinism =*flunt*=*deviennent*. 52 cause de discorde: 'variance' seems=cause of variance (not in O.E.D.); 'offence' has clearly the active sense, probably with a religious connotation; hence=*une cause de scandale*; var. *une pierre d'achoppement*.

I am poor brother Lippo, by your leave!
You need not clap your torches to my face.
Zooks, what's to blame? you think you see a monk!
What, it's past midnight, and you go the rounds,
And here you catch me at an alley's end
Where sportive ladies leave their doors ajar?
The Carmine's my cloister: hunt it up,
Do,—harry out, if you must show your zeal,
Whatever rat, there, haps on his wrong hole,
And nip each softling of a wee white mouse,
Weke, weke, that's crept to keep him company!
Aha, you know your betters! Then you'll take
Your hand away that's fiddling on my throat,
And please to know me likewise. Who am I?
Why, one, sir, who is lodging with a friend,
Three streets off—he's a certain...how d'ye call?
Master—a...Cosimo of the Medici,
In the house that caps the corner. Boh! you were best!
Remember and tell me, the day you're hanged,
How you affected such a gullet's gripe!
But you, sir, it concerns you that your knaves
Pick up a manner nor discredit you.
Zooks, are we pilchards, that they sweep the streets
And count fair prize what comes into their net?
He's Judas to a tittle, that man is!
Just such a face! why, sir, you make amends.
Lord, I'm not angry! Bid your hangdogs go
Drink out this quarter-florin to the health
Of the munificent House that harbours me
(And many more beside, lads! more beside!)
And all's come square again. I'd like his face—
His, elbowing on his comrade in the door
With pike and lantern,—for the slave that holds
John Baptist's head a-dangle by the hair
With one hand ('look you, now', as who should say)
And his weapon in the other, yet unwiped!
It's not your chance to have a bit of chalk,
A wood-coal or the like? or you should see!

Je suis le pauvre Frère Lippo, avec votre permission ! Vous
n'avez pas besoin de me fourrer vos torches sous le nez.
Morbleu ! qu'est-ce qui ne va pas? Vous croyez voir un
moine ! Quoi ! c'est minuit passé et vous faites votre ronde,
et vous me surprenez ici à l'entrée d'une ruelle où des dames 5
folâtres laissent leur porte entrebâillée? Mon cloître, c'est
le Carmel; fouillez-le à fond ! Allons ! pourchassez, s'il vous
faut montrer votre zèle, tout rat qui, là-bas, s'est trompé de
trou, et pincez tout tendron, toute petite souris blanche,
Cuic! Cuic! qui s'y est glissée pour lui tenir compagnie ! 10
Ha ! ha ! vous connaissez trop vos supérieurs? Alors vous
allez retirer cette main qui joue avec mon gosier, et vous
voudrez bien me reconnaître aussi. Qui je suis? Eh bien !
un homme, Monsieur, qui loge chez un ami dans la troisième
rue à partir d'ici—c'est un certain...comment l'appelle-t-on 15
déjà? Messire...un certain....Côme de Médicis; il habite
la maison qui coiffe l'angle de la rue. Hou ! hou ! Oui, vous
feriez bien. Souvenez-vous, le jour où vous serez pendus, de
me dire si vous avez aimé cette constriction de votre
gargamelle ! Mais vous, il vous appartient de voir que vos 20
marauds apprennent à se conduire et à ne pas vous faire
honte. Morbleu ! Monsieur, sommes-nous harengs qu'ils
pêchent les rues et considèrent comme de bonne prise tout
ce qui tombe dans leur filet? C'est Judas tout craché, cet
homme-ci ! Juste son visage ! Eh quoi ! Monsieur, vous 25
faites amende honorable. Mon Dieu ! je ne suis pas en
colère ! Envoyez vos pendards boire ce quart de florin à la
santé de la magnifique maison qui m'abrite (et bien d'autres
encore, mes garçons, bien d'autres encore !) et tout sera
arrangé. J'aimerais son visage—à celui qui joue du coude à 30
la porte, une pique et une lanterne à la main—comme
modèle pour l'esclave qui tient par les cheveux, ballante, la
tête de Saint Jean-Baptiste (comme qui dirait: 'Regardez
donc !') et de l'autre main son arme encore sanglante ! Vous
n'auriez pas sur vous un morceau de craie, de fusain, ou de 35

Yes, I'm the painter, since you style me so.
What, brother Lippo's doings, up and down,
You know them and they take you? like enough!
I saw the proper twinkle in your eye—
'Tell you, I liked your looks at very first.
Let's sit and set things straight now, hip to haunch.
           ROBERT BROWNING, *Fra Lippo Lippi.*

The passage, especially the beginning, is highly dramatic: to understand it properly one must visualize the scene and guess what the characters other than Fra Lippo are saying and doing. We have endeavoured to preserve the idiomatic, even colloquial, tone of the original, sometimes sacrificing the literal meaning of individual words to make the French appear as spontaneous as possible.

5 Var. *voici que vous me surprenez*, which is more idiomatic; but we take 'here' to be contrasted with 'there' in line 9 and accordingly prefer the literal rendering with *ici.*   7 pourchassez: not quite = 'harry out' if this = 'harass till they fall into your power'; but *capturez* would lose more of the meaning and *pourchassez et capturez* would be too explicit. Possibly 'harry' here = 'drag', sense 7 (obsolete or dialectical), O.E.D.; if so, var. *entraînez de force.*   9 pincez: cp. *La police a* pincé *le voleur.*   11 Var. *vous savez vous tenir avec vos supérieurs*; but in this and in other possible idiomatic phrases the opposition to 'You'll please to know me' would be lost. 15 comment l'appelle-t-on déjà?: *Chose* (colloquial) and *Machin* (more modern and vulgar) would be, besides inappropriate, inexact. Fra Lippo pretends he is trying to remember the name: *déjà* perhaps gives the colloquial tone sufficiently.   16 de Médicis: in 'of *the* Medici' the article is no doubt part of the name *dei Medici*; it is not used in French.   17 Oui, vous feriez bien: 'you were best' seems to imply that the watch at least look like falling back. *Oui* underlines the hint; if the watch have already fallen back, *vous faites bien* is more accurate.   20 gargamelle: has a Rabelaisian flavour which is not inappropriate.   22 harengs: the omission of the article is both archaic ('*style marotique*') and colloquial. 23 pêchent les rues: bold, but cp. *pêcher un étang*; *draguer* = 'sweep', but suggests oysters or mussels as 'the catch'.   25 Monsieur. It might be argued that the 'sir' who 'makes amends' is the 'man' referred to in the preceding line, his likeness to Judas being—in a painter's mind—sufficient amends for the rudeness of himself and the others. But we are inclined to

quelque chose d'approchant? Dommage, vous verriez!
Oui, c'est moi le peintre, puisque vous me donnez ce titre.
Eh quoi! les productions du Frère Lippo qu'on trouve çà
et là, vous les connaissez, et elles vous charment? Je le
crois! J'ai vu dans vos yeux le pétillement du connaisseur. 40
Je vais vous dire, votre physionomie m'a plu du premier
coup. Asseyons-nous et tirons cette histoire au clair
maintenant, hanche contre hanche.   P. LEGOUIS.

think that the word 'sir' is, as in l. 21, addressed to the officer who has
been trying to make an apology.   26 faites amende honorable:
slightly more formal than 'make amends', but Fra Lippo is, for one
moment, standing on his dignity.   28 maison: has both the senses of
'house', but capital M would seem odd, even with *maison = maison
princière*.   et bien d'autres, etc. The line is evidently an acknowledgment
of the thanks expressed by the 'hangdogs' who may have wished Fra Lippo
—or the Medici family?—'a happy day!' In any case the ellipse is no bolder
in French than it is in English.   29 tout sera arrangé: var. *tout est
arrangé: tout est de nouveau pour le mieux*; these would no doubt convey, like
the English, a future sense; on the other hand '*tout s'arrangera*' might
imply a lengthy process of adaptation.   30 joue du coude. The rendering "*poussant du coude son camarade*" would suggest one watchman nudging
another to attract his attention, whereas Browning intends to convey the
impression of a scramble for the nearest pot-house.   36 Dommage,
vous verriez! The 'or' implies that the constable is unable to produce any
drawing materials; hence we supply the expression of regret *Dommage!* for
clarity. The exact amount of obligation implied in 'should', is easily indicated in speech, but would require a clumsy periphrasis in print.   38 çà
et là. O.E.D. quotes this line, *s.v.* UP AND DOWN *adv.*, sense 3. Otherwise we
should have thought that the phrase came under sense 6 (now dialectal),
merely intensifying 'You know them' = *vous les connaissez à fond*.   39 Je
le crois! var. *Cela ne m'étonne pas.*   40 Var. *J'ai vu vos yeux pétiller
comme il faut!*   42 Var. *mettons les choses au point.*   43 hanche
contre hanche: a variant, perhaps permissible, for the usual *côte à côte.*

In a few minutes tea was brought. Very delicate was the
china, very old the plate, very thin the bread and butter,
and very small the lumps of sugar. Sugar was evidently
Mrs Jamieson's favourite economy. I question if the little
filigree sugar-tongs, made something like scissors, could
have opened themselves wide enough to take up an honest,
vulgar, good-sized piece; and when I tried to seize two little
minnikin pieces at once, so as not to be detected in too many
returns to the sugar-basin, they absolutely dropped one,
with a little sharp clatter, quite in a malicious and un-
natural manner. But before this happened, we had had a
slight disappointment. In the little silver jug was cream, in
the larger one milk. As soon as Mr Mulliner came in, Carlo
began to beg, which was a thing our manners forbade us to
do, though I am sure we were just as hungry; and Mrs
Jamieson said she was certain we would excuse her if she
gave her poor dumb Carlo his tea first. She accordingly
mixed a saucerful for him, and put it down for him to lap;
and then she told us how intelligent and sensible the dear
little fellow was; he knew cream quite well, and constantly
refused tea with only milk in it; so the milk was left for us.

MRS GASKELL, *Cranford.*

'Why, what a nice little lady you are, to be sure', said the
gipsy, taking her by the hand. Maggie thought her very
agreeable, but wished she had not been so dirty.

There was quite a group round the fire when they reached
it. An old gipsy woman was seated on the ground nursing
her knees, and occasionally poking a skewer into the round
kettle that sent forth an odorous steam; two small, shock-
headed children were lying prone and resting on their
elbows, something like small sphinxes; and a placid donkey
was bending his head over a tall girl, who, lying on her back,

Au bout de quelques minutes on apporta le thé. La porcelaine était très fine, très ancienne l'argenterie, très minces les tartines de beurre, et très petits les morceaux de sucre. C'était sur le sucre, évidemment, que se portait de préférence la parcimonie de Mme. Jamieson. Je doute fort 5 que la petite pince à sucre de filigrane, en forme de ciseaux, eût pu s'ouvrir assez grand pour saisir un bon gros morceau ordinaire, et, comme j'essayais de saisir à la fois deux minuscules morceaux afin de ne pas me faire remarquer en y revenant à plusieurs fois, la pince laissa bel et bien en 10 tomber un avec un petit cliquetis sec dont la malice avait quelque chose de surnaturel. Mais auparavant nous avions déjà éprouvé une légère déception. Dans le petit pot d'argent il y avait de la crème, dans l'autre plus grand il y avait du lait. Aussitôt que M. Mulliner entra, Carlo se mit 15 à faire le beau pour réclamer sa part, ce que nos bonnes manières nous interdisaient de faire, quoique nous eussions bien aussi faim que lui. Certainement, dit Mme. Jamieson, nous l'excuserions si elle servait d'abord Carlo, pauvre innocent. En conséquence, elle remplit une soucoupe et la 20 mit par terre à son intention. Et puis elle nous raconta combien ce cher petit était intelligent et avisé. Il savait très bien reconnaître la crème et il refusait toujours le thé où il n'y avait que du lait. Le lait nous fut donc réservé.

F. C. ROE.

11 cliquetis: var. *tintement.*

'Eh! quelle gentille petite demoiselle pour sûr', dit la bohémienne, la prenant par la main. Maggie la trouvait très aimable, mais l'eût désirée moins sale.

Tout un groupe était assemblé près du feu lorsqu'elles y arrivèrent. Une vieille bohémienne était assise par terre, 5 entourant ses genoux de ses bras, fourrageant de temps en temps avec une broche dans une marmite qui répandait une vapeur odorante; deux petits enfants ébouriffés étaient allongés à plat ventre, appuyés sur leurs coudes, on eût dit deux petits sphinx. Un âne placide baissait la tête au-dessus 10 d'une grande fille qui, couchée sur le dos, lui chatouillait le

was scratching his nose and indulging him with a bite of excellent stolen hay. The slanting sunlight fell kindly upon them, and the scene was really very pretty and comfortable, Maggie thought, only she hoped they would soon set out the tea-cups. Everything would be quite charming when she had taught the gipsies to use a washing-basin, and to feel an interest in books. It was a little confusing, though, that the young woman began to speak to the old one in a language which Maggie did not understand, while the tall girl who was feeding the donkey sat up and stared at her without offering any salutation.

GEORGE ELIOT, *The Mill on the Floss.*

The pine rises in serene resistance, self-contained; nor can I ever without awe stay long under a great Alpine cliff, far from all house or work of men, looking up to its companies of pine, as they stand on the inaccessible juts and perilous ledges of the enormous wall, in quiet multitudes, each like the shadow of the one beside it—upright, fixed, spectral, as troops of ghosts standing on the walls of Hades, not knowing each other—dumb for ever. You cannot reach them, cannot cry to them; those trees never heard human voice; they are far above all sound but of the winds. No foot ever stirred fallen leaf of theirs. All comfortless they stand, between the two eternities of the Vacancy and the Rock: yet with such iron will, that the rock itself looks bent and shattered beside them—fragile, weak, inconsistent, compared to their dark energy of delicate life, and monotony of enchanted pride: unnumbered, unconquerable.

Then note, farther, their perfectness. The impression on most people's minds must have been received more from pictures than reality, so far as I can judge; so ragged they think the pine; whereas its chief character in health is green

museau en le régalant d'une bouchée d'excellent foin volé. Les rayons obliques du soleil les éclairaient doucement, et la scène était à la vérité très jolie et très familière, à ce que pensait Maggie, seulement elle espérait qu'on allait bientôt 15 sortir les tasses à thé. Tout serait parfait lorsqu'elle aurait appris aux bohémiens à se servir d'une cuvette, et à s'intéresser aux livres. Ce qui était un peu déconcertant, pourtant, c'était que la jeune femme s'était mise à parler à la vieille dans un langage que Maggie ne comprenait pas, 20 pendant que la grande fille qui donnait à manger à l'âne, s'étant mise sur son séant, la dévisageait sans lui dire un mot d'accueil. F. C. ROE.

12 **régalant:** var. *gratifiant.*

Le sapin se dresse avec une sereine résistance en arbre qui se suffit, et je ne puis jamais sans vénération me tenir longtemps sous un grand escarpement de rocher dans les Alpes, loin de toute maison ou de tout ouvrage de l'homme, à regarder ses files de sapins debout sur les saillies inaccessibles et les rebords périlleux de l'énorme muraille en multitudes paisibles, chacun semblant l'ombre de son voisin— droits, figés, spectraux, comme des bandes de vaines ombres sur les murs des Enfers, s'ignorant les uns les autres—à jamais muets. Vous ne sauriez les atteindre, vous ne sauriez leur crier—ces arbres n'ont jamais perçu de voix humaine; ils dominent de haut tout autre son que celui des vents. Aucun pas humain n'a jamais remué une de leurs feuilles tombées. Ils se dressent dans leur morne désolation entre les deux éternités du vide et du roc, mais avec tant d'inflexible volonté que le roc lui-même auprès d'eux paraît ployé et fracassé,—fragile, faible, sans consistance, par contraste avec la sombre énergie de leur vie délicate et la monotonie de leur orgueil ensorcelé,—indomptables et innombrables.

Notez ensuite leur forme impeccable. L'impression qu'ils ont laissée dans l'esprit de la plupart des personnes doit plutôt provenir de tableaux que de la réalité, pour autant que j'en puis juger—tellement elles estiment le sapin déchiqueté, alors qu'à l'état de santé sa principale caractéristique est sa pleine et verte rondeur. Il se dresse compact

and full roundness. It stands compact, like one of its own cones, slightly curved on its sides, finished and quaint as a carved tree in some Elizabethan garden; and instead of being wild in expression, forms the softest of all forest scenery; for other trees show their trunks and twisting boughs: but the pine, growing either in luxuriant mass or in happy isolation, allows no branch to be seen. Summit behind summit rise its pyramidal ranges, or down to the very grass sweep the circlets of its boughs; so that there is nothing but green cone and green carpet. Nor is it only softer, but in one sense more cheerful than other foliage; for it casts only a pyramidal shadow. Lowland forest arches overhead, and chequers the ground with darkness; but the pine, growing in scattered groups, leaves the glades between emerald-bright. Its gloom is all its own; narrowing into the sky, it lets the sunshine strike down to the dew.

JOHN RUSKIN, *Modern Painters*, Part VI.

Into no other city does the sight of the country enter so far; if you do not meet a butterfly, you shall certainly catch a glimpse of far-away trees upon your walk; and the place is full of theatre tricks in the way of scenery. You peep under an arch, you descend stairs that look as if they would land you in a cellar, you turn to the back-window of a grimy tenement in a lane:—and behold! you are face-to-face with distant and bright prospects. You turn a corner, and there is the sun going down into the Highland hills. You look down an alley, and see ships tacking for the Baltic.

For the country people to see Edinburgh on her hill-tops, is one thing; it is another for the citizen, from the thick of his affairs, to overlook the country. It should be a genial and ameliorating influence in life; it should prompt good thoughts and remind him of Nature's unconcern: that

comme une pomme de pin légèrement incurvé sur les côtés, naïf et fini comme un arbre taillé dans quelque jardin élisabéthain. Loin d'avoir une expression sauvage, il forme les plus aimables des scènes forestières, car d'autres arbres montrent leurs troncs et leurs branches tordues, mais le sapin, croissant soit en masse luxuriante, soit en un heureux isolement, ne laisse pas voir de rameaux. Cime après cime, ses rangées de pyramides s'élèvent, ou jusqu'à l'herbe même ses anneaux de branches descendent, de sorte qu'il ne reste rien qu'un cône et un tapis de verdure. Et non seulement c'est un feuillage plus doux, mais en un sens un feuillage plus gai qu'un autre, car il ne projette qu'une ombre pyramidale. La forêt de plaine forme voûte sur nos têtes avec des ombres entrecoupées sur le sol, mais le sapin, poussant en groupes épars, laisse aux allées intermédiaires un éclat d'émeraude. Sa pénombre lui est toute particulière; se rétrécissant du côté du ciel, elle permet au soleil de pénétrer jusqu'à la rosée. W. THOMAS.

En aucune autre cité la vue de la campagne ne pénètre aussi profondément. Si vous ne rencontrez pas de papillon, vous aurez sûrement au cours de votre promenade une vision rapide d'arbres lointains, et la ville est pleine de trucs scéniques en fait de points de vue. Vous jetez un regard sous une arche, vous descendez des escaliers qui semblent devoir vous conduire à une cave, vous vous tournez vers la fenêtre de derrière d'un logement sordide dans une venelle— et vous voilà en face de perspectives distantes et radieuses. Vous tournez un coin de rue et voici le soleil qui se couche entre les Hautes Terres d'Écosse. Vous suivez des yeux une ruelle et vous apercevez des navires partant pour la Baltique.

Pour les campagnards c'est une chose que de voir Édimbourg sur le sommet de ses collines; c'en est une autre pour le citadin, en plein centre d'affaires, de dominer la campagne. Ce devrait être une influence géniale et réconfortante dans sa vie et qui devrait faire naître de bonnes pensées et lui rappeler l'insouciance de la Nature, que de

he can watch from day to day, as he trots officeward, how the Spring green brightens in the wood or the field grows black under a moving ploughshare. I have been tempted, in this connexion, to deplore the slender faculties of the human race, with its penny-whistle of a voice, its dull ears, and its narrow range of sight. If you could see as people are to see in heaven, if you had eyes such as you can fancy for a superior race, if you could take clear note of the objects of vision, not only a few yards, but a few miles from where you stand:—think how agreeably your sight would be entertained, how pleasantly your thoughts would be diversified, as you walked the Edinburgh streets! For you might pause, in some business perplexity, in the midst of the city traffic, and perhaps catch the eye of a shepherd as he sat down to breathe upon a heathery shoulder of the Pentlands; or perhaps some urchin, clambering in a country elm, would put aside the leaves and show you his flushed and rustic visage.

R. L. STEVENSON, *Edinburgh* (Chatto and Windus).

pouvoir jour après jour, tout en trottinant à son bureau, observer la verdure printanière qui devient plus brillante dans le bois ou le champ s'assombrir sous le soc qui se meut. L'envie me prend sous ce rapport de déplorer les médiocres facultés de la race humaine avec sa voix de flageolet enfantin, ses oreilles dures et sa vue bornée. Si vous saviez voir comme l'on verra au Ciel, si vous aviez des yeux comme on peut se les figurer pour une race d'élite, si vous pouviez noter distinctement des objets visibles non seulement à quelques mètres, mais à quelques milles de l'endroit où vous vous tenez:—songez combien votre vue serait agréablement divertie, combien vos pensées seraient aimablement distraites en parcourant les rues d'Édimbourg! Car vous pourriez faire halte, en quelque embarras de négoce, au milieu de l'agitation affairée de la ville, et rencontrer peut-être l'œil d'un berger, comme il s'assied pour reprendre haleine sur un contrefort recouvert de bruyère dans les Pentlands, ou peut-être un gamin grimpant sur un orme en plein champ en écarterait les feuilles et vous ferait voir son visage rougissant de petit paysan.

W. THOMAS.

PASSAGES OCCURRING ALSO IN THE *SUPPLEMENT**

The numbers of the passages from the Supplement are followed by their numbers here, bracketed

* See Preface to this book.

INDEX OF AUTHORS OF PASSAGES

INDEX OF TITLES OF PASSAGES

INDEX OF FIRST WORDS
OF PASSAGES

Lightning Source UK Ltd.
Milton Keynes UK
UKOW01f0939260716

279239UK00001B/9/P